D1100378

NEW WINE IN OLD SKINS

A Comparative View
of Socio-Political Structures and Values
Affecting the American Revolution

Essays Presented at an International Symposion
Held at the University of Cologne
from 19th to 21st February 1976
in Commemoration of the
American Revolution Bicentennial

Edited by

Erich Angermann, Marie-Luise Frings,
Hermann Wellenreuther

Ernst Klett Verlag Stuttgart

CIP-Kurztitelaufnahme der Deutschen Bibliothek

New wine in old skins: a comparative view of socio-polit. structures and values affecting the American revolution; essays presented at an Internat. Symposion held at the Univ. of Cologne from 19–21 February 1976 in commemoration of the American Revolution Bicentennial / ed. by Erich Angermann . . . – 1. Aufl. – Stuttgart: Klett, 1976.
    ISBN 3-12-910310-4
NE: Angermann, Erich [Hrsg.]; Universität <Köln>

Introductory Note

The title of this book needs explanation, for it might well strike prospective readers as somewhat bizarre a designation for a collection of learned essays dealing with the history of the American Revolution. It originated from two major considerations when I started thinking of a suitable way to join the forces commemorating the American Revolution Bicentennial with the interests of American History as a relatively recent field of studies in Europe and especially the Federal Republic of Germany: First, to hold a symposion was the most obvious thing to do for a group of aspiring young scholars, and if so, an allusion to the original meaning of *symposion* – a convivial meeting for drinking *and* intellectual discussion – seemed in order. Secondly, the title, after all, ought to have some bearing upon the themes we proposed to discuss, and it was to be loose enough to encompass a wide range of special topics growing out of the authors' previous studies. Put briefly, the idea underlying the title was that, all the change wrought by the American Revolution notwithstanding, the persistence of traditional institutions and behavioral patterns deserved particular scholarly attention.

Such an approach may be more obvious to the European than to the American historian. The conviction, therefore, that bringing together experts on American Revolutionary history from both sides of the Atlantic Ocean may open up new channels for future research as well as its communication, was one of the basic assumptions motivating the organization of the symposion. It appeared to us, furthermore, that a truly scholarly effort of this kind would be a meaningful and fitting way to commemorate one of the major events in World History. Last but not least, we thought to take advantage of this opportunity to show an English-speaking audience that within the last fifteen years or so some institutions in the Federal Republic of Germany, among others our Institute of Anglo-American History in Cologne *(Anglo-Amerikanische Abteilung des Historischen Seminars der Universität zu Köln),* have succeeded both in building up the institutional framework for scholarly work and in training a nucleus of dedicated students to perform it. The concept of the symposion we had in mind, however, demanded that we should not be satisfied with a mere dialogue between German and American scholars but try to bring together a truly expert group from as many European and American countries as possible. On the other hand, it was obvious that the group was to be small enough and the organization such as to encourage a lively exchange of ideas.

5

Consequently, we decided – also for reasons of economy and availability – that the symposion should last two and a half days only, 19th to 21st February 1976. This meant that, aiming as we were at a lively discussion, papers could not be read at the symposion but had to be provided well in time to all participants, and were merely to be discussed when we convened. Thus, eight papers were produced written by young scholars four of whom had been trained in Cologne, while the connection with the other contributors was established partly via Dr. Hoerder (Berlin) and partly in the course of our own work, as in the case of Dr. Hutson (Washington, D. C.).

As to the themes of the symposion, we tried to avoid copying American colloquia of a similar kind. It was not enticing to compete with American scholars in the field in such a way as would give them an unchallengeable advantage because of their readier access to source materials and superior familiarity with the cultural context of their own history. We rather aimed at trying peculiarly European approaches, as far as possible in a comparative way. We did indeed not want to study European influences upon events in Revolutionary America, as is so often expected of European scholars in the field. For although that is a perfectly legitimate concern, it had simply not been a primary interest in our work during all these years. We had, then, to cope with two difficulties. First, the studies to be presented and discussed at the symposion, even if they had to be original research papers, could in most cases not be expected to be based on research *ad hoc* conducted. So, by necessity, they had to grow out of other previous or current research projects of the authors, which implied of course that any strict topical line was out of the question. Secondly, the scarcity of scholars who are actually trained and experienced in comparative history must be obvious to anybody who has ever tried to find them in numbers – let alone among younger scholars.

Thus, while we were fully aware that we could not aspire to a consistently comparative approach in all essays, we did try to bring in as much of it and of the interaction of European and American events and ideas as possible. This is apparent in the emphasis of several of our essays on structural developments and the interplay of ideas across the Atlantic, for both lend themselves more readily to comparison than individual actions. Whereas only the first paper applies a comparative view in the strict sense, thereby largely providing the setting for many of the other topics, we attempted to expand the range of our studies in two ways: first, by bringing together a number of authors with widely differing interests and opinions, and secondly, by emphasizing the comparative and European aspects of the subjects under debate in our discussions. In both respects it proved immensely conducive to our purposes that our group included Americans and Europeans among both the authors and the commentators. For much as we wanted to bring European views to bear on American Revolutionary history, we definitely did not intend to set them against the work of American historians, but rather hoped to supplement it in a way from which both sides might profit.

The group of authors that came together turned out to be a pretty good, if certainly neither complete nor wholly representative, sample of what is going on in recent research on the American Revolution. Labeling them in a very rough-and-ready way one may say that you find an unusually wide spectrum of possible approaches: interest in changes and continuities of socio-political structures and behavioral patterns (Wellenreuther, Countryman, Kollmann), conflict-oriented revisionism of "consensus" interpretations of American Revolutionary history (Hoerder, Karsky, Kollmann), more conventional investigations of significant terms (Dippel, Kilian), and even an excursion into psycho-history (Hutson). While the essays have in fact grown out of the authors' previous or current work, they are all original pieces written especially for the occasion. This may account for a certain unevenness in some of the essays both in terms of documentation and reasoning – too young wine, as it were. It should be borne in mind, however, that they at no time pretended to perfection. They were rather supposed to reflect the process of research, to advance new ideas as they take shape in the course of such work, and to provoke a spirited debate which was bound to suggest revisions or at least qualifications.

We considered it one major condition for a successful symposion to provide a variety of fairly interesting essays as a basis for our talks – and provide them in time. But of course, it was as important to find, in addition to the authors, a likewise variegated group of commentators. Although we were unable, in spite of a circumspect search, to detect experts of American Revolutionary history in such European countries as Spain, Italy, Czechoslovakia, East Germany, and the Skandinavian countries, I dare say we were extremely lucky in bringing together an almost ideal group of commentators from ten countries. (See Notes on Participants at the end of this volume.) It proved highly representative for various backgrounds as well as differing opinions, and all our guests were extraordinarily cooperative. The latter applies not only to the good-natured willingness of all participants to comply with an all too tight and rigid schedule, that left everybody somewhat exhausted at the end of the symposion. It applies as well to the conscientious reaction to our fundamental condition that, even if we did not ask for written comments (which tend to kill a genuine debate), we did expect *all* participants to peruse *all* of the essays beforehand to ensure a well-informed and lively discussion. As one of the authors put it later on: "In reflecting on the symposium, what surprises me most is the conscientiousness of the participants; evidently, everyone read the papers in advance." It should be added that the participants proved good debaters, too, in that they succeeded in entering into an exchange of ideas in the best sense. Thus, in actual fact, the high level of the debates and the relaxed atmosphere in which they took place bore out the boldest expectations.

When all this is said, however, it must be clear that the present volume can but poorly reflect the *experience* of that symposion. Otherwise symposia of this kind were a mere waste of energy, time, and money. The essence of that experience is an intellectual intercourse that cannot be put to print. It must furthermore be clear that a group of twenty-five fairly sophisticated minds is pretty unlikely to arrive at anything even remotely resembling a consensus in any but the most trivial questions. The best they can hope for, and that justifies their toil indeed, is to perceive of and stimulate new ideas and to enhance their respect for divergent opinions – again a process that escapes the confinement of print. So, all the authors could do, in revising their essays, was to reconsider and refine their arguments and include as much as possible of what had been brought forward in both formal and informal debates. Some of the papers stand virtually unchanged, others were augmented by just a few new viewpoints, while some have been largely rewritten and greatly improved in view of the discussion. To expect more would be asking too much from an author in his own right. And I am confident that, aside from the experience of the symposion, the articles in their revised form will justify the publication of the present volume, to make our effort known to a wider audience.

It follows that the editors did not consider it their task in any way to interfere with the text of the essays or to comment on the views held by the authors. We did our best, however, to bring both text and notes in style according to the rules established by the Institute of Early American History and Culture at Williamsburg, Va. We also tried as best we could to improve the English of the German authors – with varying success, as we know all too well.

There remains the pleasant obligation to express my gratitude to all who helped in making our symposion a success and to publish the present volume. First of all, I thank the authors and commentators for all the effort they have put into the scholarly part of our experiment. Since we consider the resulting volume – notwithstanding the copyright of the individual authors – as a more or less collective achievement of the whole group, no particular acknowledgements toward individual participants are made in the several essays. Secondly, I want to thank the staff of the *Anglo-Amerikanische Abteilung* who shared the burden of the preparatory, organizational, and editorial tasks with an undefatigable dedication to the purpose; this applies above all to the co-editors, who never tired in keeping things running and in producing a printable manuscript, and Frau Doris Reichenbach, who aside from her administrative duties typed and retyped and brought in shape ever so many manuscripts.

I thank the German Research Council *(Deutsche Forschungsgemeinschaft)* that sponsored our symposion by means of a generous grant-in-aid and in a period of widespread financial distress showed an extraordinary measure of appreciation of what we had in mind. Last but not least, I want to thank the publisher, Ernst Klett Verlag Stuttgart, and in particular Dr. Adolf Dieckmann, who undertook the publication of this volume without asking for any subsidy.

One acknowledgement must not be omitted – that to the American people. Had they not started their Revolution two hundred years ago, there would be none of all these Bicentennial reminiscences, our symposion and book included.

Cologne, April 1976

Erich Angermann

Anglo-Amerikanische Abteilung des
Historischen Seminars der Universität

Contents

List of Abbreviations

AA   Peter Force, ed., *American Archives: Consisting of a Collection of Authentic Records, State Papers, Debates, and Letters and Other Notices of Public Affairs . . .* , 4th Ser., I—VI, 5th Ser., I–III (Washington, D. C., 1837–1853)

AHR   *American Historical Review*, I–   (1895–   )

EcHR *Economic History Review*, 2nd Ser., I–   (1948–   )

ib.   *ibidem,* referring to preceding title, series or periodical

id.   *idem,* referring to author of preceding book, article or quotation

JAH   *Journal of American History*, LI–   (1964–   )

JCC   Worthington C. Ford *et al.*, eds., *Journals of the Continental Congress, 1774–1789*, 34 vols. (Washington, D. C., 1904–1937)

JSH   *Journal of Social History*, I–   (1967–   )

LMCC Edmund C. Burnett, ed., *Letters of Members of the Continental Congress*, 8 vols. (Washington, D.C., 1921–1936)

PCC   Papers of the Continental Congress, National Archives, Washington, D.C. (Microfilm)

PMHB *Pennsylvania Magazine of History and Biography*, I– (1877–   )

PRO   Public Record Office, London

WMQ   *William and Mary Quarterly*, I–   (1892–   )

A View of the Socio-Economic Structures of England and the British Colonies on the Eve of the American Revolution

Hermann Wellenreuther*

When, on July 2nd, 1776, the delegates to the Continental Congress voted "that these United Colonies are, and, of right, ought to be, Free and Independent States" they did more than just cut their ties with England: with this step they established a new frame of reference within which politics, culture, religion, and economy henceforth would function in America. Thus for the historian the delegates' decision has a double meaning. It justifies the description of American historical developments after 1776 as the result of predominantly internal American forces the same way that it forces the historian to view American historical developments before 1776 within the context of the British Empire. The following paper will concentrate on the socio-economic dimension of this imperial context. In the first part of the paper the English and colonial socio-economic structures are described and compared; the second part is devoted to an assessment of the mutual influences of and links between the socio-economic and administrative and political structures on both sides of the Atlantic.

The discussion rests on two assumptions: first, that there is a direct relationship between the socio-economic and the political structures. This implies that different socio-economic structures resulted in different political structures. These are discussed in the paper. Secondly, that this relationship directly affected the capability to maintain satisfactory communication between the colonies and the mother country. Both combined become most important for the English, respectively the colonists', capability to assess each others' politics. There is, in other words, a feedback which by the middle of the eighteenth century and even more so in the following decades became of increasing importance. My theses are that as the social structures moved apart the possibility for communication decreased, the capability to assess correctly the others' politics diminished, and the danger of misconstruing the others' intentions increased proportionately. Related to this I would maintain that the colonies had evolved social and political structures of their own which they saw endangered by every new move of the mother country. The defense of these accomplishments, which the colonists viewed of course as British in the best sense, became consequently a prime motive of the Americans in the last two decades before the Declaration of Independence.[1]

I.

The term "structure" is today used with different meanings. Therefore it is necessary to state my own definition of the term. In this paper the composite term "social structure" will be used in the sense of a "unit consisting of related and weighted component parts". The units are the societies in England and in her colonies in North America. The component parts represent the various groups within these units, by which I mean people united by the force of widely shared contemporary assumptions.[2] The application of this definition in a historical analysis encounters two problems: What are these "commonly shared assumptions"? and what do I mean with the words "related and weighted"?

Both problems are intertwined in eighteenth-century *Britain*. Consider the complaint of Henry St. John: "We have now been twenty years engaged in the two most expensive wars ... The whole burthen of this charge hath lain upon the landed interest ... The men of estates have generally speaking, neither served in the Fleets nor armies, nor meddled in the public funds and management of the Treasury. A New Interest hath been created out of their Fortunes and a sort of property which was not known twenty years ago, is now increased to be almost equal to the terra firma of our island".[3] What the later Viscount Bolingbroke so much decried was the emergence of what others have called the "moneyed interest".[4] By this they meant a group within English society which derived its influence not from the amount of land owned but from the capital accumulated. Comparing the moneyed and the landed interests we can now define our condition "related and weighted" more clearly. For if we now weigh the component parts of the social structure by the amount of land owned we will have to keep in mind that this excludes a sizeable portion of English society from our analysis. This group had numerous relations with the "landed interest": it opened up new avenues for investments while at the same time it tried to gain respectability by acquiring landed property.[5]

A simple analysis of Gregory King's estimates for 1688[6] illustrates this. According to him the income of nobility, gentry, and freeholders combined represented half of the total income of the nation, while merchants, shopkeepers and craftsmen together enjoyed less than one fifth of the total income. Weighing the component parts on the basis of landownership would mean excluding this group. Since the share of this group rose probably by another 5 percent during the first half of the eighteenth century, our analysis would be even more biased.

On the other hand King's figures give us an idea of the size of the groups which received their income from land. Under the assumption that about two thirds of King's cottagers and paupers and about half of his laborers and servants were part of the rural economy, King's figures yield an estimate of 58 percent of the *population* who earned their income from working the land either by receiving rents, selling the products as owner-occupiers, sharing the profits as tenants with their landlords, or working for farmers. In reality this percentage of the population was probably considerably larger because a lot of craftsmen in rural areas were at least part-time farmers.[7] On the same basis but again without considering possible income from land by merchants, shopkeepers, and craftsmen, we arrive at the conclusion that 66 percent of the national *income* was derived from the land by nobility, gentry, freeholders, farmers, tenants, together with half of the servants and two thirds of the laborers and cottagers.

King's estimates together with other contemporary evidence provide us with an explanation why land, why income from land was considered of such importance: first, because land was the most important provider of the country, and secondly, because power and influence in England were defined according to the size of and income from landed estates.[8]

A lot has been written and said about which group owned how much land. The consensus now seems to be that the nobility and gentry together probably owned about 70 percent of the land around the middle of the eighteenth century with, since the beginning of the century, the gentry definitely losing ground to the nobility. The rest, about 30 percent, was probably owned by freeholders who in the main were owner-occupiers.[9] To put it differently, more than two thirds of the land was held by less than 5 percent of the population in the form of estates, some of which yielded their owners an income of for example £ 47,585 per year, others probably less than £ 300.[10]

It is much more difficult to arrive at an estimate of the number of freeholders. The only possible clues are provided by the size of the county electorates, since only freeholders were allowed to vote in county elections. For England and Wales together these may have numbered about 190,000.[11] There are at least two reasons why this figure must be used cautiously: first, because it is unlikely that all freeholders voted in contested elections, which are the basis for Namier and Brooke's figures, and secondly, because the incidence of fictitious freehold and copyhold votes, although illegal, may have been quite high.[12] Possibly the two factors neutralized each other. That still leaves us with the problem of the size of the population: Taking as the most conservative figure 6.14 million inhabitants,[13] we would, by using a divisor of 4.4,[14] arrive at about 1.39 million families of which the freeholders as heads of families would represent 13.62 percent of the population. If we assume on the basis of these considerations a percentage of 15 percent for the freeholders – an estimate which is probably too high – then all the arable land in England and Wales was owned by one fifth of the population. Put differently, about 30 percent of the land at the most was worked by owner-occupiers and about 70 percent of the land was leased by the nobility and gentry. Since Gregory King's figures suggest that 58 percent of the population earned their income from the land, between 35 and 40 percent of the population must have held land by one or the other form of tenure. The actual number of tenants was of course considerably higher, because a very large number of houses in villages and urban areas was owned by the same groups who monopolized the land.[15]

The social structure of English society had two distinct aspects. First, there were – on the basis of landownership – three groups, the nobility, the gentry, and the freeholders, who taken together represented one fifth of the population but owned all the land. Secondly, 35 to 40 percent of the population did not own any land but leased it from those whose property it was. While from the point of view of landownership the nobility, the gentry, and the freeholders enjoyed an independent status, a group twice their size did not.[16]

It will be interesting to compare the situation in England with that in her colonies in *North America*. Answering the same questions becomes, however, more difficult, for in America different economic circumstances, settlement patterns, and political fragmentation increased regional variations considerably. As in England landownership and capital are the factors that define the weight of the component parts within the colonial social structures. Here the similarities end. By the eighteenth century it was not the landed estate alone that was considered – by the crown at least – a sufficient stake in society, but quite generally the "good" or "substantial" estate consisting of either land or other assets. Thus the urban mercantile class in the middle and northern colonies, as well as the merchant-planters and Indian traders in the South, were part of one and the same upper social group.[17]

It is much more difficult to estimate the relative weight of the structures' component parts on the basis of property and capital. For although we have good data for some regions there are no reliable figures available for any single colony prior to 1776 with the single exception of Virginia's rent roll for 1704/05.[18]

As in England the discussion has to start with the distribution of the population. This is of singular importance for New England. In 1765 in Massachusetts for example "72.4 percent of the colony's population lived in towns of 1,000 inhabitants or more".[19] Thus in this colony as in the rest of New England, and also in southeastern Pennsylvania, farmers were a smaller proportion of the colony's population than elsewhere. In New England farmers worked their own land, but in Pennsylvania, at least in two counties, one fourth of the farms were worked by tenants.[20] New York poses different problems. Here the tenants were more numerous because big landowners owned holdings comparable to big English estates; consequently a smaller portion of the population was holding sufficient land to qualify as freeholders. A comparison between the census of 1723 for Albany City and County with the list of freeholders of 1720 for the same indicates that about 40 percent of the male white population qualified as freeholders. A similar comparison for Suffolk County for 1737 yields a percentage of 30 percent, while in the same year the freeholders constituted about 35 percent in Dutchess County. Slightly earlier, however, the freeholders constituted six out of every ten white male adults in the County of Ulster.[21]

The situation in the South is equally confusing. For Virginia the Browns have maintained that in Norfolk County, for example, two thirds of the planters held landed property of 200 acres or less and only a fraction of the people living in that county owned big estates. An analysis of the rent roll of 1704/05 suggests that this is only part of the story; for at that early date, in Norfolk County already 16.37 percent of the freeholders with estates over 601 acres owned half of all the patented land. A similar analysis of the figures given by the Browns on the basis of maximum holdings for each group indicates that by 1771 7.9 percent of the freeholders had estates of over 601 acres and controlled one third of the land.[22] In this tidewater county between 1705 and 1771 the process of engrossing land was very slow. In the end slightly more land was held by fewer persons. If this suggests a high degree of stratification it does nevertheless not invalidate the Browns' finding of a high percentage of freeholders in this county. In this respect tidewater Virginia is different from New York. At least to some extent the reverse seems to be true for the backcountry settlements of Virginia, but not for those of North and South Carolina. In Virginia a significant portion of the land was patented to a very small group who leased it to settlers. By the time of the Revolution at least in one county the tenants probably constituted between 40 and 50 percent of the frontier population.[23] In Maryland on the other hand, tenancy seems to have been much higher in the eastern counties than in the western ones, although the situation in this colony seems to be far from clear.[24]

On the whole, the weight of the individual groups within the social structures of the colonies differed from England in three respects. First, within the landowning groups – nobility, gentry, and freeholders in England, big estate owners and freeholders in the colonies – the scale heavily favored the freeholders in the colonies, who controlled up to 70 percent of the land, while in England more than 80 percent was controlled by gentry and nobility. Secondly, the freeholders constituted at least 60 percent of the white colonial male population while in all likelihood the group of big colonial landowners was not greater than 5 percent of the population. Thirdly, while two thirds of the colonial population owned land and other property, only one fifth of the English population enjoyed the same status. Another 20 percent owned other kinds of property. To sum up, the class of the propertyless may have been around 30 percent in the colonies, but it certainly was well above 60 percent in England.[25]

Measuring roughly the relative weight of the component parts within any structure is only the first step towards analyzing the more complex problem of their interdependence. Here we shall concentrate on two aspects: first, social mobility, and secondly, the context within which these relationships between the component parts are placed.

For *England* the inquiry again has to be conducted on two levels. On the one side regional studies indicate remarkably high rates of social mobility within the mercantile and professional world. Prospects for maybe 20 percent of the population were probably not too bad.[26] In a predominantly rural economy, however, the rate of social mobility within the landowning and landworking groups, but most particularly among the tenants, is significant for the whole social structure. Within this group two trends counteracted each other. On the one side the small tenants, who in the sixteenth and seventeenth centuries had declined sharply,[27] were by 1750 losing further ground. On the Gower estates 52.4 percent of the land was leased in farms of less than 100 acres between 1714 and 1720, but between 1759 and 1779 this percentage had declined to 32.8 percent.[28] This land was absorbed by tenants with independent means; thus the gap between substantial tenants and yeomen narrowed. After 1740 poor tenants on the Bedford estates found it difficult to rent a farm, while substantial tenants were courted by the estate stewards. This trend was reinforced by the landlords' increasingly successful attempts to lease new farms for a rack-rent and to shift the burden of the land tax onto the tenant. Both increased the costs of a farm, thus further contributing towards the decline of the small tenant farmer. This type of estate management followed the principle that an estate should produce as much revenue as possible for its owner.[29]

Particularly on larger estates, where the owners harbored political ambitions, this "modern" concept of estate management[30] was overshadowed by that of the estate as a social unit. This concept evolved around three terms: "obligations", "favor", and "acknowledgment". The tenant owed an "obligation", and enjoyed a special relationship with his lord. The lord, on the one hand, was expected to protect the tenant against the hostile world; the tenant in turn "acknowledged" this as a "favor" which put him under an "obligation". This the lord could use at the time, say, of an election. In the Gower and Bedford estates which I have studied closely, the first was managed with "modern" principles, the second and much larger one according to the older concept. On the Bedford estates the economic relationship between landlord and tenant formed just one aspect of the more comprehensive *feudal* framework, which in the eighteenth century still largely defined the relations between the component parts of the English social structure.[31]

The persistence of a feudal framework in England was no doubt the result of the pattern of landownership reinforced by the wage and price structure. Both involved minimal social mobility for the small tenants, the cottagers and the agricultural laborers.[32] Those who cherished higher aspirations ordinarily had but one chance to move up: They had to migrate from the country to the towns or to the English colonies in America and there sell themselves as indentured servants. But were chances indeed better across the Atlantic?

Available evidence about the wage and price structure in the *colonies* indicates that outside the South the situation was more favorable than in England. Daily wages were about three times as high for laborers in the colonies as in England, while the prices of manufactured goods were only double what they were in the mother country.[33] With increasing slave labor and indentured servitude, this was probably of little consequence outside New England. Problems related to cost and productivity of the land and the prices received for products were here of greater importance.

Most immigrants as well as colonists, who moved from old to new settlements, did not expect to rent farms but to acquire freehold land. At least up to the French and Indian War this was easy. One hundred acres of land could be bought for between £ 5 and £ 20 with terms of up to ten years for payment.[34] Since, however, a good deal of the better land in Virginia, New York, and Maryland was patented to wealthy colonists, a sizeable portion of the prospective farmers at least started out by renting a farm. They hoped no doubt to accumulate enough profit for the eventual purchase of a freehold. Realizing such expectations depended to some extent on the kind of lease the tenant had. At least in Virginia and New York long term leases were common up to the French and Indian War. Rent was moderate, certainly much below the rack-rent in England, which ranged between 5s and 15s per acre. Colonial landlords in the South and in New York expected to benefit from the improvements made by the tenants. Thus one function of tenancy was to increase the saleability of the land acquired.[35] Equally important, however, was the custom practiced by Landon Carter, but also in New York, to lease land for a limited time on a share-cropping basis.[36] Tenancy in the colonies was thus apparently a purely economic method to improve the value of land and increase profits as fast as possible. This is a far cry indeed from the English concept of the estate as a social unit.

A tenant's capability to accumulate capital, however, depended on the price he could obtain for his cash crop, on the labor force available to him, and on the productivity of the soil he worked. As the century advanced, all three factors – at least in the older settlements – worked increasingly against the tenant and the small farmer. After the 1750s the Maryland tenant was more likely to accumulate debts than capital. In the middle colonies as well as in New England, similar causes – steeply rising land prices due to the population growth, decreasing productivity of the soil, and ever smaller farming units as a result of partition – sped up migration from old to new settlements. By 1760, the chances of moving up on the social ladder had reverted to a downward social mobility in the older settlements.[37] In the newly settled areas, however, chances of social advancement were still remarkably high, if popular expectations can be credited.[38]

This comparison between England and her American colonies suggests that, in the mother country, social mobility for the large group who owned no land of their own was restricted to the tenants who rented medium to large-sized farms, and to craftsmen, shopkeepers, merchants, and the legal and clerical professions. In America, even the poorest groups with very little or no taxable property had at least a prospect of advancement by moving to new settlements. While social mobility in the older settlements was severely curtailed by the middle of the century, the economic and social situation was still marked by a greater flexibility than in England. Here stability and inflexibility were natural results of the pattern of landownership. In the colonies a different pattern produced fragmentation and flexibility.[39]

II.

Much has been written about the way colonial social structures influenced the political structures. Two contrasting interpretations have been advanced: The one maintains that the wider distribution of property led to a democratic political system;[40] the other, by pointing to the prominence of the wealthy among the political leadership, insists on the importance of social and economic stratification as the shaping force of colonial political structures.[41] Both interpretations should be modified when viewed in an Anglo-American perspective. For the trouble with the first is that by implication it insists that the stake-in-society concept had no validity, while the second presumes that the existence of a wealthy colonial political elite is sufficient evidence that the colonial political structure was basically a replica of that of England.[42] Both rest on the assumption that the Lockean union between landed property and political structure required a deferential society. Neither, however, asks what the consequences might have been if the Lockean premises had been taken seriously by the common small freeholder who then, like the gentleman in England, expected to have a share in the political decision-making process. My hypothesis is that, accepting the implications of Locke's theory, the colonists forthwith proceeded to put into effect the consequences as far as they touched their own *interests*.[43] The result was, of course, a drastic change of the English political structure in America. We will test this hypothesis by discussing briefly local administration and attitudes towards politics, especially in relation to the concept of parliamentary representation.[44]

In *England*, local administration was largely dominated by the gentry and nobility. This was certainly true for counties where, from 1732 onward, the justices of the peace had to have a yearly rental income of £ 100. They were appointed by the lord chancellor upon the recommendation of the lords lieutenants who usually made sure that the majority of the commission of the peace inclined to their political views.[45] This is also true of the other county officials, the treasurer, and the officials connected with the collection of taxes and with law enforcement, with the single exception of the coroners, who were elected by the freeholders of the county.[46]

In most boroughs, the population had a greater share in the administration of their communities. Since the Commonwealth, however, the borough corporations had hardened step by step into oligarchic bodies with ever greater restrictions on the elective process.[47] This trend characterizes as well those boroughs and villages which were administered by the

22

manor courts. For the juries, who nominated the portreeves and bailiffs, were by the eighteenth century usually not picked at random from the roll, but carefully handpicked by the stewards of the manors – at least in those boroughs where the portreeves were the returning officers at parliamentary elections.[48] The vestries in this type of borough suffered a similar fate: Being largely dependent on the cooperation of the lord of the manor, who usually enjoyed the patronage of the living, the vestry was more appointive than elective in character.[49]

In the seventeenth century, all these institutions had to varying degrees been transplanted to *America*. By the middle of the eighteenth century, however, they had undergone considerable changes. Whereas in the southern colonies the administrative bodies of the counties and parishes changed comparatively little, new forms and institutions evolved in the middle and northern colonies. In the townships of New Jersey, New York, and New England, all officers were elected by the inhabitants and freemen assembled in the town meetings. In England this was the job of the common councils and assemblies, who elected officers from amongst their own members only. In England, the communal officers were accountable to a body of which they were members, while in the colonies, the selectmen had to submit their activities to the judgement of the inhabitants in the town meetings.[50] The second major change occurred on the county level. Here the jurisdiction of the county courts was enlarged and their administrative functions were increased, while the justices of the peace as well as the sheriffs, as officers appointed by the governors, retained their close links with the central colonial executives.[51] Outside the South, the very important tax-collection machinery, however, was now put into the hands of elected officials. In New England, tax collection was controlled by the town meetings themselves, in New York, New Jersey, and Pennsylvania, the assessors, collectors, and supervisors for each county were elected annually by the freeholders.[52]

It would, of course, be wrong to infer from these changes in local administration either a democratic control or the absence of local elites. William Parsons, Justice of the Peace at Easton, Pennsylvania, dominated politics in Northamptonshire as much as the Kirkbrides in Bucks County, the River Gods in western Massachusetts, and local leading families in Virginia.[53]

In contrasting the colonies with England, two points stand out: first, the participatory level in local administrative affairs was higher in the colonies than in England; and secondly, the colonial power structures were based on and oriented towards the communities and counties themselves, while in England power structures transcended the county line in the same way as did the gentry and nobility.[54] These different orientations are a direct and very tangible result of the different social structures on both sides of the Atlantic. They are mirrored in the administrative structures of the towns, boroughs, and counties. In England, the administrative system was transregional in character, in America it was regional. In England, at least in rural areas, it was basically concentrated in a few "principal inhabitants", in "gentlemen", in the lord of the manor, in the patron. In the colonies, a large percentage of the population exercised its right to participate in the local administration by electing at least some officials. For both, the reasoning of John Locke is applicable: landed property gave a right to participate in those affairs which affected this property – in this case taxation. This quite literally was the freeholders' "interest".

The term "interest" in the eighteenth century is intimately connected with property and the rights of the inhabitants. Both are part of the fundamental laws and liberties which were much evoked on both sides of the Atlantic. What property owners in England, however, meant by "interest", and what those who owned property in America understood their interest to be, differed sharply. The English notion with its social and political implications is revealed in Robert Butcher's question when, albeit unsuccessfully, recommending his patron's candidates to the gentlemen of Launceston: "Whether the Liberties of the people are not more likely to be safe in the hands of the friends to a parsonage [i. e. personage] who has the greatest landed property in this Kingdom ... or in the hands of a Gentleman who ... may be said to be greatly inferior, both in point of weight in this Kingdom and knowledge of the World, and of mankind in general?"[55] This definition contrasts sharply with Governor Spotswood's report on the election of 1712 in Virginia that "the Mob of this Country, having tryed their Strength in the late Election and finding themselves able to carry whom they please, have generally chosen representatives of their own Class, who as their principal Recommendation have declared their resolution to raise no Tax on the people, let the occasion be what it will".[56] On the one hand we have the report of John Wynne on the election of Tavistock of 1754, pointing out "that the Tavistock people always sounded the name of Bedford without any regard to the names of the Candidates", on the other, the simple entry in the town dockets of Chesterfield township, New Jersey, of "12mo[nth] 6, 1709/10: The freeholders and Inhabetors then meet to Chues [choose] two Men wee did Chues Thomas Scoley and John Waring as Representatives for the Town according as act of Assembly Alows".[57]

In his recommendation Robert Butcher postulated a relationship between landed property and qualification to safeguard the rights and liberties of the people and at least indirectly insinuated a correlation between wealth and knowledge. In 1754 these were good enough reasons for the Duke of Bedford to nominate candidates in at least five boroughs and in one county. This reasoning has to be seen within the feudal context of eighteenth-century English society. In those boroughs where the patrons had an "interest", i. e. considerable landed property, they themselves put up the candidates at elections for the House of Commons. The patrons decided the tickets, organized and often financed the election campaign. The electors voted, when there was an opposition, not for the candidates but for the patron. After the election, electors addressed their grievances and problems not to candidates but to patrons. If someone nevertheless sent a petition to the borough's member in the House of Commons, the latter would invariably forward it to the patron of the borough. This implied, of course, that it was not the representative in the House of Commons, but the patron in the House of Lords (if he was not a Commoner himself), who was the real representative of the borough. In that case, the members of the House of Commons, who were elected by such boroughs, were free of any obligations to their electorates. Burke's concept of virtual representation no doubt had its roots in this aspect of the political structure of England. Without obligations towards their electorates, these members could justly claim to have the interest of the whole nation at heart and not only the particular interests of one borough.[58]

Only those boroughs with well-defined internal power structures and interests, and large trading towns and ports like Bristol and Liverpool, acted as their own patrons and coopted candidates who were then expected to look after the borough's interests in the House. Although such boroughs increased in importance during the eighteenth century, they certainly elected far less than half the members of the House of Commons by 1750.[59]

The report of Governor Spotswood about the Virginia election of 1712 suggests quite a different concept of representation in the colonies: According to him, not a patron but the "mob" selected candidates; and, even worse, these candidates were not selected on the basis of their landed property, but on the basis of an agreement between them and the electorate on issues the latter felt strongly about. Spotswood's complaints, which were echoed by his colleagues then and later, are evidence of a much closer relationship between the colonial constituencies and their representatives.

At least in one respect this was not very surprising, for contrary to English practice, the representatives usually came from the local communities they represented. Before their election, Thomas Scoley and John Waring of Chesterfield had served in communal offices. Jeffrey French and Richard Rigby, the candidates for Newport and Tavistock, on the other hand, had never had any connection to these boroughs before their election.[60]

Of greater import, however, is Spotswood's complaint about the preoccupation of the representatives with the interests of their constituencies to the damage of the public interests: "He is the lover of this Country who in all Controversies justifies the Virginian, and [in] all Dealings is ready to help him to overreach the Forreigner; He is the Patriot who will not yield to whatever the Government proposes, and can remain deaf to all Arguments that are used for the raising of Money".[61] In the light of these complaints, the assemblies' citations of their constituents' interests in controversies with governors and council gain a new significance.[62] By the beginning of the eighteenth century, the colonists in Massachusetts as well as in Pennsylvania, in Virginia as well as in New York, had developed distinct interests which differed from those of the crown or the proprietor.[63] Thus the General Assembly of Massachusetts, in answer to Governor Burnet's demand that they pass a civil list according to his instructions, bluntly told him in August 1728 "[that] the raising Taxes ... will be best answered without establishing a fixed Salary, and ... that we cannot in Faithfulness to the People of this Province in any other way provide for Your Excellency's Support". Very helpfully they described their position in their next message as "our native freedom and declared Judgment".[64]

These colonial "interests" were especially pronounced in questions touching either currency or taxes. They were at the root of the serious political controversies between the assemblies and the royal governors in Massachusetts, in New York, and in New Jersey, where the fight over the civil list held center stage for over a decade, and in North Carolina, where the debates over the royal quitrents paralyzed the colony for more than three years. Governor Clinton of New York unwittingly provided probably the most telling clue to this development when he remarked in 1744 that a rumored English stamp act on the colonies "might have a dangerous Consequence to his Majesty's interest" because "the People in North America are quite strangers to any Duty, but such as they raise themselves".[65]

In the 1730s, it was obvious that the Board of Trade and its legal advisers were becoming increasingly irritated by the colonial political attitudes. In this and in the following decade, the Lords in their various reports to the Privy Council again and again stressed the importance of strengthening the crown's position in the colonies in order to avert further colonial moves towards independence. In 1729, New York's Attorney General Richard Bradley suggested in his *Case Relating to Assemblys in the Plantations aiming at an independency of the Crown* that "No Assembly for the future should transact any affair in their house, without the presence of a Commissioner on behalf of the Crown."[66]

The fears of the Board of Trade that the colonies might cut their ties with Britain reveal a singular failure to understand colonial attitudes. As prisoners of their preconceived notions of English social and political structures, they could but view colonial behavior in the same way as they interpreted developments at home. Had the ordinary Englishman, the few small freeholders, and, above all, the masses of the tenants and laborers ever dreamt of taking their interests into their own hands, the Lords of Trade would have called out "anarchy". In exactly the same way they called out "independence" – a much worse charge then – when they observed similar dreadful happenings in the colonies.

The colonists, on the other side, were reacting to English policies in quite a similar fashion. Convinced that their demands, their attempts to safeguard their interests, were justified by their British birthright, they failed to grasp the significance of the English reaction. For in the eyes of colonial politicians they were but doing what their colleagues did: Meeting supposedly unjustified opposition from the crown and its governors, they resorted to available means to enforce their views. They withheld salaries from governors and other crown officials, they itemized appropriations down to the minutest details, they tagged their favorite clauses to bills the governors could hardly afford to veto.[67]

From the same premises, the colonists and the politicians in England arrived at different conclusions because, by the middle of the eighteenth century, the social and, as a result, the political structures had moved in opposite directions. The same words, when used and spoken in different political and social settings, acquired new meanings, drew forth new consequences. Ideas floating across the Atlantic, the political thought of the Commonwealthmen and of the radical Whigs, worked like firebrands in the colonial setting, while in the England of 1750 they were often nothing more than mere figures of speech.[68] Why?

On the eve of the American Revolution, in England few people owned most of the property, while in the colonies property was widely distributed. While in England few people were involved in the political decision-making process, in the colonies many had a chance to influence the course of events at least at election time. In England, few people were economically and politically independent, in the colonies, however, more than two thirds were freeholders who enjoyed the privilege of acting as *independent* members of the political community.[69] The basic characteristics of the English social and political structure were thus turned upside down in the colonies. Already in the first decades of the eighteenth century this led to serious tensions between the colonial legislatures and the crown. By the middle of the century these tensions changed into deep mistrust between the colonies and England. This mistrust was soon to turn into a constant and profound anxiety for the preservation of the colonial constitutions. Tensions, misrust, and anxiety are only stages in the process of estrangement between the colonies and the mother country, but they do not explain it. For in the final analysis all three stages, and finally the American Revolution itself, are results of the incapability of English and colonial politicians to maintain communications because each side could only evaluate and assess political and social developments on the other side of the Atlantic within a particular value system which was in agreement with colonial or English social and political structures respectively. The colonists rebelled because they wanted to preserve their own structures and value system, which they conceived of as British in the best sense, and which, one might add, were not changed materially in the course of the Revolution.

Notes

* I am grateful to Ms. Patricia Bell, Bedford County Record Office, England, and to Armin and Mechthild Frank, Göttingen, for help in writing this paper.
[1] *JCC*, V, 507. For the political dimensions of this imperial context cf. Hermann Wellenreuther, "'The Wisdom to Secure the Entire Absolute and Immediate Dependency of the Colonies': Überlegungen zum Verhältnis zwischen der Krone und den englischen Kolonien in Nordamerika, 1689–1776", in Hans-Ulrich Wehler, ed., *Zweihundert Jahre Amerikanische Revolution und moderne Revolutionsforschung*, Geschichte und Gesellschaft, special issue 2 (Göttingen, 1976).
[2] In formulating this rather simple definition I have drawn on articles published in Peter Christian Ludz, ed., *Soziologie und Sozialgeschichte*, Kölner Zeitschrift für Soziologie und Sozialpsychologie, special issue 16 (1972); Hans-Ulrich Wehler, ed., *Geschichte und Soziologie,* Neue Wissenschaftliche Bibliothek, 53 (Cologne, 1972); Walter L. Bühl, ed., *Funktion und Struktur: Soziologie vor der Geschichte*, nymphenburger texte zur wissenschaft, 20 (München, 1975). My definition has profited particularly from Henry Lefèbvre, *ib.*, 304–28.
[3] To Lord Orrery, July 9, 1709, quoted by H. T. Dickinson, "Henry St.

John, Wootton Bassett, and the General Election of 1708", *The Wiltshire Archaeological and Natural History Magazine,* LXIV (1969), 107–11, esp. 109–10.

[4] [Jonathan Swift,] *The Conduct of the Allies and of the Late Ministry in Beginning and Carrying on the Present War,* 4th ed. (London, 1711); by 1746 there were clear signs of an increasing cooperation between the monied interest and the large estate owners, cf. "On the Manner of Raising the Supply", *The London Magazine,* [XV] (1746), 631–32, which is confirmed by the correspondence of the steward of the 4th Duke of Bedford, Robert Butcher, Robert Butcher Papers, Bedford Office, London; material from this collection is quoted by permission of the Trustees of the Bedford Estates.

[5] Christopher Clay, "The Price of Freehold Land in the later Seventeenth and Eighteenth Centuries", *EcHR,* XXVII (1974), 173–89, and B. A. Holderness, "The English Land Market in the Eighteenth Century: The Case of Lincolnshire", *ib.,* 557–76; both authors stress the importance of the "bourgeois participants in the land market", cf. Holderness, 566, in their critique of H. J. Habakkuk, "The English Land Market in the Eighteenth Century", in J. S. Bromley and E. H. Kossmann, eds., *Britain and the Netherlands. Papers delivered to the Oxford-Netherlands Historical Conference, 1959* (London, 1960), 154–73; some of the social implications are discussed in D. C. Coleman, "Gentlemen and Players", *EcHR,* XXVI (1973), 92–116. P. D. Groenewegen, "A Study in the History of the Theory of Value, Production and Distribution from 1650 to 1776" (Ph. D. diss., London School of Economics, 1965), maintains that before 1700 the wealth-of-nation concept changed from the balance of trade to the productive powers of land and labor.

[6] I have used the abstract of King's data given in Lee Soltow, "Long-Run Changes in British Income Inequality", *EcHR,* XXI (1968), 17–29, esp. 17–18. A more extensive summary is printed in J. P. Cooper, "The Social Distribution of Land and Men in England, 1436-1700", *ib.,* XX (1967), 419–40, esp. 436–40.

[7] This is certainly true for a substantial number of craftsmen at Tavistock; for Bedfordshire and generally cf. Hermann Wellenreuther, "Land, Gesellschaft und Wirtschaft in England während des Siebenjährigen Krieges", *Historische Zeitschrift,* CCXVII (1974), 593–634, esp. 594 n.

[8] Important other sources of income are discussed by Christopher Clay, "Marriage, Inheritance, and the Rise of Large Estates in England, 1660-1815", *EcHR,* XXI (1968), 503–18, and Ray A. Kelch, *Newcastle. A Duke Without Money: Thomas Pelham Holles, 1693-1768* (London, 1974).

[9] These are the conclusions of F. M. L. Thompson, "The Social Distribution of Landed Property in England since the Sixteenth Century", *EcHR,* XIX (1966), 505–17, as revised by Cooper, "Social Distribution of Land" (cf. n. 6) and Holderness, "English Land Market" (cf. n. 5).

[10] The higher income is that of the 4th Duke of Bedford for the year 1751 without consideration of the expenses for the estate and without considering the substantial profits from the sale of wood as given in the rentals in the Russell Papers, Bedford and Devon County Record Offices; materials from these collections are quoted by permission of the Trustees of the Bedford Estates. The small income is that of George W. Bewes of Newport, Cornwall, who sold his estate to Bedford in 1753.

[11] Sir Lewis Namier and John Brooke, *The History of Parliament. I: The*

House of Commons 1754-1790 (London, 1964), I; cf. John Cannon, *Parliamentary Reform,* 1640-1832 (Cambridge, 1973), 29-33.

[12] E. g. Ralph J. Robson, *The Oxfordshire Election of 1754: A Study in the Interplay of City, County, and University Politics,* Oxford Historical Series, British Series (Oxford, 1949).

[13] Phyllis Deane and W. A. Cole, *British Economic Growth, 1688-1959: Trends and Structure* (Cambridge, 1964), 6.

[14] This figure represents the assumed size of a family in the eighteenth century, cf. Richard Wall, "Mean Household Size in England from Printed Sources", in Peter Laslett and Richard Wall, eds., *Household and Family in Past Time* (Cambridge, 1972), 159-203.

[15] I do not know any reliable estimates of the number or ratio of tenants to the whole population. In the light of King's figures and the discussion of Thompson, "Social Distribution of Landed Property" (cf. n. 9), my estimate seems justified. The figure of 40 percent is too low when tenants in urban areas are included. Thus the Duke of Bedford owned 70 percent of the houses in Tavistock, [John Wynne,] "Fieldbook of Tavistock, c. 1753", T 1258M/M I (187), Russell Papers, Devon County Record Office. For London cf. Donald J. Olsen, *Town Planning in London: The Eighteenth and Nineteenth Centuries,* Yale Historical Publications, Miscellany 80 (New Haven, Conn., 1964).

[16] This summary neglects the merchants, shopkeepers, and craftsmen which with one exception will be the rule for the rest of this paper. At least with reference to the figures given by King it will be possible, however, to construct corrected estimates for the whole population.

[17] Cf. Leonard Woods Labaree, *Royal Government in America: A Study of the British Colonial System before 1783* (New Haven, Conn., 1930, repr. New York, 1958), ch. IV; one index for this colonial development are the descriptions by colonial governors of the social positions and economic status of persons recommended for appointment to the councils, cf. Governor William Burnet to Lords of Trade, New York, June 17, 1722, and Governor George Clinton to the same, New York, Nov. 18, 1743, E. B. O'Callaghan, ed., *Documents Relative to the Colonial History of the State of New York* (Albany, N. Y., 1853-87), V, 649, VI, 248-49; James High, "The Origins of Maryland's Middle Class in the Colonial Aristocratic Pattern", *Maryland Historical Magazine,* LVII (1962), 334-45; Philip M. Brown, "Early Indian Trade in the Development of South Carolina: Politics, Economics, and Social Mobility during the Proprietary Period, 1670-1719", *South Carolina Historical Magazine,* LXXVI (1975), 118-28, esp. 118-26; Hermann Wellenreuther, *Glaube und Politik in Pennsylvania, 1681-1776: Die Wandlungen der Obrigkeitsdoktrin und des Peace Testimony der Quäker,* Kölner Historische Abhandlungen, ed. Theodor Schieffer, 20 (Cologne, 1972), 184-87, 442-47, and Gary B. Nash, "The Free Society of Traders and the Early Politics of Pennsylvania", *PMHB,* LXXXIX (1965), 147-73. In South Carolina as well as in Pennsylvania these merchants secured early sizeable land-grants. Land-grants to New York Indian traders early became a political issue, Thomas Elliot Norton, *The Fur Trade in Colonial New York, 1686-1776* (Madison, Wis., 1974), ch. 6, and Patricia U. Bonomi, *A Factious People: Politics and Society in Colonial New York* (New York, 1971), 60-68.

[18] Published by Thomas J. Wertenbaker, *The Planters of Colonial Virginia* (New York, 1959), 183-247.

[19] David Grayson Allen, "The Zuckerman Thesis and the Process of Legal Rationalization in Provincial Massachusetts", *WMQ*, 3rd Ser., XXIX (1972), 443–60, esp. 450. In the large towns the percentage of the propertyless seems to have been larger than in rural areas, cf. James A. Henretta, "Economic Development and Social Structure in Colonial Boston", *ib.*, XXII (1965), 75–92; Peter J. Parker, "Rich and Poor in Philadelphia, 1709", *PMHB*, XCIX (1975), 3–19. Both studies are based on tax assessment lists and measure the distribution of certain types of property only. Jackson Turner Main has pointed out that a considerable number of those with no property were sons of taxpayers.

[20] Since no county-wide tax assessment list analysis is available, more detailed statements are impossible. The analysis of tax assessment lists of individual townships indicates considerable stratification particularly in the older townships, cf. Kenneth Lockridge, "Land, Population and the Evolution of New England Society 1630–1790", *Past & Present*, XXXIX (Apr. 1968), 62–80. Lockridge's conclusions are based on too few case studies and must, therefore, be treated with great caution; of more value are *id., A New England Town: The First Hundred Years, Dedham, Massachusetts, 1636–1736* (New York, 1970); Edward M. Cook, Jr., "Social Behavior and Changing Values in Dedham, Massachusetts, 1700 to 1775", *WMQ*, 3rd Ser., XXVII (1970), 546–80; Philip J. Greven, *Four Generations: Population, Land, and Family in Colonial Andover, Massachusetts* (Ithaca, N. Y., 1970); J. M. Bumsted, "Religion, Finance, and Democracy in Massachusetts: The Town of Norton as a Case Study", *JAH*, LVII (1970–71), 817–31. Chester and Lancaster Counties are the subject of James T. Lemon, *The Best Poor Man's Country: A Geographical Study of Early Southeastern Pennsylvania* (Baltimore, Md., 1972), ch. 1, 2; some of Lemon's results for western Pennsylvania are comparable with those of Charles S. Grant, *Democracy in the Connecticut Frontier Town of Kent*, Columbia Studies in the Social Sciences, 601 (New York, 1961); urbanization in Pennsylvania is analyzed by James T. Lemon, "Urbanization and the Development of Eighteenth-Century Southeastern Pennsylvania and Adjacent Delaware", *WMQ*, 3rd Ser., XXIV (1967), 501–42; *id.*, and Gary B. Nash, "The Distribution of Wealth in Eighteenth-Century America. A Century of Change in Chester County, Pennsylvania, 1693–1802", *JSH*, II (1968–69), 1–24, have analyzed tax assessment lists of one of Pennsylvania's oldest counties.

[21] Sung Bok Kim, "A New Look at the Great Landlords of Eighteenth-Century New York", *WMQ*, 3rd Ser., XXVII (1970), 581–614; Bonomi, *Factious People* (cf. n. 17), ch. VI; the percentages are computed from tables given in E. B. O'Callaghan, ed., *The Documentary History of the State of New York* (Albany, N. Y., 1849–51), I, 241–246, 471 (Albany City and County); 472, IV, 132–34 (Suffolk County); I, 472, IV, 134–36 (Dutchess County); I, 471 (census of 1731), III 586–87. My assessment differs considerably from that of Staughton Lynd, *Anti-Federalism in Dutchess County, New York: A Study of Democracy and Class Conflict in the Revolutionary Era* (Chicago, Ill., 1962), 41–42. Lynd maintained that the percentage of freeholders in Dutchess County was "75 %o in 1713–1714, 11 %o in 1740–46, and 38 %o in 1771–75" which according to him is clear evidence that the participatory role of the population in the political decision-making process was low in this county. In computing his percentages, Lynd ignored the limitation of the New York census which lists "adult white males over 16 years", and not those of 21 years. Thus the corrected percentage for 1771–75 would be 48.01 percent in this

county, where large estates were more numerous than in other parts of the colony. In the election of 1768 the candidates of the wealthiest landowner of the county, Henry Beekmans, were resoundingly defeated by the freeholders!

[22] Robert E. and B. Katherine Brown, *Virginia 1705-1786: Democracy or Aristocracy?* (East Lansing, Mich., 1964), 13; Wertenbaker, *Planters* (cf. n. 18), 201-04.

[23] Willard F. Bliss, "The Rise of Tenancy in Virginia", *Virginia Magazine of History and Biography*, LVIII (1950), 427-41; Harry Roy Merrens, *Colonial North Carolina in the Eighteenth Century: A Study in Historical Geography* (Chapel Hill, N. C., 1964), 25-27, 140; Richard Maxwell Brown, *The South Carolina Regulators* (Cambridge, Mass., 1963), 15. Jackson T. Main has suggested that tenancy was less important in the southern colonies than I assume.

[24] David Curtis Skaggs, *Roots of Maryland Democracy, 1753-1776,* Contributions in American History, 30 (Westport, Conn., 1973), ch. 3, 4, presents a more negative picture of Maryland's distribution of property than can be found for other colonies. Generally less than half of the white male population seem to have owned land. Skaggs' findings contrast with the brighter description of Paul G. E. Clemens, "From Tobacco to Grain: Economic Development on Maryland's Eastern Shore, 1660-1750" (Ph. D. diss., Rutgers University, New Brunswick, N. J., 1974).

[25] There are insufficient data to be more specific about stratification within the large group of colonial freeholders. Skaggs, *Roots of Maryland Democracy* (cf. n. 24), 43, table 6, suggests that about 60 percent of the landowners held less than 249 acres; in Prince William County, Va., 55.5 percent of the landowners held less than 300 acres in 1754, Brown and Brown, *Virginia 1705-1786* (cf. n. 22), 14, table B. The percentages for the other groups support the impression that the smallest landowners and the big ones with holdings over 1,000 acres represented tiny fractions of the colonial societies. Stratification within the freeholders was probably of less importance than the gap between freeholders and those who owned no property. This, in turn, would suggest, that assessments of the functioning of the colonial political systems based on the assumption of marked stratification within the colonial societies have to be viewed with considerable scepticism, cf., too, n. 21.

[26] Detailed studies indicate a trend similar to that within the group of tenants. In hard times the small craftsmen suffered much more than the well-off entrepreneurs, cf. Julia de Lacy Mann, *The Cloth Industry in the West of England from 1640 to 1880* (Oxford, 1971); D. B. Huffer, "The Economic Development of Wolverhampton, 1750-1850" (M. A. thesis, University of London, 1957), 163 ff.; Marie B. Rowlands, "Industry and Social Change in Staffordshire 1660-1760. A Study of the Probate and Other Records of Tradesmen", Lichfield and South Staffordshire Archaeological and Historical Society, *Transactions, 1967-1968* (1968), 37-58, found impressive evidence for upwards mobility.

[27] Margaret Spufford, *Contrasting Communities: English Villagers in the Sixteenth and Seventeenth Centuries* (Cambridge, 1974), 3-167.

[28] J. R. Wordie, "Social Change on the Leveson-Gower Estates, 1714-1832", *EcHR*, XXVII (1974), 593-609, esp. 596. In the Trentham agency of the same estate the overall number of tenants increased between 1730 and 1770 from 82 to 103, that of the small tenants climbed from 41 to 45. But the number of cottagers, who are not included in the figure of all tenants mentioned above,

jumped from 67 to 123, D 593/G/2/2/8, D 593/G/2/4/20, Sutherland Papers Stafford County Record Office; material from this collection is quoted by the permission of the Rt. Hon. the Countess of Sutherland.

[29] My statements are based on an intensive analysis of the Gower and Bedford estates. Modern management principles were mostly introduced in small and medium sized estates at first, cf. B. A. Holderness, "The Agricultural Activities of the Massingberds of South Ormsby, Lincolnshire, 1638–c.1750", *Midland History*, I, No. 3 (Spring 1972), 15–25; R. A. C. Parker, *Coke of Norfolk: A Financial and Agricultural Study, 1707–1842* (Oxford, 1975), 53–57 *et passim*. "Rack-rent" represents the actual yearly rental value of an object.

[30] Cf. Wellenreuther, "Land" (cf. n. 7), 602 n.

[31] Cf. Peter Laslett, *The World We Have Lost*, 2nd ed. (London, 1971), chap. 3, and 186–88; G. E. Mingay, *English Landed Society in the Eighteenth Century*, Studies in Social History, ed. Harold Perkin (London, 1963), 14–15. Mingay displays here like other students of English rural society in the 18th century a remarkable disregard for the social consequences of economic practices and methods which he, like Parker, *Coke of Norfolk* (cf. n. 29), views from the point of view of efficiency and management, cf. in this context G. E. Mingay, "The Large Estate in Eighteenth-Century England", *First International Conference of Economic History, Stockholm 1960* (Paris, 1960), 367–83, and the different interpretation of V. M. Lavrovsky, "The Great Estate in England from the Sixteenth to the Eighteenth Centuries", *ib.*, 353–65. The term "feudal" does here not only describe the legal relationship between lord and tenant but likewise the mutual bond which obliged both to *serve* each other within the framework of a deferential hierarchy, cf. Heide Wunder, ed., *Feudalismus*, nymphenburger texte zur wissenschaft, 17 (München, 1974). Cf. n. 39 below.

[32] Mingay, *English Landed Society* (cf. n. 31), 253. The concept of the estate as a social unit provided more protection for the lowest groups.

[33] E. W. Gilboy, *Wages in Eighteenth-Century England*, Harvard Economic Studies, 45 (Cambridge, Mass., 1934); Wellenreuther, "Land" (cf. n. 7), 604 n., 625–26; Samuel McKee, *Labor in Colonial New York*, Empire State Historical Publications, 38 (New York, 1935, repr. Port Washington, N. Y. [1965]); Robert E. Brown, *Middle-Class Democracy and the Revolution in Massachusetts, 1691–1780* (Ithaca, N. Y., 1955), 11–13; Cadwallader Colden's report of 1723, in O'Callaghan, ed., *Documentary History of the State of New York* (cf. n. 21) I, 489; R. W. Kelsey, ed., "An Early Description of Pennsylvania: Letter of Christopher Sower, Written in 1724", *PMHB*, XLV (1921), 243–54, esp. 251. Prices: E. T. Rogers, *History of Agriculture and Prices in England, 1259–1793* (Oxford, 1866–1902), VII; Lord Beveridge *et al.*, *Prices and Wages in England from the Twelfth to the Nineteenth Century* (London, 1939); Arthur Harrison Cole, *Wholesale Commodity Prices in the United States, 1700–1861* (Cambridge, Mass., 1938, repr. New York, 1969).

[34] Cf. Cadwallader Colden's report on the "State of the Land in the Province of New York in 1732", in O'Callaghan, ed., *Documentary History of the State of New York* (cf. n. 21), I, 249–55, esp. 253; Merrens, *Colonial North Carolina* (cf. n. 23), 61–62; Alfred P. James, *The Ohio Company: Its Inner History* ([Pittsburgh,] 1959), 40–41; Lemon, *Best Poor Man's Country* (cf. n. 20), 67–69. In England a hundred acres of the worst kind of land could certainly not be bought for less than £ 75 at 1s per acre at 15 years' purchase. Another important distinction between England and her colonies is the

absence (except for New York) of copyholds in the latter. While copyholders were denied the right to vote, tenants with a lease for 21 years enjoyed the franchise.

[35] Bliss, "Rise of Tenancy" (cf. n. 23), 427–41; Richard Beale Davis, ed., *William Fitzhugh and His Chesapeake World, 1676–1701: The Fitzhugh Letters and Other Documents,* Virginia Historical Society Documents, III (Chapel Hill, N. C., 1963), 189–90, 248–50.

[36] Jack P. Greene, ed., *The Diary of Colonel Landon Carter of Sabine Hall, 1752–1778, ib.,* IV–V (Charlottesville, Va., 1965), I, 258, 277, 302, 309; II, 708, 855, 878, 1035–36; Bonomi, *Factious People* (cf. n. 17), 191–95; this lease was in use also in Maryland, cf. Edward C. Papenfuse, Jr., "Planter Behavior and Economic Opportunity in a Staple Economy", *Agricultural History,* XLVI (1972), 297–311.

[37] Cf. Papenfuse, Jr., "Planter Behavior" (cf. n. 36); Skaggs, *Roots of Maryland Democracy* (cf. n. 24), 39–53, but for more positive assessments Clemens, "From Tobacco to Grain" (cf. n. 24), and Benjamin Franklin, "Observations Concerning the Increase of Mankind, Peopling of Countries, &c.", in Leonard W. Labaree *et al.,* eds., *The Papers of Benjamin Franklin* (New Haven, Conn., 1959–), IV, 227–234, esp. 228. For New England cf. n. 20 above, and the discussion of the rate of migration in Massachusetts by Douglas Lamar Jones, "The Strolling Poor: Transiency in Eighteenth-Century Massachusetts", *JSH,* VIII (1974–75), 28–54, esp. 29–32. The interdependence of land price, price of staple products and profitability of farming is the subject of Papenfuse, Jr., "Planter Behavior" (cf. n. 36), of Louis De Vorsey, Jr., ed., *De Brahm's Report of the General Survey in the Southern District of North America,* [South Carolina] Tricentennial Edition, 3 (Columbia, S. C., 1971), 162, and of Merrens, *Colonial North Carolina* (cf. n. 23), 63–65.

[38] Grant, *Kent* (cf. n. 20), 34–35; "Report of Governor William Tryon on the State of the Province of New York, 1774", in O'Callaghan, ed., *Documentary History of the State of New York* (cf. n. 21), I, 503–20, esp. 517.

[39] It is obvious that my conclusions directly contradict those reached by Kenneth A. Lockridge, "Social Change and the Meaning of the American Revolution", *JSH,* VI (1972–73), 403–39. Lockridge does not seem to be well informed about English social structure and seems to rely too heavily on the development in the eastern New England townships where, as elsewhere, marked social tensions characterize only towns with a population of over 2,500 inhabitants. But only 6 percent of the colonial population lived in such urban areas! Lockridge's second example is Maryland, where again the evidence is less than clear (cf. above n. 37). Neither his description nor his conclusions are applicable to New York, New Jersey, Pennsylvania, Virginia, the Carolinas, or Georgia. Similar objections apply to Rowland Berthoff and John M. Murrin, "Feudalism, Communalism, and the Yeoman Freeholder: The American Revolution Considered as a Social Accident", in Stephen G. Kurtz and James H. Hutson, eds., *Essays on the American Revolution* (Chapel Hill, N. C., and New York, 1973), 256–88. The authors argue that a "feudal revival" (p. 264) largely influenced political and social developments in Maryland, Pennsylvania, South Carolina, Virginia, New Jersey, and New York (pp. 264–74); this "feudal revival" the authors pit against the colonial and revolutionary "doctrine of equality" (p. 282), which triumphed during the Revolution destroying in its course the "feudal revival" (p. 272). This argument is less than convincing: (a) increased prof-

its of allegedly feudal lords like Carteret, Fairfax, Baltimore, and Penn (pp. 265–68) are not as such indicators of a "feudal revival" but results of territorial expansion with resulting remarkable increases in the number of people who bought lands and paid quitrents; (b) the political controversies in Maryland and Pennsylvania (pp. 268–69) are not the result of such "feudal revivals" but of attacks by the legislatures of both colonies on the feudal overlordships of Baltimore and Penn. These disputes originated in Maryland in the debate over the proprietary reforms of 1733 (cf. Charles Albro Barker, *The Background of the Revolution in Maryland*, Yale Historical Publications, Miscellany 37 [New Haven, Conn., 1940, repr. 1967], chap. VII), and in Pennsylvania in the controversy over the payment of expenses for conferences with Indian tribes (cf. Wellenreuther, *Glaube und Politik in Pennsylvania* [cf. n. 17], 167 n., 222–24). In both instances Berthoff and Murrin simply reverse the relationship between cause and effects. Only two colonies, New Jersey and New York, saw tendencies towards a "feudal revival". But such tendencies in two out of twelve colonies do not seem to warrant the sweeping generalizations and hypotheses the authors advance.

[40] Brown, *Middle-Class Democracy* (cf. n. 33); Brown and Brown, *Virginia 1705–1786* (cf. n. 22); the debate on Massachusetts has been summed up by James A. Thorpe, "Colonial Suffrage in Massachusetts: An Essay Review", *Essex Institute Historical Collections*, CVI (1970), 169–81, and Skaggs, *Roots of Maryland Democracy* (cf. n. 24), 4–9.

[41] There is no doubt that politicians tended to be wealthy and of old stock, cf. Robert Zemsky, *Merchants, Farmers, and River Gods: An Essay on Eighteenth-Century American Politics* (Boston, 1971), ch. II; Bonomi, *Factious People* (cf. n. 17), ch. III, VI; Wellenreuther, *Glaube und Politik in Pennsylvania* (cf. n. 17), 169–193; Jack P. Greene, "Foundations of Political Power in the Virginia House of Burgesses, 1720–1776", *WMQ*, 3rd Ser., XVI (1959), 485–506. But cf. above n. 21 and n. 25.

[42] So James A. Henretta, *The Evolution of American Society, 1700–1815: An Interdisciplinary Analysis,* Civilization and Society. Studies in Social, Economic and Cultural History, ed. Theodore K. Raab (Lexington, Mass., 1973), ch. III, esp. 93–95, and earlier J. R. Pole, "Historians and the Problem of Early American Democracy", *AHR*, LXVII (1961–62), 626–46, esp. 634–38. Pole's discussion poses a more fundamental problem: How far can literary evidence produced by one group of the society, e. g. the colonial upper class, be taken as evidence of societal attitudes and behavior of other groups of the same society? Could it not be argued that this kind of evidence says very little about the other groups but a lot about the social aspirations and views of the group which produced such literary evidence?

[43] To my knowledge the proposal to analyze the colonial political structure from the point of view of "interest" was first advanced by Michael G. Kammen, *Empire and Interest: The American Colonies and the Politics of Mercantilism* (Philadelphia, 1970), 8–14 *et passim,* and by Joseph Albert Ernst, "Ideology and the Political Economy of Revolution", *Canadian Review of American Studies*, IV, No. 2 (Fall 1973), 137–48. Michael Kammen drew my attention to this article. The function of "interest" in the colonial legislative process is the subject of J. R. Pole, *Political Representation in England and the Origins of the American Republic* (London, 1966), ch. II. *et passim.* Richard Buel, Jr. considers John Locke's role for colonial political thought grossly exaggerated. I

have three reasons for my position: 1. There is considerable evidence that Locke was known and cited by colonists, cf. Lawrence H. Leder, *Liberty and Authority: Early American Political Ideology, 1689–1763* (Chicago, Ill., 1968), 38–45; Alice M. Baldwin, *The New England Clergy and the American Revolution* (New York, 1958, 1st ed. 1928), ch. III; e. g. William Livingston *et al.*, *The Independent Reflector,* ed. Milton M. Klein (Cambridge, Mass., 1963), esp. Nos. IV, XXXIII, XXXVI–XXXIX. 2. There is considerable evidence that Locke's ideas were popularized through the London magazines which were quite regularly read in the colonies and the political writings of Whigs, cf. e. g. [John Trenchard and Thomas Gordon,] *Cato's Letters: Or, Essays on Liberty, Civil and Religious, and other Important Subjects,* 6th ed. (London, 1755), Nos. 69, 84, and Bernard Bailyn, *The Ideological Origins of the American Revolution* (Cambridge, Mass., 1967), *passim.* 3. While it is quite true, as J. G. A. Pocock, "Machiavelli, Harrington, and English Political Ideologies in the Eighteenth Century", *WMQ*, 3rd Ser., XXII (1965), 549–83, pointed out, that James Harrington was more important for the English 18th-century notion of property and power (but not for the colonial notion which Pocock does not discuss in this article!), it is of equal importance that contemporaries associated the popularized notion most readily with Locke, cf. Paschal Larkin, *Property in the Eighteenth Century with Special Reference to England and Locke* (1st ed. 1930, repr. New York, 1969), 90–125.

[44] In developing my hypothesis I have profited from Bernard Bailyn, "Political Experience and Enlightenment Ideas in Eighteenth-Century America", *AHR,* LXVII (1961–62), 339–51; Pole, *Political Representation* (cf. n. 43), 341–44, 503–39; Gordon S. Wood, "Rhetoric and Reality in the American Revolution", *WMQ,* 3rd Ser., XXIII (1966), 3–32; Jack P. Greene, "An Uneasy Connection: An Analysis of the Preconditions of the American Revolution", in Kurtz and Hutson, eds., *Essays* (cf. n. 39), 32–80. Each of these authors points to important colonial developments which set the colonies apart from England. Pole, however, is the most successful in integrating specific colonial interests and the colonial concept of representation into a stimulating interpretation of the American Revolution. Likewise all these authors are to a varying degree aware of the colonists' rather curious perception of English politics. And all authors list the weaknesses in the imperial administration of the colonies. But none of them pits the concrete social and political structure of England on the one side and of her colonies on the other against each other as a starting point for interpreting political behavior in its individual social context.

[45] Bertram Osborne, *Justices of the Peace 1361–1848: A History of the Justices of the Peace for the Counties of England* (Shaftesbury, 1960), 164; Ester Meir, *Local Government in Gloucestershire, 1775–1800,* Bristol and Gloucestershire Archaeological Society, *Publications,* Records Section, 8 (Gateshead, 1969), 41–69. The political importance of the justices of the peace in connection with the Broad Bottom Government is discussed in Add. Mss. 35,602, fol. 34, 46, 50, Hardwicke Papers, British Museum.

[46] W. R. Ward, *The English Land Tax in the Eighteenth Century,* Oxford Historical Series. British Series (Oxford, 1953); *id.,* "The Administration of the Window and Assessed Taxes, 1696–1798", *English Historical Review,* LXVII (1952), 522–42. Correspondence relating to the election of Coroners Richard Ward and Dixie Gregory of Bedfordshire is in VII/27/24, 68, 81, Robert Butcher Papers, Bedford County Record Office.

[47] This is based on my study of Launceston, Newport, Camelford (all Cornwall), Okehampton, Tavistock (all Devonshire), Bedford (Bedfordshire), Lichfield and Newcastle-under-Lyme (all Staffordshire). Cf. H. A. Merewether and A. J. Stephens, *The History of the Boroughs and Municipal Corporations of the United Kingdom from the Earliest Times to the Present Time* (1st ed. 1835, repr. Brighton, 1972).

[48] Jarvis Knight to Robert Butcher, Tavistock, Sept. 8, 1741, L 1258/A/Devon Letters/Bdle. 4, and further correspondence relating to the selection of the juries and portreeves *ib.*, Bundles 3, 6a, Russell Papers, Devon County Record Office; cf., too, "Manor of Sheriffhales, Court Roll, 1747–1748, 1759," D 593/ J/17/3/8, Sutherland Papers, Stafford County Record Office. A returning officer had two functions in elections: He received the writ of election, supervised the election itself which included examination of the voters' qualifications, and returned the writ to the high sheriff.

[49] W. E. Tate, *The Parish Chest: A Study of the Records of Parochial Administration in England,* 3rd ed. (Cambridge, 1969), 13-25. The term "living" is used here in the sense of a "benefice".

[50] Michael Zuckerman, *Peaceable Kingdoms: New England Towns in the Eighteenth Century* (New York, 1970), but cf. the critique of Allen, "Zuckerman Thesis" (cf. n. 19); Lockridge, *A New England Town* (cf. n. 20), ch. 7.

[51] George Lee Haskins, *Law and Authority in Early Massachusetts: A Study in Tradition and Design* (New York, 1960), 176–77; Paul M. McCain, *The County Court in North Carolina before 1750,* Historical Papers of the Trinity College Historical Society, Ser. 31 (Durham, N. C., 1954); [Maryland Province,] *A Compleat Collection of the Laws of Maryland* (Annapolis, 1727), 97 (Evans No. 2897); George Webb, *The Office and Authority of a Justice of the Peace. And also the Duty of Sheriffs, Coroners, Church Wardens, Surveyors of Highways, Constables, and Officers of Militia* (Williamsburg, Va., 1736), 106 (Evans No. 4101); the exception to the rule is New York, cf. Julius Goebel, Jr. and T. Raymond Naughton, *Law Enforcement in Colonial New York: A Study in Criminal Procedure* (New York, 1944). The power and function of sheriffs in Pennsylvania is described in Labaree *et al.,* eds., *Papers of Benjamin Franklin* (cf. n. 37), IV, 410–11. Cf. Edward Channing, *Town and County Government in the English Colonies of North America,* Johns Hopkins University Studies in Historical and Political Science, 2nd Ser., 10 (Baltimore, Md., 1884), 47.

[52] In the South the sheriffs collected the taxes with the help of the constables, cf. [Maryland,] *Laws of Maryland* (cf. n. 51), 16-23, 99-100; John Mercer, *An Exact Abridgment of All the Public Acts of Assembly of Virginia in Force and Use* (Williamsburg, Va., 1737), 156 (Evans No. 4204); Marvin L. Michael Kay, "The Payment of Provincial and Local Taxes in North Carolina, 1748-1771", *WMQ,* 3rd Ser., XXVI (1969), 218–40; [New York Province,] *Acts of Assembly Passed in the Province of New-York, from 1691 to 1725. Examined and Compared with the Originals in the Secretary's Office* (New York, 1726), 6-7 (Evans No. 2785); parish levies were, however, collected by the constables, *ib.,* 24; E. R. L. Gould, "Local Self-Government in Pennsylvania", *PMHB,* VI (1882), 156–173, esp. 164–65, and "Answers to Criticisms of the Supply Bill" [March 21, 1757], in Labaree *et al.,* eds., *Papers of Benjamin Franklin* (cf. n. 37), VII, 149–50; in New York as well as in Pennsylvania the poor rate was under the care of the county courts. Donald L. Kemmerer, *Path to*

Freedom: The Struggle for Self-Government in Colonial New Jersey, 1703–1776 (Princeton, N. J., 1940), 45–46.

[53] John W. Jordan, "William Parsons, Surveyor General, and Founder of Easton, Pennsylvania", *PMHB*, XXXIII (1909), 340–46, and William Parsons' description of the power structure in Northamptonshire, Labaree *et al.*, eds., *Papers of Benjamin Franklin* (cf. n. 37), IV, 410–11. Wellenreuther, *Glaube und Politik in Pennsylvania* (cf. n. 17), 190–92; Zemsky, *Merchants, Farmers and River Gods* (cf. n. 41), *passim;* Dirk Hoerder, *Society and Government 1760–1780: The Power Structure in Massachusetts Townships* (Berlin, 1972); Charles S. Sydnor, *Gentlemen Freeholders: Political Practices in Washington's Virginia* (Chapel Hill, N. C., 1952).

[54] In some colonies, notably in Virginia, Maryland and South Carolina, a small group of wealthy colonial politicians by the middle of the 18th century had developed "interests" in more than one county. Hans-Christoph Schröder has pointed out that this assessment somewhat neglects the role played by the local gentry in England. The function of this gentry is, however, severely circumscribed by the patronage powers and the right of appointment usually enjoyed by the leading families of the county.

[55] Robert Butcher to ?John Carpenter, Bath, Apr. 10, 1754, L 1258/Election Add./Launceston/Bdle. 1, Russell Papers, Devon County Record Office.

[56] Governor Spotswood to the Board of Trade, Oct. 15, 1712, R. A. Brock, ed., *The Official Letters of Alexander Spotswood, Lieutenant-Governor of the Colony of Virginia, 1710–1722*, Virgina Historical Society, *Collections*, N. S. I–II (Richmond, Va., 1882–85), II, 1–2.

[57] John Wynne to Robert Butcher, Tavistock, Apr. 28, 1754, L 1258/LP/Bdle. 32, Russell Papers, Devon County Record Office. Carlos E. Godfrey, ed., "Town Dockets of Chesterfield Township, Burlington County, New Jersey, Dec. 15, 1692 to Dec. 2, 1712", *PMHB*, XXXV (1911), 211–22, esp. 218.

[58] I have here summarized some findings to be published in my forthcoming study on English political structure. John Brooke has pointed out that the rejection of Butcher's offer to the gentlemen of Launceston as well as the defeat of Bedford's candidates in Newport would seem to indicate that my distinction between the patron and the electorates would not only fit the wealthiest members of the nobility. This point is substantiated by an analysis of the function of Sir Humphrey Morrice in Newport and Launceston, and the Phillips family in Camelford, to cite just two examples. As I shall show elsewhere, patronage functions have to be seen within the context of and in relation to the social structure of the respective borough.

[59] Cf. e. g. W. E. Minchinton, ed., *Politics and the Port of Bristol in the Eighteenth Century: The Petitions of the Society of Merchant Venturers, 1698–1803*, Bristol Record Society, *Publications*, XXIII, ed. D. Douglas (Bristol, 1963); K. A. Macmahon, ed., *Beverley Corporation Minute Books (1707–1835)*, The Yorkshire Archaeological Society, *Record Series* CXXII for the Year 1956 (London, 1958), xxii, 2–3, 5–6, 12, 33, 36, 38, *et passim*. Beverley was, like Bedford, a small borough, which had a well-defined power structure of its own. According to Namier and Brooke, *House of Commons, 1754–1790* (cf. n. 11), I, there were 101 boroughs with an electorate with less than 199 voters, 41 boroughs with less than 499 voters and 53 boroughs with more than 500 voters. The first two groups elected 57 percent of all members of the House of Commons. From the point of view of power structure versus domination by a polit-

ical patron two other criteria are important: the type of franchise and the economic structure of the borough.

[60] Cf. "Memorandum of some Grounds and Reasons to Hope that His Majesty will be Graciously Pleased to Grant his Royal Assent to the Act for Frequent Election of Representatives [1738]", in O'Callaghan, ed., *Documentary History of the State of New York* (cf. n. 21), IV, 159–63. Bruce E. Steiner, "Anglican Officeholding in Pre-Revolutionary Connecticut: The Parameters of New England Community", *WMQ*, 3rd Ser., XXXI (1974), 369–406, esp. 376 for statistical data on Anglican delegates to the General Court who before had held offices within their townships.

[61] Governor Spotswood to the Board of Trade, Dec., 29, 1713, Brock, ed., *Official Letters of Spotswood* (cf. n. 56), II, 50; Governor Gabriel Johnston to the same, Edenton, Oct. 15, 1736, William L. Saunders, ed., *Colonial Records of North Carolina, IV: 1734–1752* (Raleigh, N. C., 1886), 173–78, esp. 178.

[62] Cf. esp. John C. Rainbolt, "The Alteration in the Relationship between Leadership and Constituents in Virginia, 1660 to 1720", *WMQ*, 3rd Ser., XXVII (1970), 411–34; Wellenreuther, "Wisdom to Secure" (cf. n. 1).

[63] Cf. e. g. "Report of the Committee of Propositions and Grievances of North Carolina Assembly to Governor G. Johnston, Oct. 7, 1736, and the Governor's Answer Thereto", in Saunders, ed., *Colonial Records of North Carolina* (cf. n. 61), IV, 236–39.

[64] *Journals of the House of Representatives of Massachusetts*, vol. VIII: *1727–1729* ([Boston,] 1927), 269, 304. For a statistical analysis of legislation in Massachusetts and New York relating to the governors' function in the administration of provincial finances and military affairs cf. Wellenreuther, "Wisdom to Secure" (cf. n. 1).

[65] Governor George Clinton to Duke of Newcastle, Nov. 13, 1744, in O'Callaghan, ed., *Documents Relative to the Colonial History of the State of New York* (cf. n. 17), VI, 268–69.

[66] *Ib.*, V, 901–03. For a more detailed discussion of the crown's attempts to secure her prerogatives in the colonies between 1720 and 1749 cf. Wellenreuther, "Wisdom to Secure" (cf. n. 1).

[67] Cf. Jack P. Greene, *Quest for Power: The Lower Houses of Assembly in the Southern Royal Colonies, 1689–1776* (Chapel Hill, N. C., 1963).

[68] Cf. Bernard Bailyn, "The Central Themes of the American Revolution: An Interpretation", in Kurtz and Hutson, eds., *Essays* (cf. n. 39), 3–31. Bailyn believes that the colonists in the face of "an organized pan-Atlantic effort of highly placed autocrats to profit by reducing the free way of life the colonists had known ... were led by the force of these ideas [developed by Commonwealthmen, radical Whigs], now integrated as they had not been before and powerfully reinforced by Continental writings on the laws of nature and of nations and by the latest formulations of the English radicals, into resistance and revolution" (p. 10). At the same time he dismisses "those mysterious social strains that seem to beguile the imaginations of historians straining to find peculiar predispositions to upheaval" (p. 12). I disagree with this interpretation: Bailyn does not take into account that ideas do not operate as such but in the minds of human beings, minds, which are shaped and influenced by the social climate, by political as well as economic, religious and cultural circumstances surrounding the person. A tract written in England defending the established church in New England applied to a dissenting church; the terms "freeholder"

or "electorates" had a different political reality and significance in the colonies and in England because they were part of different socio-economic realities. Thus an appeal to the freeholders in England meant an appeal to less than 20 percent of the population but an appeal to the freeholders in the colonies meant addressing more than two thirds of the colonial population (slaves and indentured servants excluded). Furthermore, it does seem rather questionable to me to exclude factors like sudden severe economic crises as reasons why ideas become relevant. But this is exactly what Bailyn seems to propose.

[69] Duncan J. MacLeod has pointed out the importance of the notion of James Harrington that property not only was the basis of power but of independence. Our analysis of the socio-economic structure would illustrate the remarkably independent behavior of colonists within their sphere of politics. This interpretation would help in understanding the colonists' behavior in the years before the Declaration of Independence.

Socio-Political Structures and Popular Ideology, 1750s–1780s

Dirk Hoerder

"For if the Representation be *unequal*, the Government will not long continue *equal*," the inhabitants of Beverly, Mass., lectured the state legislature in 1778, when the new constitution was formed. John Adams, committed to the theory of popular sovereignty, had foreseen such criticism. Actual submission of the draft constitution to the sovereign people would merely "divide and distract them," he grumbled. These conflicting views might be taken as evidence for a division of society into two antagonistic groups, the "people" vs. the "natural aristocracy" or "better sort." But to do so would mean to "focus too much on an immediate dualization of society with fairly direct political consequences" (Lockridge).[1]

Two other dualisms, once considered to be of great explanatory value for the Revolutionary period and the war of independence are no longer convincing. As to the whig-tory dichotomy, both groups drew on the same authorities for their political beliefs (Bailyn), both were fearful of the corrupting influence of luxury, both had similar attitudes to property. Nor can their struggle be reduced to a contest for offices. Either group included many men who never held offices and who because of their social position were ineligible for higher offices.[2]

Similarly, the antagonism between Britain and the colonies can no longer be understood simply in the dualistic terms of an "imperial" interpretation. Independence was "in the womb of time" (Bumsted) rather than a new concept evolving after the Stamp Act crisis. Formal reality in 1776–1783, it required a "second war of independence", in 1812–1815 to end continuing British encroachments and discriminatory economic practices. Before the 1770s, few colonial "patriots" thought of independence, and the sixties can and have to be explained without the hindsight that independence was approaching. External and internal developments were closely entwined and many of these could have gone either way. Two important factors were the lack of give in the British government and the emergence of a – still colonial – society able to organize and defend itself on its own. Social and economic structures had changed and political structures had to be changed accordingly. Demands for such changes were widespread in the sixties and came from whigs and tories, from "articulate" and "inarticulate". The purpose of this essay is to examine the complex societal conditions governing the relations between social groups and classes within the American mainland colonies and within the imperial system during the transition period from colonial to national political structures. Particular attention will be paid to expressions of popular ideology.[3]

I.

The "new imperial policy", which had been in preparation since the thirties and forties, its implementation after 1763, and colonial opposition against it have eclipsed the intra-colonial causes for changes in internal and external political structures and relations.[4] Crown appointed colonial administrators like Thomas Pownall, Francis Bernard, and Thomas Hutchinson perceived them and tried to influence their course by submitting extensive proposals for reform to the British ministry.[5] Colonists, too, tried to come to grips with social and economic changes and to translate them into new institutions and imperial relations. This is evidenced by concern about independence particularly from the thirties to the early sixties (Bumsted), by the demands for royal government from conservative colonial groups, and by the social and political concepts surfacing in reaction to the Stamp Act.

As to the first of these three issues, J. M. Bumsted has pointed out that the main themes of the argument for or against independence were imperial and economic. Economic self-sufficiency, contended the English economist Josiah Tucker, would lead to demands for political self-sufficiency. In the colonies, where semi-independence had long been political practice, British attempts to interfere in political and economic matters met with opposition on the grounds that the colonists were Englishmen and that they therefore were entitled to the same rights and privileges as those living in Britain. The unresolved issue in these debates was the question whether Britain should benefit from the colonies. Mercantilism and classic concepts of colonization considered economic benefits the main purpose of acquiring colonies. Lacking in the debates was a clear analytical distinction between colonies of exploitation and colonies of settlement. The original motivation, exploitation of natural resources with labor provided by a subjected native population, came to naught as Edmund Morgan has graphically shown for Virginia. In consequence the English immigrants could not consider themselves representatives of their native country over a conquered people slaving for the benefit of Britain. They had to do the work themselves and consequently had different attitudes about to whom should accrue the profit from their labor.[6]

While the scope of the economic activities was regulated by Parliament, while political institutions were regulated by charter and controlled by imperial institutions no such official regulations existed for the social sphere. In the middle and southern colonies tenancy and use of slave labor established a social hierarchy. The situation was more complex in the New England colonies. Subsistence farming and local self-government did not prevent the development of elites but retarded this process considerably. By the middle of the eighteenth century, however, demographic expansion and economic diversification had brought about an enormous increase of the gap between farmers and large landholders, between journeymen mechanics and merchants. Many of those who had gained began to desire institutionalization of their superior positions. Little support for such a demand could be found within colonial societies and only the southern planter elite had some success. Therefore sections of the "better sort" began to look for allies elsewhere. To shift power from local communities to the top of provincial society, i. e. to themselves, they demanded more royal control.

In retrospect this might appear as a self-defeating proposal. But contemporary advocates paid only limited attention to the imperial consequences, they looked to internal advantages, to their immediate self-interest. They wanted nothing less than the creation of a colonial nobility. In Massachusetts there were pleas for royal appointment of councillors from established elite and from placemen. In Connecticut Anglican forces expected more influence with crown appointment of governors. Well-placed Rhode Islanders, often merchants, contemplated favors the King might bestow on them and petitioned for a change of government. Of course, this conservative elite comprised only a small part of the population, but what counted was their great influence and power. The call for an American nobility, whether for life or even hereditary, was not limited to crown supporters. John Adams and many others agreed that an independent upper house should counter popular influence. In Pennsylvania the Quaker party, discontent with proprietary politics and seeing its internal influence wane hit upon royal control as a remedy, too.[7]

Another group of political leaders was ready to curtail connections with Britain if political interference continued. This became evident during the Stamp Act crisis. Rhode Island politicians thought that resistance might have to be carried to great length and wondered whether crowd leaders from the lower classes would rise to influential positions. Emissaries from the New York Sons of Liberty toured New England to enquire about preparations for military resistance. In Massachusetts it was rumored again and again in the years after 1765 that armed resistance was planned.[8]

On the part of the lower classes in general there is little evidence for long harbored grievances against the British, with the important exception of sailors and the waterfront community (impressment). The strict enforcement of the customs acts against petty smuggling which sailors practiced to improve on their meagre wages began only after 1763 and did hardly cause any friction earlier. The Stamp Act was considered a grievance because bonds for debt, judicial documents etc. were taxed, which was "unconstitutional". There was also the general opposition to "placemen". The feeling was that they did not work but pocketed high fees. The hatred against them and the ideology that motivated it had surfaced before. At the time of the Stamp Act, an external "irritant" which affected the population of all colonies at the same time, opposition to placemen was transferred to sections of the complacent and self-confident colonial elite. Many supporters of the plans for a colonial aristocracy became targets of crowd action. The opposition to imported luxuries was added to the anti-British and sometimes anti-upper class feelings. In the country simple living according to traditional precepts played an important role in the support for non-importation. Anger surfaced when merchants abandoned this policy from self-interest.[9] In brief, reaction to these impositions was the first phase of a general process of mobilization for sections of the population whose influence on politics was relatively low, but which did feel the economic and social changes and had to articulate an attitude toward them.[10] Significant earlier phases of mobilization had been socially and geographically limited. The change to general opposition was of crucial importance for the subsequent course of events.

The process of mobilization as described here raises two intricate questions. Which specific groups within the social hierarchy were involved? Did a west-east antagonism exist and if so, was it intensified during the development toward statehood? The concept of social classes has been derived from sources about the eastern urban communities, but only about six percent of the total population lived in towns of more than 2500 inhabitants. Is the concept applicable to farmers? In the larger towns "lower classes" (sometimes: "orders" or "ranks"), "middling interest" and "better sort" had separate interests and diverging ideological viewpoints. The members of the two higher strata felt they spoke for those below. Thus the upper sorts had the connections, the leisure, the educational possibilities, the personality structure to dominate the sociopolitical system in addition to the economic one, and they were convinced that they spoke for the "public interest" which a class or an interest could not. Definitions of these strata, whether by property owned, by political, or by economic function, immediately extend the problem beyond the urban areas. The argument for the primacy of the coastal towns is that political and economic power was concentrated there, that the British governors resided there as well as colonial legislatures, that dense settlement and better communications brought about a higher capacity for quick action. From 1765 to 1770 most of the militancy and maneuvering was confined to the coastal towns. This changed and was in some cases changed deliberately in the seventies.

In the country, with widespread property ownership, even if limited in size, most male white inhabitants would belong to the "middling interest", if stratification is defined by property and the consequent political right to vote. But subsistence farmers – or perhaps "marginal participants in the market" – were not only considered "rabble" by the large landowners as were the lower classes in the towns, they also had different interests again as had their lowly urban counterparts. Their place in the market – whether it was major or minor – had consequences for their political outlook. Up to the sixties small farmers and the propertyless urban dwellers could see government mainly through its demands for taxes and as being oppressive, while other groups were already getting more out of government. In the formative period of the national constitution these differing views of government were of even more fundamental importance. They did not remain static but changed in time according to perceived changes in interest. There was artisan and farmer support for the Constitution, but there also were uprisings against the unresponsive eastern authorities.

The predominance of the cities as far as market participation, decision making etc. rather than mere concentration of population goes was challenged repeatedly by rural areas. Reversal of political domination, often shortlived, sometimes brought about an accomodation of differing interests. The increasing urban orientation also brought about increased concern about the roles of both merchants and urban lower classes. In the subsequent debates about representation, whether of individuals or property or both, or of communities, the majoritarian principle was on the winning side with separate safeguards for property.[11]

II.

In Massachusetts the target of the mobilizing lower classes was Thomas Hutchinson, native of the province and royal governor. As "acquisitive bourgeois" (Bailyn) he was part of an elite "that was a stabilizing element" (Ernst). The political system of the New England colonies permitted a considerable amount of popular participation via town meeting and annual election of many officials. Deferential patterns, however, offset many of the elective features. Election of men of property and standing into the most influential offices and their re-elections was customary. This also gave the crown the advantage that representatives in the lower houses could be brought into the fold of its supporters with lucrative appointments. This patronage system and the appointees' quest for "dignity" which meant submission of the lower orders, was partly countered by the "quest for power" of the lower houses of assembly when crown or parliamentary rights were concerned. Nevertheless election patterns made such appointees long-term assets. John Adams once observed that even in New England a semi-hereditary pattern of office-holding had developed to some degree. As long as opportunities were abundant this caused only limited friction, but in the middle of the eighteenth century with a definite scarcity of unsettled lands in New England and elsewhere such positions were eyed rather unfavorably by those who had to support them with fees and taxes.[12]

It was at this point that acquisitiveness and potentially revolutionary discontent could begin to interact and did so in 1765 on a "national" scale. Earlier there had only been the latent problem of the corporate notion of property entailing social responsibility, and the concept which considered property merely a means for individual advance or to enhance an already elevated social position.[13] The latter was in the process of being changed into the liberalist notion of private property and its sanctity (as opposed to mere security). The governor of Massachusetts failed to discern this difference. Hutchinson himself admitted that the lower classes hated him for his stand on monetary politics and policies. He profited in an almost unprecedented manner from lucrative offices which he felt were his just due. He thus again collided with the lower classes. He was also at odds with many politicians. Some considered his accumulation of offices corrupting and unconstitutional, others coveted the same positions and were in no mood to show deference. Thirdly, the governor alienated merchants and speculators. When forced to choose between enforcing British policies or following entrepreneurial or capitalist interests he did the former, trying to benefit personally from the policies. Given the changed circumstances, particularly the growing group-consciousness of (whig) merchants and mechanics, Hutchinson undermined the position of the old elite (*"ancien régime"*) including his own. Entangled in the web of patronage politics and mercantile gentlemen's agreements he could not respond vigorously to criticism and attacks. Vigor, in his opinion, was the behavior of *nouveaux arrivés* but not of men of property and traditional standing.[14]

Maryland, by the middle of the eighteenth century, also had experienced several decades of declining opportunities. As in most of the middle colonies widespread tenancy as well as the cultivation of cash crops distinguished it from the northern colonies. The port of Baltimore had not yet achieved economic importance. Large parts of the land were in the hands of a few wealthy families and concentration of landholding was increasing. Contrary to Massachusetts, Maryland was a proprietary colony, but the political system was similar in one respect at least. Influential men, who owed their position to election and re-election, were brought over to the side of the court party by patronage, i. e. by being bribed with lucrative offices. While Massachusetts had only the merchant patricians of the seaboard and the River Gods of the Connecticut Valley, Maryland had a landed gentry which to a considerable degree consisted of favorites of the proprietor. As in Massachusetts there were numerous men from among the better sort whose ambitions were thwarted. Among the lower classes discontent was also looming large. From 1690 to 1760 movement up the economic scale was "glacially slow" (Land, Skaggs) for those who began at the bottom. Land grants being made by the proprietor and slave labor being cheaper than that of white men, most indentured servants found themselves with no property at all and little prospect for obtaining land once their indenture was over.

The politically active citizens were split into a country and a court party, the latter under increasing criticism since the fifties. By 1768, influential members of the country party refused offices from the proprietor, certain that they could enhance their position or at least keep their influence without relying on the unpopular politics of Lord Baltimore. The role of the lower classes increased with the necessity to oppose British placemen. Crowd action forced the stamp master to resign and to leave the colony in 1765. "Swamp men and Shingle Makers" were the allies of a respectable church vestry disputing the proprietor's right to name the rector of a parish (another of the many sinecures in the colony). From 1770 to 1773 the "fee controversy" brought matters to a break. The lower house demanded a downward revision, the councillors, benefiting by the fees, stalled. The stalemate resulted in a unilateral declaration of the governor continuing the old fee-table. As a result another argument of the imperial debate was transferred to intra-colonial affairs. The fees, considered taxes not approved by the legislature, brought about the by now well-known cry "no taxation without representation." At the next elections, 1773, the court party lost what influence it had left. Just as in other colonies the (whiggish) country party then split into several groups, conservatives, men on the rise, advocates of more popular participation. These splits materially influenced politics once the British lost control.[15]

In the plantation society of South Carolina social differences were even more obvious than in Maryland. Only a tiny minority of the population was of political influence, the majority consisted of black slaves. Within the white minority power was concentrated among planters and merchants, sometimes called the "squirearchy", but a growing frontier community provided a class of small farmers. Their interests were so little heeded by the established groups that it took the Regulator movement to focus attention on the back country as well as to establish the propertied groups there over outlaws and the lowly. Once the Regulators had achieved this purpose, a Moderator movement headed by a number of justices of the peace, who had met with opposition from the Regulators, used their links to the low country and to political institutions to repress Regulators.[16]

As so often, local grievances were linked with imperial issues. The one problem which Regulators and Moderators could not solve was that of representation in the lower house. Fearful of the power of the assemblies the home government insisted on limiting the number of representatives and forbade governors to admit members from new parishes or counties, usually recently settled western regions. Nevertheless the lower house was the most important institution in South Carolina politics. Like other assemblies it had consciously extended its power. While in other colonies this involved a struggle with the upper house or its weaning from British influence nothing of the kind was required in South Carolina. After 1756, the British ministry had attempted to get a pliable council by packing it with dependent placemen. In result it had lost respect and power to a degree that men with political ambitions preferred to remain in the lower house.[17]

While the legislature was the domain of the better sort, the Charlestown mechanics as those of other port towns were a force to be reckoned with. The element of journeymen among them was probably smaller than elsewhere because master craftsmen could rely at least partially on slave labor. The independent artisans formed a "Mechanics Party" in 1762

and for over a decade pursued a policy combining their economic interests with opposition to British taxation. In Massachusetts lower class
participation had been curbed by Samuel Adams' consensus politics based
on the past ideal of corporate cohesiveness with no separate interests. In
Maryland artisan forces were negligible. Popular aspirations therefore
lacked opportunity and capacity to emerge continuously and openly,
though a close reading of town meeting or parish records, of petitions or
court proceedings reveals a striking degree of differences of ideology and
interest. In South Carolina mechanics did assert their interests, particularly colonial manufactures against overseas commerce. However, they
did not change the system of elite domination. Mechanics did not sit in
the lower house, they had better placed spokesmen there which, of
course, had interests of their own. During the years of change small
farmers also became a political force in all three colonies.[18]

In these colonies, representing different sections and their respective
social structures, growing alienation from Britain was obvious. In each of
them some political institutions with internal as well as external functions were no longer operating smoothly by the sixties when the ministry
openly changed its policies. The governors of Massachusetts were losing
much of their political power, as did the Maryland court party and the
South Carolina council. At the same time two social groups were increasing their influence. Men on the rise, particularly merchants, felt
impeded by patronage politics and placemen, by economic restrictions
and by blocked social mobility. Together with disaffected sections of
established elites they wielded considerable power.[19] Secondly, the lower
classes articulated their grievances and interests more openly. Their
socio-economic position was precarious, their interest in land and labor
outspoken, their number sufficient to force political recognition.[20]

III.

The brief outline of some elements of the social and political systems of
three selected colonies might suggest that there was more diversity than
similarity between the settlements on the American mainland. But when
economic, social, and political structures are compared to those existing
at the beginning of the colonial ventures the similarities had definitely
increased, those between the thirteen colonies as well as those between
American and British institutions. Both, the Anglicization and Ameri-
canization were accompanied by the development of a kind of self-
awareness in the colonies. At first couched in a language of equality

with British Englishmen and sometimes with British institutions and thus implicitly negating the subordinate colonial position, it burst forth into a separate national consciousness once it became obvious that Parliament and the British ministry thought little of the "rights of Englishmen" when these were mere colonists.

This "Americanism" took different forms and cannot simply be subsumed under "community symbols."[21] One aspect was the growing demand for a reduction of restraints on American manufactures, voiced where mechanics produced for American markets and where they succeeded in expressing their group interest. Another aspect was the discontent of many, particularly northern merchants about the Navigation Acts, now considered restraining rather than beneficial.[22] Socio-political elites found British interference and arrogant placemen more and more difficult to accept. When British administrators called for a crown appointed nobility to guarantee social stability, American whigs were thinking of a "natural aristocracy."

On the opposite end of the social ladder the lower classes found elite conduct and demands, whether British or American, the more difficult to bear the more opportunities for their own advancement decreased. In the deferential New England societies where the virtuous character of frugal living was expounded again and again; in an environment where considerable saving was necessary to set up for oneself; in colonies where scant attention was paid to the necessities of frontier communities, fee-gobbling officials, a wealthy upper class, and the display of numerous symbols of superior rank brought about an articulation of already latent discontent and a political alignment sometimes bearing similarities to class-conscious politics.[23] But to avoid over-simplification it has to be stressed again that self-consciousness of specific groups was not the same all over the continental colonies. Nor were interests. Massachusetts mechanics were less interested in American manufactures than their South Carolina brethren because their main employment was the building of ships on British orders. Similarly the interests of planter elites often did not coincide with those of merchant patricians. Within these two groups the degree of indebtedness to British mercantile firms and abilities to repay credits caused friction and differences in attitude.[24]

In the years before 1776, however, local, regional, colonial, and sectional rivalries seemed secondary to the clash of interests with Britain. Whig ideology, much more than mere propaganda, as an earlier generation of scholars thought, provided a convenient frame of reference to articulate grievances and conflicts. What appeared as a preponderance of political arguments in this contest was rather a reflection of the factor that colonial societies were sufficiently sophisticated that all conflicts, political or not, were mediated via political institutions. This is true even for the non-importation schemes. Politicians repeatedly argued for them in stronger terms than merchants. Also, none of their advocates expected them to bring about changes automatically. Rather the petitions of British merchants losing business and the discontent among unemployed lower classes in England were to induce Parliament to change its political stance.

Once British authority came to an end with the Declaration of Independence in 1776; once the war placed considerable strain on the economy and once new institutions had to be designed and tested, whig ideology was no longer able to fulfill its role as unifying factor, as even Bailyn admitted. Different social and economic groups asserted their interests, different concepts of political organization competed with each other, and the new constitutions reflected some compromises but more so the dominance of mercantile or planter interests and their ideology.

The period of interim government between the demise of the pre-Revolutionary political systems and the development of new permanent institutions was characterized by an influx of new men into government. These came mainly from rising groups or from established but politically excluded sections of a colony's population. A second characteristic was popular aspirations for more equal or more responsive government. An analysis of officeholding in interim institutions (committees, conventions, congresses) shows that actual gains were only made by men who previously had already occupied an elevated position. Among whigs, as earlier among tories, the gentlemen of property and standing acted according to interest rather than according to ideology once threats to their interest and position passed a certain threshold level.[25] Contrary to the advocates of a colonial nobility in the sixties, they could not appeal to the center of the empire for support. They could and did use institutional devices to strengthen their position and they could rely on a concept of property that furthered their aims rather than those of the whole community. But they also – more so than in earlier decades – had to appeal for popular support and were thereby forced to compromise with popular demands. Such recourse to the people had a mobilizing effect in addition to other factors working in this direction. Lower classes and middling interest became more articulate when their positions were concerned.

IV.

Different interests and the resulting different concepts about future political structures were particularly obvious during the extensive constitutional debates in Massachusetts. For historians these debates provide extraordinary insights into contemporary ideologies. The formative period, 1774 to 1780, may be divided into four successive stages of structural and argumentative development: (1) The spontaneous interim government based on local committee rule and regional conventions. (2) The attempt of the leadership, purged of tory elements, to avoid debates about political structures and to use a higher ranking institution to sanction established forms of government and thereby their own position. (3) Agitation and direct action of broad sections of the population for a new constitution including a bill of rights and emphasizing protection against arbitrary rulers. (4) The actual establishment of new political structures with its social and – to a lesser degree – economic consequences.

In 1775, the delegates to the Massachusetts Provincial Congress, though less distinguished in social status and economic position than the representatives of the last colonial legislature, attempted to restore the old institutions without appealing to the people for approval. Only after long hesitation did they decide that election warrants from the British military governor should not be obeyed. Only after Lexington and Concord did they declare the governor inimical and thus no longer a source of legitimacy and authority. Only then did they substitute as higher authority to appeal to for legitimization the Continental Congress, the national level of extra-legal interim government, elected indirectly and established by the old colonial legislatures or by provincial conventions.

Asking for its "recommendation for this colony to take up and exercise civil government," the Massachusetts leadership also suggested the answer: resumption of the Crown Charter of 1691. Popular political thought, particularly in the west, favored resumption of the original Charter which contained more participatory elements. The leadership first argued that immediate and vigorous government was necessary because of the external threat to the province posed by the British military force. But it was also fearful of internal upheaval: "There are, in many parts of the Colony, alarming symptoms of the abatement of the sense in the minds of some people of the sacredness of private property, which is plainly assignable to the want of civil government." Congress advised to resume the Charter of 1691. Among the first moves of the new legislature based on this recommendation were an address to the people, congratulating them on their popular government; a resolve confirming the decisions of the non-Charter based provincial congresses; and an assertion from the council of "the supremacy of the Charter over natural rights."[26]

Particularly in western Massachusetts opposition to this proceeding was outspoken and supported by crowd action. Criticism was also voiced in the east, but probably because of the higher concentration of property, demands were different. While the west stressed the necessity for a constitution approved by the people and particularly for a bill of rights and safeguards against arbitrary exercise of power by the rulers, the east emphasized a government of checks and balances, particularly a separate representation of property as a check on representation of persons. In the west small farmers predominated, in the east merchants and lawyers. A draft constitution of the legislature was rejected overwhelmingly by the towns in 1778. A second draft, mainly the work of John Adams, submitted for ratification 1780, met with innumerable objections. But "ingenious" tabulating of votes by the delegates of the convention brought about a majority for the constitution.[27] While phases (2) and (4) will receive no further attention here – they have been dealt with elsewhere – we want to use some of the arguments brought forward during the formative period, the high mark of articulated popular opinion, to analyze different concepts of state government. To focus the debate we will concentrate on the six frames of government produced during this period, the constitutions of 1778 and 1780, the plans of "The People the Best Governors" (1776) and of the "Essex Result" (1778), the propositions of the towns of Ashfield, Hampshire Co., and of Middleborough, Plymouth Co., both of 1776.[28]

The inhabitants of Ashfield, 628 persons in 1776, of whom about 25 percent, the free white adult males, could vote, demanded a governmental structure that could hardly be more simple and direct. It knew no intricate system of separation of powers or of checks and balances. Its foundation was to be the "Law of God." On the provincial level there was to to be a "States Ginaral", seemingly with executive functions, and a unicameral assembly. All other magistrates, whether town or judicial officials, were to be elected on the township level. The legislature was to be a replica of the town meeting. The response to the draft constitution of 1780 showed that the Ashfield people could accept more sophisticated government without deserting their basic premises, local control, no property qualifications, unicameral legislature. The reasoning proceeded from a notion that a simple form of government "is the Natural Right of the Commonwilth" tempered with practical arguments like "advantagius to the Commonwilth" and not so oppressive to the "widdow and fatherless."

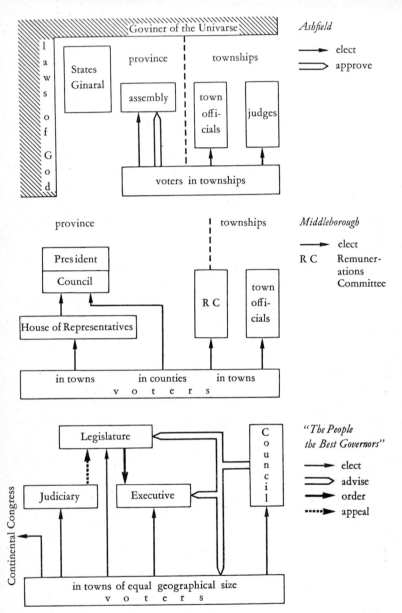

Ashfield

Goviner of the Univarse

laws of God

States Ginaral

province — assembly

townships — town officials — judges

voters in townships

→ elect
⇒ approve

Middleborough

province

President
Council

House of Representatives

townships — R C — town officials

voters — in towns — in counties — in towns

→ elect
R C Remunerations Committee

"The People the Best Governors"

Continental Congress

Legislature — Judiciary — Executive — Council

voters — in towns of equal geographical size

→ elect
⇒ advise
→ order
·····▶ appeal

Note: The role of the „States Ginaral" is not clear. It may be an executive branch replacing the governor. It could also be a separate body to consult with the other North American states.

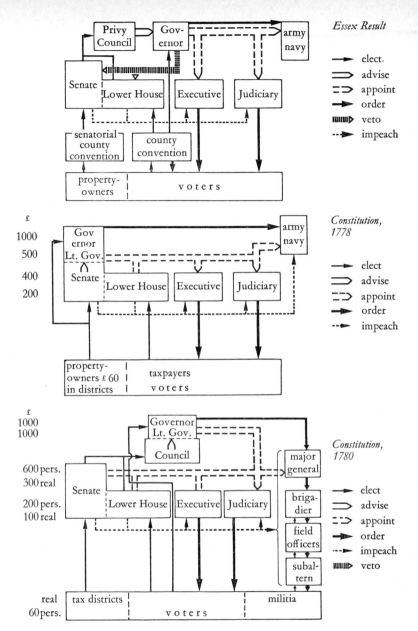

Note: The preceding graphs are simplified. They do not include residence requirements; power to pardon; power to establish additional courts or other institutions; election of officials (e.g. councillors) from a select few only (e.g. senators).

The figures to the left of the graphs are to property qualifications necessary for voting or holding office.

Middleborough, incorporated in 1669, with more than 4000 inhabitants and ranking eleventh in property assessed for taxation of towns in 1780, expressed vociferous opposition to the constitution of 1780, arguing from the concept that a complex government would offer opportunities to officials to further their private interests rather than the public good: "Voting money from the Comunity into their own Pockets . . ." Therefore a major purpose of the constitution should be to prevent ambitious individuals, a "Venal and Most Wretched Set of Villains," from plural officeholding, continuous holding of the same office, and financial misconduct. Annual popular election of officials would safeguard the people from infringements on their rights. Any other form, whether appointment or indirect election, would not be "Consistant with the Right of Nature." Contrary to Ashfield, wishing for simple and direct government, the inhabitants of Middleborough aimed at strong popular control over a somewhat more complex government. They perceived the emergence of separate interests, in this case those of the rulers, and realized that offices meant opportunities to strengthen cohesion of one social group and its members' personal positions to the detriment of others. In modern terms: political advancement of some meant downward mobility for less well-placed sections of the population.

The People the Best Governors: or a Plan of Government Founded on the Just Principles of Natural Freedom was published anonymously in 1776 and addressed itself to the "honest farmer and citizen." (Note the term "citizen" – as contrasted with the French term "bourgeois" – with its implication of informed political activity, whether in or out of office, in the interest of the whole.) Hierarchical tendencies were strongly condemned, "the people," that is "Tent-makers, cobblers and common tradesmen," "best know their own wants and necessities." The structures of government were no more complex than those of the Middleborough plan, but the separation of powers into a legislative, executive, and judicial branch was more explicit. Personal property was rejected as a qualification for voters or officials, rather "the liberties of a person" were to be the guiding principle for all decisions. The election districts (townships) were to be of about equal size and land was to be the basis of taxation. The author felt that only "popular government" based on "natural rights" would secure "freedom" "against the sly insinuations and proposals of those of a more arbitrary turn."

These three forms of government are similar in that they all assume a unicameral legislature without even bothering to deal with the question of two houses. They may be called "popular governments," or, with some reservations about the modern implications of the term, "populistic democracies" (Dahl). In his *Preface to Democratic Theory* Dahl contrasts "Madisonian democracy," a system of checks and balances as outlined in *Federalist* No. 10, with the former. He considers Madison's theory "inadequate" as a system (though not as an ideology) mainly because of its "inability to reconcile two different goals." The "idea that all the adult citizens of a republic must be assigned equal rights, including the right to determine the general direction of government policy" was irreconcilable with the intention "to erect a political system that would guarantee the liberties of certain minorities whose advantages of status, power, and wealth would... probably not be tolerated indefinitely." To protect such minorities and not ethnic or religious ones, "majorities had to be constitutionally inhibited."[29]

The "Essex Result," a criticism of the constitution of 1778 by a dozen towns from the eastern county of Essex, probably authored by the "conservative" Newburyport lawyer Theophilus Parsons (Handlin) represented the most restrictive plan of government proposed in this period. Property was to be represented in a second legislative house. A complicated system of indirect elections ("doubly refined" officials) even for the lower house was devised, introducing structural property qualifications for all parts of government. Higher officials had to serve in lower capacities first to become even more "refined." This would have promoted an *esprit de corps,* reduced the number of candidates to chose from, and barred effectively expression of popular demands via regular institutional channels. Salaries were to be fixed by the constitution, to prevent legislators from pressuring executive and judicial officers into compliance by means of low "stipends" as they had done with obnoxious British officials. Judicial officers were to be appointed by the governor, remain in office during "good behavior," i. e. practically for life, and to be removable only by impeachment. Opposition to a judicial system with appointments "during pleasure" had been an integral part of the struggle against the arbitrary power of British officials. Social groups and individuals advocating a participatory form of government had voiced demands for direct (annual) election of judges. But in the "Essex Result" anti-egalitarian beliefs were stated quite openly. "Yet... we are to look further than to the bulk of the people, for the greatest wisdom, firmness, consistency, and perseverance. These qualities will most probably be found among men of education and fortune."

The draft constitutions of 1778 and 1780 were based on similar premises, the structural consequences of which were bicameral legislature, stringent property qualifications for voters and officials, large appointive powers for the legislators (1778) or the governor (1780), "permanent and honorable" fixed salaries, tenure during "good behavior" for judicial officials, removal of magistrates only by impeachment. Similar restrictive elements appeared in the constitutions of other states.

Maryland's new constitution "was designed specifically to insure the continuance of elitist rule." The three branches of government "were firmly controlled by a small ruling class of wealthy men." After the court party had been shattered, the leaders of the popular party wanted to enjoy power and its benefits without interference from the proprietor. Drawn into the imperial dispute and fearing "a revengeful democracy" or civil war they joined with the long established elite to enact radical tax reform measures to appease the people. Even Charles Carroll of Carrollton accepted this as "the price of Revolution," and, according to Ronald Hoffman, the wealthy acquiesced to insure the survival of their class.[30]

In South Carolina the conservative wing of the legislature bitterly fought for indirect election for the upper house. When this could not be achieved, Governor John Rutledge, who had earlier told the representatives to use their "influence and authority to keep peace and good order" among their constituents, vetoed the constitution explaining that "democratic power" had been found to be "arbitrary, severe, and destructive." A new governor signed the instrument of "democratic power," which required that voters have a fifty acre freehold or pay taxes equal to those on such an estate. Candidates had to own 500 acres plus 20 slaves or £ 1000 estate (House), £ 2000 settled freehold and estate (Senate), £ 10.000 freehold or a plantation (governor). In addition the governor was elected indirectly by the legislature as was the executive council. Residence requirements were dropped for candidates whose freehold exceeded £ 3500 (House) or 7000 (Senate). These were the better placed spokesmen for the mechanics. Equality of representation was not intended.[31]

The constitutions of other states were basically similar (W. P. Adams). Rhode Island, with a popularly elected governor already under British domination, continued its traditional system for another sixty-five years until a "rebellion" against the suffrage limitations occurred (1841/42). It was crushed but suffrage was extended. About the same time a "rebellion" was necessary in New York to change economic conditions having survived from pre-Revolutionary times in only slightly modified form. During the Revolution Robert Livingston, belonging to the elite of the state, had pointed out that it was necessary to swim with the torrent if the elite wanted to control it. During the formation of the national Constitution similar principles prevailed, but wealthy merchant-financiers, speculators, and some politicians voiced economic interest as opposed to social status and gentlemanly leisure more explicitly than in the seventies. These men had realized early that the integrating political function of the Constitution for the new nation also furthered their commercial and financial interests.[32]

Although the term "natural aristocracy" was used in none of the constitutions, the concept of a hierarchical social order determined the forms of the new governmental structures. Demands for "popular government" voiced by small farmers and artisans were brushed aside. The principle of "mixed government" in which democratic, aristocratic, and monarchical components were integrated into a system of countervailing powers was replaced by the principle of "balanced government" in which the interests of a leadership that considered itself "natural" and those of a propertied minority were protected against demands for equality and broad political participation by a system of checks and balances.[33]

V.

The process of mobilization and increasing militancy after 1765 changed with the ratification of the state and federal constitutions. Until then large sections of the population had been drawn into political or, later, war-related activities. Only the crown supporters had been eliminated or had changed sides. Within the whig leadership differences over hierarchical and participatory concepts, between corporate and liberalist organizational forms continued to exist and led to the Federalist-Antifederalist split and to popular protest against taxation, unjust authority, high pay and status for army officers. Democratic-republican societies drawing support mainly from mechanics opposed unresponsive and arrogant leaders. Government remained the domain of "gentlemen of property and standing" who continued their quest for power to the detriment of the new sovereign, the people.

Nevertheless, a number of important changes took place. In the middle states the resurgence of feudal customs was stopped. In accordance with the stage of economic development property was now defined in a liberalist rather than in a corporate sense at least in commercial circles. Thus the foundation for an economic development according to Hamiltonian principles with their social and political concomitants was laid. The "possessive individualism" inherent in the Lockean tradition came into its own. As Robert Morris phrased it, the interests of "moneyed men" and of government had to be combined. Pre-Revolutionary developments like the "regionally selective commercialization [which] amounted to a geographic concentration of wealth" (Lockridge) and the increase of poverty, "thwarted aspirations... and undernourishment" in the cities (Nash) were further accelerated.[34]

While the poor had no power at all, the lower middle class and sections of the lower class had to be appeased or accomodated to some degree. An important means was legislation, which moved "a colony or state tax system closer to the often stated colonial ideal that taxes ought to be distributed according to each man's ability to pay." This included (1) diminution or abolishment of the poll tax, (2) a change from single rate taxes to an *ad valorem* base, (3) inclusion of previously untaxed property, especially unimproved lands, and (4) taxing luxury items higher than necessities. Many of these reforms were undertaken under threats of direct action. Massachusetts crowds destroyed expensive imported carriages, Maryland crowds opposed tax collectors. But such state level reforms "reinforced the belief of many prominent Americans that a stronger national government was urgently needed to restrain state legislatures." President Washington saw "combustibles" – reasons for popular discontent and uprisings – in many states.[35]

Massachusetts set the pattern for rebellion: The movement of the western farmers in 1786 was quelled militarily, but later a number of reforms embodying some of the popular demands were enacted. Temporarily even the most elitist groups or parties had to appeal to popular support for their policies by more than election rhetoric. Popular ideology in its different forms and the willingness to act on these principles among small farmers and mechanics speeded up structural changes in the political system. Structural changes in the economic sphere on the other hand impeded the long-range development of an independent popular ideology including agrarian as well as urban elements and its legitimation by tradition. Representation remained unequal and, as the people of Beverly had foreseen, government remained unequal, too. State constitutions and Madisonian government were not designed to achieve equality.

Notes

[1] Oscar and Mary F. Handlin, eds., *The Popular Sources of Political Authority: Documents on the Massachusetts Constitution of 1780* (Cambridge, Mass., 1966), 293; John Adams to James Warren, [May] 3, 1777, *Warren-Adams Letters* (Massachusetts Historical Society, *Collections*, LXXII-LXXIII [Boston, 1917-1925]), I, 322, cf. also 234, 242-243; John Adams, *A Defense of the*

Constitutions of Government of the United States of America (London, 1787); Kenneth A. Lockridge, "Social Change and the Meaning of the American Revolution", *JSH*, VI (1972-1973), 403-439, esp. 404.

[2] Bernard Bailyn, *The Ideological Origins of the American Revolution* (Cambridge, Mass., 1967), 23, 28-31; Dirk Hoerder, *People and Mobs: Crowd Action in Massachusetts during the American Revolution, 1765-1780* (Ph. D. diss., Free University of Berlin, 1971), 588-589.

[3] J. M. Bumsted, "'Things in the Womb of Time': Ideas of American Independence, 1633-1763", *WMQ*, 3rd Ser., XXXI (1974), 533-564; see also Jack P. Greene, "An Uneasy Connection. An Analysis of the Preconditions of the American Revolution", in Stephen G. Kurtz and James H. Hutson, eds., *Essays on the American Revolution* (Chapel Hill, N. C., 1973), 32-80. "In the womb of time" cannot be taken in a deterministic sense (Schulte Nordholt). But several commentators pointed out – and this author agrees – that the possibilities for westward expansion, for manufacture, for demographic increase, and the growing self-consciousness of the English settlers made it likely that the question of independence would have been raised at some point of time.

[4] The term "structures" as used here simply means the complex network of institutions and organizations together with social traditions and stratification that are part of a political and social system. The structures are not static but are affected by constant changes.

[5] Bernard Bailyn, *The Ordeal of Thomas Hutchinson* (Cambridge, Mass., 1974); Edmund S. and Helen M. Morgan, *The Stamp Act Crisis: Prologue to Revolution* (Chapel Hill, N. C., 1953), 11-20; Edmund S. Morgan, "Colonial Ideas of Parliamentary Power, 1764-1766", *WMQ*, 3rd Ser., V (1948), 311-341.

[6] Bumsted, "Independence" (cf. n. 3), 544; Edmund S. Morgan, "The Labor Problem at Jamestown, 1607-1618", *AHR*, LXXVI (1971-72), 595-611.

[7] Charles Paxton to Townshend, Dec. 22, 1764, Paxton Letters, Massachusetts Historical Society, Boston; Israel Williams to Thomas Hutchinson, May 8, 1771, Massachusetts Archives CLIV, 90, Massachusetts State Archives, Boston; Francis Bernard to William Wildman, Viscount Barrington, Dec. 15, 1761, Sparks MSS., 4th Ser., II, 23, Houghton Library, Harvard University, Cambridge, Mass.; *Boston Newsletter*, May 3, 1764; Morgan, *Stamp Act* (cf. n. 5), 16, 50-52, 150, 243; James H. Hutson, *Pennsylvania Politics 1746-1770: The Movement for Royal Government and Its Consequences* (Princeton, N. J., 1972); Joseph Dorfman, "The Regal Republic of John Adams", *Political Science Quarterly*, LIX (1944), 227-248.

[8] L. H. Butterfield, ed., *Diary and Autobiography of John Adams*, 4 vols. (Cambridge, Mass., 1961), I, 300; Bernard Friedman, "The Shaping of the Radical Consciousness in Provincial New York", *JAH*, LVI (1969–70), 781-801, esp. 791n; Hoerder, *People and Mobs* (cf. n. 2), 270, 281, *passim*.

[9] Marc Egnal and Joseph A. Ernst, "An Economic Interpretation of the American Revolution", *WMQ*, 3rd Ser., XXIX (1972), 3-32, esp. 21-24.

[10] For the mobilizing effect of the Stamp Act see Hoerder, *People and Mobs* (cf. n. 2), ch. 4; of the tea duty (committees of correspondence), Richard D. Brown, *Revolutionary Politics in Massachusetts: The Boston Committee of Correspondence and the Towns, 1772-1774* (Cambridge, Mass., 1974); of the war (militia), John Shy, "The American Revolution: The Military Conflict Considered as a Revolutionary War", in Kurtz and Hutson, eds., *Essays* (cf. n. 3), 121-156. On the term "unconstitutional", its development and implications see

Gerald Stourzh, *Vom Widerstandsrecht zur Verfassungsgerichtsbarkeit: Zum Problem der Verfassungswidrigkeit im 18. Jahrhundert* (Graz, 1974).

[11] The paragraphs on the urban-rural relationships and on stratification are based on comments by Richard Buel, Jr., Edward Countryman, Joseph A. Ernst, Duncan J. MacLeod, Jackson T. Main, and H.-C. Schröder. But the responsibility for the summary rests with the author.

[12] For deference see J. R. Pole, "Historians and the Problem of Early American Democracy" *AHR*, LXVII (1961-62), 626–646, esp. 646. Jack P. Greene, *The Quest for Power: The Lower Houses of Assembly in the Southern Royal Colonies, 1689–1776* (Chapel Hill, N. C., 1963); Jackson T. Main, *The Upper House in Revolutionary America, 1763–1788* (Madison, Wisc., 1967); Dirk Hoerder, *Society and Government: The Power Structure in Massachusetts Townships, 1765–1780* (Berlin, 1972).

[13] The difference of these notions was particularly obvious in the disputes between absentee landholders and settlers (Schröder). There was always some acquisitiveness (Ernst), but in this author's opinion the public interest was more than a mere overlay.

[14] Bailyn, *Ordeal of Hutchinson* (cf. n. 5); Dirk Hoerder, "*Crowd Action in a Revolutionary Society: Massachusetts 1765-1780*, Studies in Social Discontinuity, ed. Charles Tilly and Edward Shorter (forthcoming: New York, 1976); Butterfield, ed., *Diary of John Adams* (cf. n. 8), I, 261; James Henretta, "Economic Development and Social Structure in Colonial Boston", *WMQ*, 3rd Ser., XXII (1965), 75–92; Allan Kulikoff, "The Progress of Inequality in Revolutionary Boston", *ib.*, XXVIII (1971), 378–412; John J. Waters and John A. Schutz, "Patterns of Massachusetts Colonial Politics: The Writs of Assistance and the Rivalry between the Otis and Hutchinson Families", *ib.*, XXIV (1967), 543–567. On intra-legislative socio-political structures cf. Robert M. Zemsky, "Power, Influence, and Status: Leadership Patterns in the Massachusetts Assembly, 1740-1755"; *ib.*, XXVI (1969), 502–520. For the "corporate" structures in Massachusetts see Michael W. Zuckerman, "The Social Context of Democracy in Massachusetts", *ib.*, XXV (1968), 523–544, and critiques by David G. Allan, "The Zuckerman Thesis and the Process of Legal Rationalization in Provincial Massachusetts", *ib.*, XXIX (1972), 443–468, and Hoerder, *People and Mobs* (cf. n. 2), 64–68.

[15] Aubrey C. Land, "Economic Base and Social Structure: The Northern Chesapeake in the Eighteenth Century", *Journal of Economic History*, XXV (1964–1965), 639–659; David C. Skaggs, "Maryland's Impulse toward Social Revolution: 1750–1776", *JAH*, LIV (1967–1968), 771–786, esp. 774, 778; James H. Haw, "Politics in Revolutionary Maryland, 1753–1788" (Ph. D. diss., University of Virginia, 1972); Ronald Hoffman, *A Spirit of Dissension: Economics, Politics and the Revolution in Maryland* (Baltimore, Md., London, 1973). As to "sinecures", rectors were not even required to reside in their parish and often hired lower paid substitutes. However, church vestries unrelentingly opposed such practices and had done so for a long time.

[16] Richard M. Brown, *The South Carolina Regulators* (Cambridge, Mass., 1963); M. Eugene Sirmans, *Colonial South Carolina: A Political History, 1663 to 1763* (Chapel Hill, N. C., 1966); Robert M. Weir, "'The Harmony We Were Famous For': An Interpretation of Pre-Revolutionary South Carolina Politics", *WMQ*, 3rd Ser., XXVI (1969), 473–501; B. D. Bargar, *Royal South Carolina, 1719–1763* (Columbia, S. C., 1970); Peter H. Wood, *Black Majority: Negroes*

in South Carolina (New York, 1974).

[17] See n. 12; Richard Walsh, *Charleston's Sons of Liberty: A Study of the Artisans, 1763-1789* (Columbia, S. C., 1959).

[18] *Ib.;* other case studies are Staughton Lynd and Alfred F. Young, "The Mechanics and New York City Politics, 1774-1801", *Labor History*, V (1964), 215-276, and Charles S. Olton, *Artisans for Independence: Philadelphia Mechanics and the American Revolution* (Syracuse, N. Y., 1975).

[19] For the conceptualization of the position of "men on the rise", of an "ancien régime", etc. see Crane Brinton, *The Anatomy of Revolution* (New York, 1938), and Alexis de Tocqueville, *L'ancien régime et la révolution* (Paris, 1962 [orig. publ. 1856]).

[20] See n. 18; Alfred F. Young, "Pope's Day, Tar and Feathers, and 'Cornet Joyce, jun.': From Ritual to Rebellion in Boston, 1745-1775", unpubl. ms. prepared for the Anglo-American Labor Historians Conference, Rutgers University, April 1973 (forthcoming). I am grateful to Alfred Young for sending me his comments on an earlier draft of this paper. Marcus Wilson Jernegan, *Laboring and Dependent Classes in Colonial America, 1607-1783*, repr. ed. (New York, 1960).

[21] John M. Murrin, "Anglicizing an American Colony: The Transformation of Provincial Massachusetts", (Ph. D. diss., Yale University, 1966); Richard L. Merritt, *Symbols of American Community, 1735-1775* (New Haven, Conn., 1966).

[22] There are numerous studies of the impact of the Navigation Acts on the colonies as well as on trade patterns. Lacking is an acceptance of the fact that perceived restraints (ideological level) may have more weight than actual benefits (economic level).

[23] As for the lower classes, "class consciousness" is meant in the sense of E. P. Thompson's "moral economy" (cf. his "The Moral Economy of the English Crowd in the Eighteenth Century", *Past and Present*, L [Feb. 1971], 76-136); cf., too, Alfred F. Young's investigation of lower class behavior (cf. n. 20); and this author's research on the tradition of crowd action (cf. n. 2, 14). For accomodation or appeasement of middle and lower class interests see Robert Becker's work on taxation (cf. n. 35); for friction and conflict cf. the studies of E. James Ferguson, *The Power of the Purse* (Chapel Hill, N. C., 1961), and *id.*, "Currency Finance: An Interpretation of Colonial Monetary Practices", *WMQ*, 3rd Ser., X (1953), 153-180, and Joseph A. Ernst, *Money and Politics in America: A Study in the Currency Act of 1764 and the Political Economy of Revolution* (Chapel Hill, N. C., 1973).

[24] Jackson T. Main, *The Social Structure of Revolutionary America* (Princeton, N. J., 1965), and case studies by Henretta, "Economic Development" (cf. n. 14), by Kulikoff, "Progress of Inequality" (cf. n. 14), by Land, "Economic Base and Social Structure" (cf. n. 15), by James T. Lemon and Gary B. Nash, "The Distribution of Wealth in Eighteenth-Century America. A Century of Change in Chester County, Pennsylvania, 1693-1802", *JSH*, II (1968-1969), 1-24; Emory G. Evans, "Planter Indebtedness and the Coming of the Revolution in Virginia", *WMQ*, 3rd Ser., XIX (1962), 511-533, and *id.*, "Private Indebtedness and the Revolution in Virginia, 1776 to 1796", *ib.*, XXVIII (1971), 343-374.

[25] The concepts implied in these terms have been developed by Leonard Richards, *"Gentlemen of Property and Standing". Anti-Abolition Mobs in Jack-*

sonian America (London, 1970), and Theodore M. Hammett, "Two Mobs of Jacksonian Boston: Ideology and Interest", *JAH*, LXII (1975–1976), 845–868.
[26] Elisha P. Douglass, *Rebels and Democrats: The Struggle for Equal Political Rights and Majority Rule during the American Revolution* (Chapel Hill, N. C., 1955); J. R. Pole, *Political Representation in England and the Origins of the American Republic* (London, New York, 1966), 33–75, 172–249, esp. 177 (on interest), 176 (on property) and *passim;* Hoerder, *People and Mobs* (cf. n. 2), 556–557; "Proclamation of the General Court, Jan. 23, 1776", in Handlin, ed., *Popular Sources* (cf. n. 1), 65–69.
[27] Samuel E. Morison, "The Struggle over the Adoption of the Constitution of Massachusetts, 1780", Massachusetts Historical Society, *Proceedings*, L (1916–1917), 353–412.
[28] Handlin, ed., *Popular Sources* (cf. n. 1), 111–112, 533–537 (Ashfield), 125–127, 396–397, 693–699 (Middleborough), 324–365 (Essex Result), 190–201 (Constitution of 1778), 441–472 (Constitution of 1780); *The People the Best Governors*, in F. Chase, *History of Dartmouth College* (Cambridge, Mass., 1891), I, 654–663.
[29] Robert A. Dahl, *A Preface to Democratic Theory*, repr. ed. (Chicago, 1966 [orig. publ. 1956]), esp. 31.
[30] Hoffman, *Spirit of Dissension* (cf. n. 15), 269–272.
[31] Willi Paul Adams, *Republikanische Verfassung und bürgerliche Freiheit: Die Verfassungen und politischen Ideen der amerikanischen Revolution* (Darmstadt, 1973), and *id., Republikanismus und die ersten amerikanischen Einzelstaatsverfassungen* (Ph. D. diss., Free University of Berlin, 1968), 58–64, 347.
[32] Marvin Gettleman, *The Dorr Rebellion: A Study in American Radicalism* (New York, 1973); David M. Ellis, *Landlords and Tenants in the Hudson-Mohawk Region, 1790–1850* (Ithaca, N. Y., 1946).
[33] There is a difference between the original theory of mixed government and the American variant "balanced government". In England, there was alienation of "men on the rise" (Brinton) from authority, too. But its expression and demands for changes were suppressed by the crown, the hereditary aristocracy, and the established church (Brooke). Mixed government was the reflection of an organic stratified society with strong social barriers, balances were necessary where no official hereditary separation of classes existed, where "artificial" barriers had to be created (MacLeod). Such artificial barriers in time can become accepted as natural (Schulte Nordholt). The socially conservative whigs were looking for such barriers (Hoerder). Though John Adams rejected a proposal for appointment of an American nobility by the British crown (Pole), he thought about a "natural aristocracy" and "regal republic" (Joseph Dorfman, "Regal Republic" [cf. n. 7]).
[34] Rowland Berthoff and John M. Murrin, "Feudalism, Communalism, and the Yeoman Freeholder: The American Revolution Considered as a Social Accident", in Kurtz and Hutson, eds., *Essays* (cf. n. 3), 256–288; Curtis P. Nettels, *The Emergence of a National Economy, 1775–1815* (Toronto, London, 1962); E. James Ferguson, *Power of the Purse* (cf. n. 23); C. B. Macpherson, *The Political Theory of Possessive Individualism: Hobbes to Locke* (Oxford, 1962); Hans-Christoph Schröder, "Das Eigentumsproblem in den Auseinandersetzungen um die Verfassung von Massachusetts, 1775–1787", in Rudolf Vierhaus, ed., *Eigentum und Verfassung: Zur Eigentumsdiskussion im ausgehenden 18. Jahrhundert,* Veröffentlichungen des Max-Planck-Instituts für Geschichte, 37

(Göttingen, 1972), 11–64; Stephen E. Patterson, *Political Parties in Massachusetts* (Madison, Wis., 1973); Lockridge, "Social Change" (cf. n. 1), 408; Egnal and Ernst, "An Economic Interpretation" (cf. n. 9); Gary B. Nash, "Social Change and the Origins of Revolution in the Cities", unpublished paper, Sept. 1974, forthcoming *Journal of Interdisciplinary History* (1976); Ramon S. Powers, "Wealth and Poverty: Economic Base, Social Structure, and Attitudes in Pre-Revolutionary Pennsylvania, New Jersey and Delaware" (Ph. D. diss., University of Kansas, 1971).

[35] Robert A. Becker, "The Politics of Taxation in America, 1763–1783" (Ph. D. diss., University of Wisconsin, 1971), xi, ii, 414–415, cf. *Dissertation Abstracts International. A. The Humanities and Social Sciences,* vol. 32, No. 5 ([Ann Arbor, Mich.] 1971), 3193, and Robert A. Becker, "Revolution and Reform: An Interpretation of Southern Taxation, 1763 to 1783", *WMQ,* 3rd Ser., XXXII (1975), 417–442; Nettels, *National Economy* (cf. n. 34), 86.

The Revolutionary Transformation of New York

Edward Countryman[*]

Supporters of the thesis that there was a revolution in America as well as a movement for independence have rarely sought to buttress their argument by reference to purely institutional history. Crowd behavior, conflict within the revolutionary movement, popular loyalism, ideological dispute and political economy have all provided good evidence for suggesting that America underwent profound internal upheaval between 1760 and 1790 but, on the surface, the record of the institutions that ruled men and women does not. Governors, bicameral legislatures and courts were found both before and after Independence, and if the king was metaphorically killed in 1776 the adulation that had once been his was only transferred to another man named George. The archetype of the revolution, in institutional terms, lay in Connecticut and Rhode Island, where royal charters became state constitutions with little more than the stroke of a pen. Nothing could be farther, it would seem, from the experience of France after 1789, of China in 1911 and of Russia in 1917.

It is, for many reasons, time that this view was challenged, time that the institutional history of two places in New England ceased to govern our understanding of that of the rest of America. We know, for instance, that the rapid mobilization of whole groups of Americans into public life in the 1760s and 1770s burst the bounds of the old order, making politics the "universal topic" and leading to the creation of revolutionary committees and congresses and ultimately of a Revolutionary army.[1] And as one political scientist puts it, "the political essence of revolution is the rapid expansion of political consciousness and the rapid mobilization of new groups into politics at a speed which makes it impossible for existing political institutions to assimilate them."[2] We know, too, that however much new institutions might have looked like old ones a period of intensely creative thought led to a whole new theoretical basis for authority even in the most conservative states.[3] We know that institutional proposals of a very radical kind were bruited in many places and adopted in some.[4]

New York, the subject of this essay, is a particularly suitable place for a new look at the institutional side of the Revolution. In formal terms it changed little. The royal governor was succeeded by a chief magistrate chosen for a lengthy term by a limited electorate and armed with considerable power. The royal council gave way to a small state senate, chosen by the same small group. The state assembly can be seen as merely a reincarnation of its provincial predecessor. But, as I have recently argued, the gulf between the two sets of institutions was far deeper than it was wide, for during the independence crisis New York underwent a nearly complete social and political collapse. Turning His Majesty's province into a sovereign state meant both a sweeping redefinition of what New York was and a complicated and creative process of coping positively with the demands of a mobilized populace.[5] That study probed the depth of the gulf; this will survey the terrain on the gulf's two sides. The essay's goal will be to compare the institutions of the province with those of the state, not in formal terms but rather in terms of the relationship between people charged with exercising authority and people who were governed. In doing so it will develop four major propositions about the differences between the old order that collapsed in 1775 and the new one whose creation had only begun when its constitution was proclaimed in 1777.

Proposition I: The state and provincial orders rested on radically different assumptions about who, or what, should be represented and about the proper attitude of men in authority towards criticism by ordinary people.

The colonial assembly of New York was small and ill-apportioned. At its maximum size, which it enjoyed for less than half a decade, it consisted of only twenty-seven men, chosen from an idiosyncratic patchwork of constituencies. The busy, populous city of New York was allowed four representatives but every county, no matter how small or how empty, was able to choose at least two. This meant that between them tiny Kings and Richmond had as many votes (two each) as the city itself. And, in another carry-over of practice from the unreformed House of Commons, the privilege of electing a single member was given to the Hudson Valley manors of Rensselaerwyck, Livingston and Cortlandt, to the county borough of Westchester and to the town of Schenectady. Until 1775 voters in these special constituencies had the legal privilege of voting in elections for county delegates as well.

This patchwork may have provided a rough and ready system of apportionment, giving as it did four members to growing Westchester County and five to Albany, which was the most well-peopled county in the province, but the absence of representation for the rest of the manors, for the nonmanorial great patents and for such significant towns as Poughkeepsie, Newburgh and Kingston would suggest the irrationality of the system. Its patchwork nature is further illustrated by the way that assemblymen were paid. All salaries came out of the provincial treasury, but at rates that were fixed when a constituency's delegates first took their seats. By 1773 representatives from some counties were being paid twice as much as those from others.[6] Such practices and the presence in both houses of the legislature of generation after generation of Livingstons, Morrisses, Johnsons, DeLanceys and Van Rensselaers suggest that the provincial legislature may best be understood not as a modern representative institution but rather as one of those eighteenth-century "constituted bodies" in which the tendency was "more toward the *Geburtsstand* than toward free association."[7]

Any attempt to rationally explain this system was bound to rip itself apart on contradiction. The representation of Schenectady but not of Newburgh, of Cortlandt Manor but not of Philipse Manor, could be justified in terms of the doctrine of virtual representation. That, as the Englishman Thomas Whately explained to protesting Americans in 1765, maintained that any special interests could be as well represented by a delegate from one group that possessed them as by a delegate from another.[8] The equality, with two seats each, of empty Richmond and Charlotte and of populous Ulster and Dutchess counties could be explained in terms of the need to represent the corporate whole, not the separate individual, and in New York the corporate whole was the county. "If a County was made and there were but 5 Freeholders in it, I would vote for a representation for it", observed William Smith, Jr.[9] But, again like the House of Commons, the assembly was based on an uneasy mixture of both principles.

The representatives considered that criticism of themselves or their institution was a crime; in this they were at one with assemblies throughout America.[10] Their insistence that they were above ordinary folk showed itself in such small things as their oft-repeated warning that "no other person" besides their official printer "presume to print" the assembly's journal. It showed itself in larger things, like the treatment meted out to writers, printers and even private correspondents who did criticize, whether intentionally or inadvertently. In 1756 the assembly resolved that by publishing a letter in their newspaper its official printers had attempted "by false and malicious Misrepresentations, to irritate the People . . . against their Representatives" and that both author and publishers were guilty of "a high Misdemeanour and a Contempt of the Authority of this House." The printers crawled to get the assembly's pardon, one of them declaring "that he humbly confesses his Fault . . . that he had no Design to give Offence . . . promises to be more circumspect for the future, and humbly begs the Pardon of the Honourable House." His sycophancy saved his official appointment, but though he had "long experienced the Kindness of the Honourable House" the assembly let him languish in jail for another full week after this self-abasement.[11]

Other writers were forced to bow as deeply in the 1750s[12], and in the following decade, when critics were both more serious and more careful with their identity, the assembly's response was shrill. It declared that one piece was "Libellous, Scandalous and Seditious, containing many indecent and insolent Expressions, highly reflecting on the Honour, Justice and Authority of and an high Insult and Indignity to this House."[13] A mild pamphlet published in London by the wretchedly unpopular lieutenant governor of the province, Cadwallader Colden, "tended to destroy the confidence of the People in two of the Branches of the Legislature ... to render the Government odious and contemptible; to abate that due Respect to Authority so necessary to Peace and good order."[14] And when Alexander McDougall was identified as the author of the truly abusive broadside *To the Betrayed Inhabitants of the City and Colony of New York* in 1770 he was imprisoned at the assembly's order and told that his refusal to plead to its charges could bring him to the "long hard penalty" of being crushed to death.[15] When McDougall tried to gain his freedom with a writ of *habeas corpus* from the supreme court the assembly had the records of the House of Commons searched in order to find precedents proving that "the Prisoners committed by us, cannot be taken from us."[16]

Neither archaic concepts of representation nor such legislative arrogance survived the Declaration of Independence. The constitution of 1777 replaced special seats and county equality in the assembly with a system of apportionment giving counties as few as two seats and as many as nine. Elections, which could take place under the old order as much as seven years apart, became annual. The appointive royal council, with its maximum of twelve members, was replaced by a senate of twenty-four and the constitution required a census and legislative reapportionment septennially. The assembly could grow with reapportionment to a maximum of three hundred members and the senate to one hundred.[17] All of these things meant that men who were far more "ordinary" found themselves in positions of power and that they held their power for much shorter periods.[18]

The constitution abolished acts of attainder, save for the duration of the War of Independence, and though the assembly briefly continued the old practice of appointing an official printer and warning lest any other "presume to print" its journals that was soon dropped. A bill of rights adopted in 1787 forbade the imprisonment of people save under indictment or presentment by a grand jury and, by declaring the sanctity of the right of petition, safeguarded citizens from legislative persecution for daring to ask for what they wanted.[19] These changes, and a new sense of self-restraint on the part of legislators, provided the climate in which Hamilton's "Phocion" letters and *The Federalist* could be freely published, for the old government would have seen these as the veriest libel. And no longer did its constituents address the legislature in the language of servility.

Proposition II: The provincial government was at most semi-consultative in its relationship with the public. The state government was much more fully responsive to public demands.

The old order was not a closed system, a "black box" within which arbitrary decisions were taken. On the contrary, there were numerous ways in which the people at large could both find out what their representatives were doing and put pressure on them. Moreover, these mechanisms increased in number and strength as the provincial period drew to its close. As early as 1754, when the question of whether King's College should be Anglican was the topic of the day, the assembly decided that its best course was prudence, voting to postpone deliberations and in the meantime to publish the bill "that ... we may have the opportunity of knowing the general sentiments of our Constituents, on this great and important Concern."[20] Nor was this the only time that public opinion was invited on serious issues and, for that matter, on local and trivial ones.[21]

The assembly's journal was available to the public, and between 1750 and 1775 the amount of significant information that it contained increased dramatically. In the late 1750s it contained very few roll-call votes and the information provided about these gave little idea about the content of the division. But by the 1770s the assemblymen were dividing frequently – they took fifty divisions in the last session alone – and the text of the journal gave a careful reader a complete picture of what the members were doing. From 1769 onwards the assembly's chamber was open to the public. Due deference, including removal of hats, was required of visitors, and though we have no way of finding out how many men or what sort of men attended we do know that the radical merchant Alexander McDougall was frequently there.[22] By 1774 an interested observer, especially one who lived in New York City, could know fully the assembly's business. And when assemblymen sponsored bills that were clearly calculated to build electoral support they showed that they knew as much as any modern American congressman about "pork-barrel politics."[23]

But in other ways the system was not so open. The *Assembly Journal*, for instance, was sold rather than distributed to localities. Privileged folk like Sir William Johnson, Bart., read it regularly and carefully and discussed the assembly's affairs with their correspondents. Johnson himself, however, noted that his neighbors in the Mohawk Valley "have no knowledge of what is doing at the Capital" and that the members who were supposed to represent them "[res]ide at a distance and have contrary interests."[24] And the rhetoric of submission, the crawling of offending printers, the humility of petitions and the intense interest of assemblymen in the privileges of their house all demonstrated that the men in power were masters and those outside were subjects.

The other two branches of the government, the governorship and the council, made no pretence at being "popular", for the governor was the king's vicegerent and the council kept all of its proceedings secret. The diary that William Smith, Jr., kept during his eight years as a councillor and confidant to several governors demonstrates how one official thought those branches ought to act. Smith, son of another councillor, codifier of New York's laws, historian of the province and author of outspokenly whiggish essays, was no defender of arbitrary authority, but to his mind the distance between rulers and ruled ought to be great. When the council passed a bill to prevent trials by justices of the peace in the taverns that many of them kept, Smith and the governor had a good laugh at "the thought of our submitting to humour the Tavern Keepers." When a sheriff was turned out of office despite petitions for his retention and was told that "the Petitions should be of no service for the People had no Right to interpose with respect to Offices", Smith thought that "sound doctrine." When a newly appointed governor told the historian that "he meant to consult the Interest of the Province but should not steer by the Popular Voice", Smith told him that he was right. *Noblesse* could, of course, *oblige*. During a dispute on a minor point Smith told his fellow councillors that "it greatly magnified an Admn. to promote the public good unsolicited by the People, and still more, when thro' Blindness they opposed what being for their Good, they would afterwards approve." But when, at the very end of the colonial period the legislature passed laws to benefit the New York City construction industry and the province's Scots immigrants Smith noted scornfully that "these two Bills owe their Success to Condescensions to the Carpenters and seceders to get votes at the next Elections — shameful Principles to act upon."[25]

Yet for all its stridence the assembly became less and less able to uphold its self-proclaimed superiority in the last ten years of its life. An anonymous letter in 1765 told the assemblymen to "be not so conceited as to say or think that other People know nothing about Government you have made these laws and say they are Right but they are Rong and take a way Leberty, Oppressions of your make Gentlemen make us Sons of Liberty think you are not for the Public Liberty."[26] McDougall's diatribe of 1769 brought him imprisonment and threats of torture but one prescient assemblyman replied laconically to the threat to crush McDougall to death with the observation that the house might throw its prisoner "over the Bar, or out of the Windows, but that the public would judge of the justice of it."[27] Seven years later that assemblyman would be elected revolutionary governor of New York State; meanwhile McDougall, by his proud defiance, turned his imprisonment into a propaganda victory, focussing public anger about jobs, and depression, and the hated British garrison onto the assembly itself.[28]

The last five years of the old assembly saw a barrage of publications in the same spirit. The house was reviled as the "general Assembly of Liliput," whose members should not be asked to think lest they be consigned to "a task for which nature, and long disuse, have rendered some of you unfit" and lest the effort "cruelly anticipate the future punishment of others."[29] The heavy accent of assemblyman John DeNoyelles, McDougall's chief tormentor, was mocked in public.[30] And by 1775 New Yorkers were being told that they needed no assembly at all, for it, like Parliament, had become a tool of tyranny and had been superseded by the better form of revolutionary congresses and committees in which "the people have all the weight and influence they ought to have."[31] Perhaps the disparity between the claims of the assembly to supremacy and its ability, after 1765, to enforce them demonstrates that the assembly itself was withering and that the "power vacuum" which some students see as the surest sign of imminent revolution was setting in.[32]

Independence and the chance to create a new structure turned the trends in the old towards openness into a rush and virtually wiped out its elitism. The secret deliberations of the council were replaced by open senate sessions recorded in a published journal. The assembly's journal, naturally, continued to be published as well.[33] By the late 1780s the newspapers were publishing the proceedings and even the actual debates of the legislators.[34] As a result of the vicissitudes of war the legislature met between 1777 and 1783 not in New York City, its traditional venue, but rather in Peekskill, Newburgh, Poughkeepsie, Kingston and Albany, and one may infer that its close presence helped to demythologize it in the minds of both townsmen and farmers in the neighboring countryside.

There were parallel changes in the spirit of the government's operations. Public appointments, both military and civilian, were vested by the constitution in a body made up of the governor and of four senators, who were chosen by the assembly. This was not the direct popular election for which some called,[35] but the council of appointment, as the body was called, acted as if the people had a right to a say about their officials. On the first occasion that the question arose, when a militia colonel was attacked for gross corruption and for misuse of his powers, the council resolved that it was "reduced to an absolute Necessity in point of Duty to hear every Complaint of Misbehaviour in Officers of the Militia and to displace where there are just grounds for it." And when it ordered a dismissal it was on the ground "that the Pleasure of the People of this State . . . determines the tenure of his Office."[36]

During the dark days of 1779, when militant loyalism, economic crisis and food shortage converged in such a general crisis that crowds took to the streets and revolutionary committees formed anew, Governor George Clinton, who had once warned the colonial assembly that the people would judge its treatment of McDougall, advised the state legislators to pay close attention to what the people were telling them. They did, passing a series of highly popular laws that punished loyalists, that imposed taxation according to the radical principle of "circumstances and other abilities to pay taxes, collectively considered," that imposed price controls and that embargoed precious grain and flour from leaving the state.[37] Some of these laws marked direct turn-arounds from policies that the legislature had previously followed, and such direct responsiveness, especially in matters of taxation and property, would have been inconceivable under the old order. In 1781 the two houses jointly published an unprecedented address to the people, taking care to see that it appeared repeatedly in the newspapers and that copies circulated in every township of the state. Popular complaints were still running high about many things and the legislators told their "Friends and Fellow-Citizens" that "the representatives of a free people cannot be inattentive to the opinions of their constituents." They stressed that some evils were unavoidable and could not be changed but that it was nonetheless fitting for them, "the temporary representatives of the majesty of the people, to prosecute this address in a stile which free men ought to use to their equals."[38] The legislature had not become an automatic rubber stamp for the popular will, but it was no longer a "shameful principle" for it to respond to pressure from outside.

Proposition III: Officials and men in positions of social and political privilege regularly used the public machinery of the old order to achieve their private ends. This was much less the case under the new order.

The record of the late provincial period shows instance after instance in which officials used power for their own purposes, sometimes with disastrous public results. Many officials considered their offices as private possessions, which they held for their own good rather than for the service of either king or country. In 1764 Lieutenant Governor Colden involved himself in a nasty squabble with the captain of a sloop of war over a seizure that the sloop had made in New York Harbor. Such raids caused great distress, but that was not Colden's concern. The captain informed the lieutenant governor that "he intended to claim one half for himself, officers and crew", but Colden replied that "by the statute by which the ship and cargoe are forfeited one third is given up to the Governor and that I could not consent to give up the Rights of the Governor."[39] Nor could he consent to give up his share of the loot. Six years later, when Colden yielded command to the Earl of Dunmore he and the noble lord had a typically eighteenth-century dispute over whether Dunmore should receive half of "the Emoluments of Government received by [Colden] since the date of [Dunmore's] Commission."[40] When the earl was transferred to Virginia he disgraced himself before his successor and the provincial council in a drunken tirade, shouting "damn Virginia – did I ever seek it? Why is it forced upon me? I asked for New York – New York I took, and they have robbed me of it without my consent."[41]

One reason for Dunmore's anger at losing New York may be found in what Colden did in 1774 and 1775, when the lieutenant governor was once again in charge. The tea crisis had broken, the empire was on the brink of destruction, but much of Colden's time was spent on other things. In an effort to quiet the fierce conflicts in the Green Mountain area which had resulted from long confusion about whether the area belonged to New York or New Hampshire the Board of Trade had awarded the region to New York but had forbidden the province to make any further land grants there. But when Colden resumed control he announced to his council that he would begin to hand out lands freely in "the Grants," despite his instructions. "Observe this well," noted Councillor William Smith, who hated Colden and who was only too glad to have evidence that the lieutenant governor was a crook. Smith remonstrated again and again in the council against granting the lands; not only did it break the king's instructions, but by putting more New York grantees into the area it was almost certain to ruin whatever faint hopes existed of settling the dispute peacefully. For the next year Smith's diary records his lonely opposition to grants for the Speaker of the assembly, for the governor's son-in-law, and for the members of various great families, all in the tens of thousands of acres. Even where he stood to gain himself he voted against the grants.[42] But at the very beginning of the land grab, writing to his friend Philip Schuyler, Smith showed how limited was his sense of the proper role of a king's servant: "Colden is granting Lands in the Face of the last instructions . . . the seal is ready if the Money is laid down – I intend to sport away about £ 1000 as I suppose it will be the last chance . . . I shall buy lands that I opposed the Grant of – Is there any Thing Wrong in this? – Have I not discharged my Duty when I voted agt. a Petition in which I was myself concerned . . . apply soon for the next Packet may close the present Scene in which the Kings Property is to be disposed of agt. his Will – Let all this be a secret."[43] Lord Dunmore, himself heavily involved in northern New York speculations, had known what he was losing.

The entire political program of the majority in the last assembly, which sat from 1769 to 1775, rested on assumptions similar to those of Colden, Dunmore and Smith. The party moved quickly to consolidate its power after the election of 1769, using both the letter of the law and the privileges of the assembly for its own gain. Though much of what it did was, in technical terms, progressive enough, the problem lay in the spirit in which it was done. A law passed to prevent justices of the supreme court from sitting in the assembly was a step towards the separation of powers, but its purpose was to keep Justice Robert R. Livingston from taking the seat to which he was repeatedly elected.[44] Another law, requiring representatives to live in their constituencies, presaged future American practice and pointed towards a need for close identification between representatives and constituents. The law was passed, however, solely for the sake of evicting two of the minority from their seats.[45] In 1775 the majority abolished the double vote in the special constituencies of Albany County, where its opponents were strong, but not in those of Westchester, where it had more support.[46] In the name of parliamentary privilege it bullied opposition candidates who challenged the elections of its members, and electoral officials who presented the returns from opposition constituencies.[47] And it defended all that it did as "an Exertion of that Right which the Constitution had lodged in the Representatives of the People."[48]

Lesser officials, too, considered office as private property. One step taken by the "popular whigs" – as they had been until they gained power in 1769[49] – was the sacking of office-holders to make room for their own men. This was hardly unique in American political history; what is interesting is William Smith's comment that one of those fired, the sheriff of Westchester County, was "a Widows Son" who acquired the shrievalty "by the resignation of his Uncle." This, thought Smith, gave the sheriff a legitimate claim; Smith himself, after all, had gained his seat on the council by the resignation of his father.[50] And when residents of southern Albany County protested against the assembly's nomination of a Van Rensselaer as road commissioner on the ground that it would encourage his "extravagant Claims and Encroachments" against "their ancient Township" the protest had no effect.[51]

The record of the post-Independence government was hardly spotless. Governor Clinton, in a flash-back to the powers of his predecessors, once threatened to prorogue the legislature rather than let it consider the independence of the Green Mountains, now become Vermont. Clinton had some land claims there and his political ally James Duane had many more.[52] After 1791 he and his followers "proceeded to dispose of land on a scale that might have made the most generous Royal governor . . . blush" and even earlier his land policies had delivered "more land into the hands of speculators than to actual settlers."[53] But Clintonian land policy did differ significantly from what went on before. The land laws were rewritten again and again in the 1780s, but three things that contrasted sharply with earlier practice remained constant. One was the openness of the process of handing land out; the maps on which grants were recorded were to be accessible and lands were to be sold at public vendue rather than in private deals.[54] Another was the reduction to almost nothing of the fees involved. William Smith had thought it a magnificent gesture on the part of Governor Tryon when the governor forgave fees of £ 1300 due from one great family and he applauded again when Tryon promised to distribute 100,000 acres among his councillors without fees[55], but a law of 1784 limited fees to a mere £ 3 for the governor and £ 5 for the surveyor.[56] The third was the provision of a chance for smaller people to get land directly from the state. The land law of 1785 provided that people could make locations of up to five hundred acres at the rate of four shillings per acre, which meant a payment of only £ 100 for the maximum grant, and that of 1786, dividing lands into townships of 64,000 acres, provided that every fourth township was to be sold in individual lots of six hundred and forty acres each.[57] Surveys were, moreover, regularized, with a pattern of townships, as nearly square as possible, to replace the haphazard irregularities which had made colonial grants a surveyor's nightmare and a lawyer's bonanza. The Revolution in New York did not wipe out speculation by any means, but it did at least change it from a gentleman's privilege to a citizen's opportunity.

There would be abuse enough of parliamentary power in the later legislative history of New York, but in the decades following Independence, at least, its handling was in line with the principle of popular rather than partisan sovereignty. State legislators were expelled several times. One victim was the militia colonel already mentioned, who had a seat in the senate, and his expulsion was due to his misuse of the power that he held. Another was a Hudson Valley senator who was both a perennial absentee and a Baptist lay preacher. His lay preaching, the senate resolved, did not make him a minister and thus did not disqualify him under the clause of the constitution that denied seats to the clergy, but he was expelled when he escaped on horseback from the custody of the officer who had been sent to bring him to account for his absences. [58] Both of these men were re-elected after their expulsions and were given their seats. The naming in 1787 of Alexander Hamilton to the Philadelphia convention, which he supported but which most of his fellow legislators did not, and the scornful refusal by Governor John Jay in 1800 of a plan to steal the presidential election from Jefferson were later indications that post-Revolutionary New Yorkers did not accept the right of a party to use privilege in order to crush its opponents.

Proposition IV: The legislation passed by the provincial government frequently reflected the interests of the elite at the expense of ordinary people. The laws passed by the state government came much closer to being either socially "neutral" or anti-elitist.

Historians have paid great attention to the spectacular battles fought by the factions of colonial New York, but they have spent much less effort on understanding what those factions did with power when they had it. A complete study of the laws they passed is impossible here, but a careful look at two sensitive categories, taxation and tenancy law, shows a persistent pattern of class legislation, regardless of what faction was in control.

Let us look first at taxation. The day-to-day expenses of colonial New York were met from three permanent taxes, a duty on imports, a series of excise laws and the license fees paid by hawkers and pedlars. The impost could be quite significant, reaching £ 10,346 in 1760, when many goods were being imported for the army, and standing at £ 5200 in 1774. As the historian of colonial taxation suggests, this reliance on imposts and excises meant that the burden of supporting the government rested on consumers in a way quite unrelated to their actual ability to pay. Poor and middling people inside the market economy paid more, proportionately, than the rich.[59]

The province resorted to land taxes only in time of war, when loans had to be floated, and throughout the colonial period practice in taxing land was governed by a law passed as early as 1693. But war was endemic in early America and land taxes were in use on and off throughout the eighteenth century; between 1759 and 1762 alone the legislature voted the hefty sum of £ 252,000. These land taxes were set out on a county quota basis, and each time a new tax was passed each county's quota was determined by bargains and alliances in the assembly. Usually this "log-rolling" meant that the two cities, New York and Albany, bore disproportionate amounts of the tax; in 1693 £ 1450 out of a total tax of £ 6000 was to be paid by New York City and in 1759 the metropolis was billed for £ 3000 out of a total tax of £ 9000. In the latter year Albany was to pay another £ 1500. By contrast, the large, populous and, in agricultural terms, valuable county of Dutchess was to pay a mere £ 642 in 1759, barely more than it had paid in 1693, when it was raw frontier.[60] Within the counties taxes were assessed "on estates real and personal" and assessors always took real estate to mean improved real estate. The vast empty tracts held by speculators and on great estates would pay no taxes until they were settled, and even then the terms of leases would require tenants to pay them.

Colonial New Yorkers made sporadic attempts to tighten up the tax system, but always on a piecemeal basis. In 1758, for instance, a law established one method of assessment for all of New York City "that persons of Equal Estates in the different Wards may be Rated in their assessments at Equal Sums."[61] Another law, passed in 1764, tried to equalize taxation in Orange County by requiring a stringent oath from assessors, but by providing that the assessors should rate estates "according to the Value by Improvements thereon" it meant that the great speculations called Minisink, Kakiate and Wawayanda would continue untaxed. That no doubt pleased the past and future assemblymen, the urban merchants and the attornies who were heavily involved in these patents.[62] Yet another attempt at reform, in 1775, provided a stiff rate on improved lands in Orange but again made no mention of taxing unimproved lands.[63] These laws were typical: none applied to the whole province and though they tried to cope with the system's inefficiency none attacked its structural problems.

Taxation changed drastically after Independence. In its first two sessions the state legislature passed tax laws that operated on a wholly different basis, setting specific rates for real and personal property and for the first time requiring the taxation of unimproved real property.[64] In the third session, that of 1779–1780, the legislature reverted to the older system of county quotas, but with the significant addition of the clause for assessment according to "circumstances and abilities." Here was a radical piece of work! Assessors were now free to ignore the clauses in leases by which landlords had imposed on tenants the duty of paying taxes and to set their rates on the basis of the figure a man cut, the kind of clothes he wore and cutlery he used and furniture he sat on, and the speculative property he held. In short the legislature had passed a tax on wealth. The "cirumstances and abilities" clause was to be bitterly debated by many subsequent legislatures, but it remained a very popular law for year after year.[65]

Tenancy was a second subject of class legislation, and never more strikingly than in an act passed in 1774 "for the better security and more easy Recovery of Rents, and Renewal of Leases, and to prevent Frauds committed by Tenants." This act was passed by an assembly dominated by the "urban" legislative group centered on the DeLancey family, the "popular whigs" of the 1760s, but no law could have been more favorable to the great landholders. Its chief effect was to allow landlords to distrain the goods, chattels and crops, harvested or growing, of tenants who owed them rent. The goods were to be appraised and sold at public vendue, the proceeds going to the landlord. The law dealt with the age-old custom of "rescuing" goods that authority had seized by providing for triple damages to the landlord if this happened or, for that matter, on any breach of impoundment. Tenants, for their part, were to be entitled to double damages for unlawful acts committed by persons in the act of distraining their goods, but unlawful acts during a seizure would not make the distraint illegal. The tenant, moreover, would be entitled to no damages at all if the landlord made "tender of amends." Tenants caught in the act of rescuing distrained goods received no equivalent privilege; they would pay their triple damages. Goods carried off the tenant's premises were subject to distraint within thirty days of their removal and the law allowed a landlord, in the company of a constable, to enter and break open any places that he believed contained goods hidden to avoid distress. The law also provided that any tenant refusing to deliver up his land at the end of a lease was to be liable to double rent. And "whereas great Inconveniences may happen to Lessors and Landlords in Cases of Re-entry for non-payment of Rent, by reason of the many niceties that attend re-entries at Common Law" those "niceties" were wiped out as far as tenants were concerned. Instead a very simple procedure would allow the landlord to serve his notice and evict the tenant.[66]

This act was part of a barrage of bills in 1773, 1774 and 1775, all having in direct object the establishment of a secure position for New York's landlord class. One "for the Recovery of Possessions by Ejectment upon a Title under Sixty Years" of age was rejected by Governor Tryon. William Smith, who had married into the landholding Livingston family, took issue with the veto, complaining that the governor's only objections were "that a Right of Action over and over again for the same lands, would force the poor occupant to give up to the Rich Plaintiff and that at this Juncture the Ministry would consider [the bill] as a Mean to ruin and distress the Claimants [in the Green Mountains] under New Hampshire." Councillor James DeLancey, like Smith, knew better, for DeLancey had been told that the bill "was requisite to enable the Proprietors of the Manor of Cortlandt to recover old possessed lands." DeLancey was "considerably interested" in that manor.[67] Another striking class law was the riot act by which New York tried in 1774 to put down the agrarian insurgency in the Green Mountains. The act imposed capital attainder upon eight of the insurgency's leaders by name and again and again it specified the death penalty for offenses committed in the region of strife.[68] And as a final gesture, the assembly also enacted a law forbidding the crown to challenge any land title in any way more than sixty years after the original grant.[69] The hostility of the crown to the existence of the great tracts was well known[70] but by passing the law the assembly had made the landlords as secure against attacks from above as from below. It was, however, 1775.

The laws passed by the state government did not turn the tables completely. Great estates, like Livingston and Rensselaerwyck, survived the Revolution, not to fall until the antirent upheaval of the 1840s. Landlordism even spread westwards; in the 1800s a minister travelling in what had been the Iroquois country noted that "the same evil operates here ... as in many parts of this country – the lands are most of them leased."[71] But in some significant ways hostility to the great holdings was written into the laws. Moreover by 1790 the cards in the legal deck were no longer stacked against the tenant. One step, as shown above, was the enactment for the first time of tax laws that could strike at landlords where it hurt, in their unimproved holdings. Another, likewise a response to immense popular pressure, was the passage in 1779 of a law confiscating the estates of many prominent loyalists, whom it named, and providing for easy action against others by grand juries. In order that "no advantage may be taken of mere matters of form," the confiscation act loaded procedure against loyalist landholders as fully as the tenancy act of 1774 had loaded it against tenants. And in an ominous though vague final clause, the confiscation act declared "the sovereignty of the people of this state in respect of all property within the same."[72] The bill of rights adopted in 1787 prevented any possibility of a repetition of the 1774 tenancy law by prohibiting the eviction of any person from "his or her franchise or freehold" or the seizure of any person's "goods and chattels unless he or she be duly brought to answer and be fore-judged of the same by due course of law."[73] The Revolution had thus destroyed a sizable proportion of the landlord class, brought punitive taxation of the assets of those who had survived and guaranteed to tenants the same procedural rights that the law gave to landlords. There would still be evictions and violent class strife, but tenants and landlords alike would enjoy the benefit of "the many niceties" of the law.

It remains to relate these four propositions to the recent historiography of the Revolution and to tentatively raise some new possibilities for exploration. An increasing number of studies are developing the idea that the pre-Revolutionary structure was an inefficient, vacillating, class-dominated "old order." One student sees county courts, appointed from above, as taking power away from town governments, elected from below, in Massachusetts.[74] Another notes the inability of the provincial government there to cope with rioting and sees in its "unwillingness to accept responsibilities" a syndrome "typical of an 'ancien régime'."[75] Profound disquiet and fading self-confidence have been noted within Virginia's ruling class in the 1760s.[76] Yet another student finds his evidence in the remarkably ineffective taxation policies which the colonies adopted.[77] And a study of the courts of provincial New York concludes that they simply could not do the job of enforcing the law, that, in other words, government was not good at governing.[78] All of these points lead one to infer that the colonial elite was proving inadequate for the task of governing a developing society. Even unsuccessful reforms like those propounded at various times by Archibald Kennedy, Thomas Hutchinson, William Smith and Joseph Galloway bear the point out, for the roads to the great revolutions are littered with the names of similar reformers, likewise astute, likewise impotent.

Such a situation might be described as one of "political decay"[79] and it may be that this decay reflects the inability of the colonial regime to even cope with, let alone guide, social development and political mobilization. The contrast in larger terms between pre-Revolutionary and post-Revolutionary New York is instructive. The student of the former must explain things like Leisler's Rebellion, the vicissitudes of Anglo-

American politics, slow population growth and land-rioting.[80] The student of the latter, by contrast, discusses a state with a surging population and booming prosperity, with an advanced transportation network, with the ability to make a successful transition from grain-based agriculture to dairy farming, market gardening and industrialization. One need only mention the Erie Canal system to indicate the vital role that an efficient state government played in the making of the Empire State, but even before the canal one finds evidence that the state was playing a vital role. The vitality stems, one suspects, from the close relationship between government and people that developed during the Revolutionary period. The Revolutionary movement, in its many facets, had mobilized the populace politically in a way which the old institutions could not stand and the result had been decay. Post-Revolutionary society, with its expectation of commercial success for every man, saw demands on the political system continue and even increase, but the new system could cope.

Partly this reflects the existence of new means of communication, especially political parties and newspapers. But equally it reflects new acknowledgement of the right of people "outside the walls" to get action from their government when they wanted it. The old order was not closed; there was room for popular participation on many issues. But it was a "shameful principle" not an honorable one, for officials and legislators to do what their constituents wanted because their constituents wanted it. By contrast both in actions and in words the men who occupied the new institutions demonstrated that they believed they had a duty to be responsive, even if that meant telling the people that what they wanted could not be done. As an outstanding political science theorist suggests, "the acceptance by superordinates of the obligation to be responsive, in however limited a way, is probably as great a watershed in democratic political development as the right of people to choose representatives, which is to say to participate at all."[81] When New York's rulers accepted that principle in the first years of independence it was very new wine indeed.

Notes

* I wish to thank Michael W. Doyle, Dirk Hoerder and Duncan MacLeod for criticisms of earlier drafts of this essay.
1 See Pauline Maier, *From Resistance to Revolution: Colonial Radicals and the Development of American Opposition to Britain* (New York, 1972); Patricia U. Bonomi, *A Factious People: Politics and Society in Colonial New York* (New York and London, 1971); and Richard A. Ryerson, "Political Mobilization and

the American Revolution: The Resistance Movement in Philadelphia, 1765 to 1776," *WMQ*, 3rd Ser., XXI (1974), 565–588.

[2] Samuel P. Huntington, *Political Order in Changing Societies* (New Haven and London, 1968), 266.

[3] See Gordon S. Wood, *The Creation of the American Republic, 1776–1787* (Chapel Hill, N. C., 1969), and J. R. Pole, *Political Representation in England and the Origins of the American Republic* (London, 1966).

[4] See "The Respectful Address of the Mechanicks in Union, for the City and County of New York, represented by their General Committee," *AA*, 4, VI, 895–896, and Dirk Hoerder, "Socio-Political Structures and Popular Ideology, 1750s–1780s" in this volume.

[5] Edward Countryman, "Consolidating Power in Revolutionary America: The Case of New York, 1775–1783," *Journal of Interdisciplinary History,* VI (1975–1976), 645–677.

[6] These comments are drawn from a reading of the *Assembly Journal* from 1750 to 1775. C. O. 5/1216–1220, PRO. On assemblymen's pay see Guy Johnson to Sir William Johnson, 23. Feb., 1773, James Sullivan and Alexander C. Flick, eds., *The Papers of Sir William Johnson,* 14 vols. (Albany, N. Y., 1921–1965), VIII, 722.

[7] Robert R. Palmer, *The Age of the Democratic Revolution, I: The Challenge* (Princeton, N. J., 1959), 29.

[8] Whately, "The Regulations Lately Made ... Considered" in Edmund S. Morgan, ed., *Prologue to Revolution: Sources and Documents on the Stamp Act Crisis, 1764–1766* (Chapel Hill, N. C., 1959), 17–23.

[9] William H. W. Sabine, ed., *Historical Memoirs From 16 March 1763 to 25 July 1778 of William Smith,* 2 vols. in 1 (New York, 1969), I, 135.

[10] See Mary Patterson Clarke, *Parliamentary Privilege in the American Colonies* (New Haven, Conn., 1943).

[11] *Assembly Journal,* 19–30 March, 1756, C. O. 5/1216, PRO.

[12] *Assembly Journal,* 16–24 March, 1758, C. O. 5/1216, PRO.

[13] *Assembly Journal,* 29 Nov., 1765, C. O. 5/1217, PRO.

[14] *Assembly Journal,* 30 Dec., 1767, C. O. 5/1218, PRO.

[15] Alexander McDougall, *To the Freeholders and Freemen of the City and Colony of New York,* Broadside (New York, 1770, Evans No. 11710).

[16] *Assembly Journal,* 19 Jan.–16 Feb., 1771, C. O. 5/1219, PRO.

[17] "The First Constitution of the State of New York," in Robert C. Cumming et al., eds., *The Constitution of the State of New York with Notes, References and Annotations* (Albany, N. Y., 1884), 42–55.

[18] See Jackson T. Main, "Government by the People: The American Revolution and the Democratization of the Legislatures," *WMQ*, 3rd Ser., XXIII (1966), 391–407.

[19] *Laws,* of the State of New York, microfilm ed., in William Sumner Jenkins, ed., *Records of the States of the United States* (Washington, D. C., 1949), N. Y. B2, Reel 6, Unit 2, 10th sess., Ch. 1.

[20] *Assembly Journal,* 26 Nov., 1754, C. O. 5/1216, PRO.

[21] See the correspondence of Sir William Johnson with Hugh Wallace, James DeLancey and John Watts on a proposed division of Albany County, in Sullivan and Flick, eds., *Johnson Papers* (cf. n. 6), VII and VIII, *passim.; Assembly Journal,* 16 Jan., 18 Febr., 1756, C. O. 5/1216, PRO.

[22] For the rules governing visitors see *Assembly Journal,* 6 Dec., 1769, C. O.

5/1219, PRO; on McDougall see Roger J. Champagne, *Alexander McDougall and the American Revolution in New York* (Schenectady, N. Y., 1975), 18.

[23] *Assembly Journal*, 7 Apr., 19 May, 1769, C. O. 5/1218, PRO.

[24] Sir William Johnson to Hugh Wallace, 12 Feb., 1771, Sullivan and Flick, eds., *Johnson Papers* (cf. n. 6), VII, 1136; Sir William Johnson to James De-Lancey, *ib.*, 100–101.

[25] Sabine, ed., *Historical Memoirs of William Smith* (cf. n. 9), I, 119, 55, 118, 132, 212.

[26] *Assembly Journal*, 29 Nov., 1765, C. O. 5/1217, PRO.

[27] McDougall, *To the Freeholders and Freemen* (cf. n. 15).

[28] See Champagne, *Alexander McDougall* (cf. n. 22), Ch. 2, 3.

[29] *A Letter to the Majority of the General Assembly of Liliput*, Broadside (New York, January 1772, Evans No. 12433).

[30] *Debates on Dividing Orange County*, Broadside (New York, 1774, Evans No. 13239).

[31] *"A Poor Man" to the Citizens of New York, 30 December, 1775*, Broadside (New York, 1775).

[32] Chalmers Johnson, *Revolutionary Change* (Boston and Toronto, 1966).

[33] The constitution of 1777 specified merely that the journals of both houses be printed in the same manner as that of the colonial assembly. The first two sessions of the state assembly issued normal warnings to nonofficial printers but thereafter the practice was dropped. The senate never issued such warnings.

[34] But compare this argument with that in Linda Grant DePauw, *The Eleventh Pillar: New York State and the Federal Constitution* (Ithaca, N. Y., 1966), 24–25.

[35] Certain local officials, most notably assessors of taxes, were elected both before and after Independence, but all policy officials were appointed from above under both the old and new orders.

[36] *Minutes of the Council of Appointment April 2, 1778–May 3, 1779* (New York Historical Society, *Collections*, LVII–LVIII [New York, 1925]), 18, 72.

[37] This is discussed fully in Countryman, "Consolidating Power" (cf. n. 5).

[38] "An Address from the Legislature of the State of New York to their Constituents," *Assembly Journal*, microfilm ed. in William Sumner Jenkins, ed., *Records of the States* (cf. n. 19), N. Y., A. 1b., Reel 4, Unit 1, 13 March, 1781.

[39] Colden to R. Monckton, 20 Jan., 1764, *Colden Letter Books*, I (New York Historical Society, *Collections*, IX [New York, 1877]), 281.

[40] Colden to Arthur Mairs, 12. Nov., 1770, *Colden Letter Books*, II (*ib.* X [New York, 1878]), 235–236.

[41] Sabine, ed., *Historical Memoirs of William Smith* (cf. n. 9), I, 107.

[42] *Ib.*, 185 ff.

[43] Smith to Philip Schuyler, 9 July, 1774, *ib.*, I, 188–189.

[44] *Assembly Journal*, 23 Nov., 1769, C. O. 5/1219, PRO; *The Address of Mr. Justice Livingston to the House of Assembly in Support of his Right to a Seat*, (New York, 1769, Evans No. 11313).

[45] *Assembly Journal*, 12 May, 1769, C. O. 5/1219, PRO; Lawrence H. Leder, "The New York Elections of 1769: An Assault on Privilege," *Mississippi Valley Historical Review*, XLIX (1962–1963), 675–682.

[46] Sabine, ed., *Historical Memoirs of William Smith* (cf. n. 9), I, 215.

[47] *Assembly Journal*, 29 Apr., 1769, 7 Dec., 1769, 21 Dec., 1769, C. O. 5/1218–1219, PRO.

⁴⁸ *Assembly Journal,* 25 Jan., 1771, C. O. 5/1219, PRO.

⁴⁹ See Bonomi, *A Factious People* (cf. n. 1), 237–239.

⁵⁰ Sabine, ed., *Historical Memoirs of William Smith* (cf. n. 9), I, 68, 34–39.

⁵¹ *Assembly Journal,* 8–17 Jan., 1770, C. O. 5/1219, PRO.

⁵² *Senate Journal,* microfilm ed., in William Sumner Jenkins, ed., *Records of the States* (cf. n. 19), N. Y. A. 1a, Reel 2, Unit 1, 21 February, 1781; E. Wilder Spaulding, *His Excellency George Clinton, Critic of the Constitution,* 2nd ed. (Port Washington, N. Y., 1964), 143–144.

⁵³ Alfred F. Young, *The Democratic Republicans of New York: The Origins, 1763–1797* (Chapel Hill, N. C., 1967), 243, 232.

⁵⁴ *Laws* of the State of New York (cf. n. 19), 7th sess., Ch. 60.

⁵⁵ Sabine, ed., *Historical Memoirs of William Smith* (cf. n. 9), I, 146.

⁵⁶ *Laws* of the State of New York (cf. n. 19), 7th sess., Ch. 60.

⁵⁷ *Ib.,* 8th sess., Ch. 66; 9th sess., Ch. 67.

⁵⁸ *Senate Journal* (cf. n. 52), 30 June, 1778 to 8 Feb., 1779, 27 May, 1780 to 15 Mar., 1781.

⁵⁹ Robert Arthur Becker, "The Politics of Taxation in America, 1763–1783," (Ph. D. diss., University of Wisconsin, 1971), 58–59, 114, 68.

⁶⁰ *The Colonial Laws of New York* (5 vols., Albany, N. Y., 1894), Ch. 30 (1693), I, 315–321; Ch. 1059 (1758), IV, 215–235.

⁶¹ *Ib.,* Ch. 1076 (1758), IV, 306–309.

⁶² *Ib.,* Ch. 1263 (1764), IV, 826–827. In the following year the law was changed to provide for taxation of "every part" of the real and personal estates of residents and absentees. "Woodlands," however, were excepted and a continuing loophole was thus provided. *Ib.,* Ch. 1289 (1765), IV, 884–886.

⁶³ *Ib.,* Ch. 1740 (1775), V, 858–862.

⁶⁴ *Assembly Journal* (cf. n. 38), 25 Feb.–27 Mar., 1778.

⁶⁵ *Ib.,* 31 Jan., 1780, 21 June, 1781, 8 Nov., 1781, 5 Feb., 1783.

⁵⁶ *Laws* of the State of New York (cf. n. 19), 7th sess., Ch. 60.

⁶⁷ Sabine, ed., *Historical Memoirs of William Smith* (cf. n. 9), I, 142–143.

⁶⁸ *Colonial Laws* (cf. n. 60), Ch. 1660 (1774), V, 647–655.

⁶⁹ *Ib.,* Ch. 1738 (1775), V, 850–856.

⁷⁰ See Bonomi, *A Factious People* (cf. n. 1), 182.

⁷¹ "Journal of Rev. John Taylor's Missionary Tour Through the Mohawk and Black River Countries in 1802," Edmund Bailey O'Callaghan, ed., *The Documentary History of the State of New York* (4 vols., Albany, N. Y., 1849–1851), III, 1136.

⁷² *Laws* of the State of New York (cf. n. 19), 3rd sess., Ch. 25.

⁷³ *Ib.,* 10th sess., Ch. 1.

⁷⁴ John M. Murrin, "Review Essay," *History and Theory,* XI (1972), 226–275.

⁷⁵ Dirk Hoerder, *People and Mobs: Crowd Action in Massachusetts during the American Revolution, 1765–1780* (Ph. D. diss., Free University of Berlin, 1971), 207.

⁷⁶ Gordon S. Wood, "Rhetoric and Reality in the American Revolution," *WMQ,* 3rd Ser., XXIII (1966), 3–32.

⁷⁷ Becker, "Politics of Taxation" (cf. n. 59).

⁷⁸ Douglas Greenberg, "The Effectiveness of Law Enforcement in Eighteenth-Century New York," *American Journal of Legal History,* XIX (1975), 173–207.

⁷⁹ Samuel P. Huntington, "Political Development and Political Decay," *World Politics,* XVII (1965), 386–430.

[80] See Thomas J. Archdeacon, *New York City, 1664–1710: Conquest and Change* (Ithaca and London, 1976); Stanley Nider Katz, *Newcastle's New York: Anglo-American Politics, 1732–1753* (Cambridge, Mass., 1968); Bonomi, *A Factious People* (cf. n. 1); and Edward Countryman, "'Out of the Bounds of the Law': Northern Land Rioters in the Eighteenth Century," in Alfred F. Young, ed., *The American Revolution: Explorations in the History of American Radicalism* (DeKalb, Ill., 1976).

[81] Ted Robert Gurr, personal communication, 25 July, 1975. See also Ted Robert Gurr and Harry Eckstein, *Patterns of Authority: A Structural Basis for Political Inquiry* (New York, 1975).

Agrarian Radicalism in the Late Revolutionary Period (1780–1795)

Barbara Karsky

> Because they were poore therefore
> they were determined to do them-
> selves justice ... poor Men were
> always oppressed by the Rich.

> Let it stand as a principle that govern-
> ment originates from the people; but
> let the people be taught ... that they
> are not able to govern themselves.

Nothing better illustrates the conflict inherent in the American Revolution than these two diametrically opposed statements. In the first a New
York tenant farmer, William Prendergast, defended the Great Rebellion
of 1766; the second was the reflection of Jeremy Belknap, New Hampshire delegate to the Constitutional Convention two decades later.[1] If
the Revolution established popular sovereignty in principle, as the
statement of Jeremy Belknap attests, it was the firm hope of some
that it remain a principle only. The crisis of the Revolutionary years
brought into full evidence the internal dissension within the patriot
cause. At its inception a movement for independence, the revolutionary
nature of the colonial fight was quickly revealed in the struggle for the
repartition of power.

This struggle was defined as a question of "who should rule at home" by
the progressive historian Carl L. Becker at the beginning of the twentieth
century. In his study of New York politics Becker suggested that colonial
society was predominantly aristocratic in tone. Becker's statement of
the problem was contested during the Cold War period by consensus
historians who argued that American society was essentially democratic
in spirit from colonial times on, thus casting doubt on the revolutionary
nature of the struggle with Great Britain.[2] More recent studies have
challenged these later arguments by pointing out certain changes occur-
ring over the eighteenth century which transformed the nature of
colonial society from one of relative egalitarianism to one of increasing
economic and social differentiation. Developments in this direction were
the rising importance of county institutions in decision making processes
to the detriment of corporate democracy at the town level and the general evolution of power away from the local gentry into the hands of a

more cosmopolitan colonial elite. Other tendencies were the moves to revive feudal privileges in many colonies, with concomitant demands for the creation of permanent upper chambers. These transformations were significant of the growing economic and social polarization of American society. The changes suggested by Kenneth Lockridge – "increasing population density, land shortage, migration, interpersonal and interregional concentration of wealth, social differentiation and commercial dependency" – are indicative of this trend and have led him and others to view the Revolution as a "social accident."[3]

The contributions of recent scholarship have carried the debate on the meaning of the American Revolution "beyond Becker," yet his original statement of the problem remains central to this debate. Recent works on popular radicalism and crowd behavior in the revolutionary era, as well as attempts to approach the problem from below, have underlined the significance of Becker's question, while enlarging the field of discussion on the internal revolution.[4]

What is the role of agrarian radicalism in the context of this debate? The numerous incidents of rural discontent throughout the colonial period attest to the basic disequilibrium of American society from its origins. In the last half of the eighteenth century agrarian uprisings, regardless of their intent and nature, contribute to the development of a growing popular self-consciousness. Increasingly the old social relationships of privilege and deference are challenged and the desire for new definitions of the body politic are affirmed.

Concerted radical action occurred increasingly before the Revolution. Richard M. Brown noted forty-four cases of rioting between 1760 and 1775 although twenty-eight of these were urban.[5] Among the major instances of rural radicalism were the New Jersey tenant riots (1745–1754), the Pennsylvania frontier uprisings (1755–1764), the movements for Regulation in the Carolinas (1765–1771), the New York anti-rent wars (sporadic but repeated from the 1750s through the 1770s) and the war of the New Hampshire Grants (1769–1791). These movements are not necessarily comparable in terms of participants, motives or goals, but all are indicators of social change and of increasing tension within the colonies. Whatever the local conditions of rural discontent, whatever the specific complaints and demands – land problems, heavy taxes, currency shortages, inadequate representation – the movements both of the colonial and the early national periods share a common denominator of social conflict and search for alternative solutions to contemporary problems other than those sustained by the ruling political order.

A number of concepts basic to agrarian politicization can be observed developing in these movements. Attempts to define the relationship between labor and property, emphasis on fraternity of interests and unity of action are especially notable. In the Great Rebellion, the recognition of distinct class interest is evidenced in Prendergast's defense which underlined the inadequacy of the judiciary to deal equitably with problems of the landless and the yeomen. Upstate farmers expected to receive the support of the urban poor in their projected march on New York (1766) and called themselves "the rural Sons of Liberty." But no such link between urban and rural proletariat existed as yet either in the Great Rebellion or later in the Shays Rebellion, nor was it easy to form so long as some promise of available land and of economic opportunity held forth the possibility of upward mobility.[6] As for the New York Sons of Liberty, this group denied any association with the upstate farmers and have been shown to be solidly middle class in composition. Their attitude towards the Great Rebellion was similar to that which the old whig leaders in Massachusetts later displayed towards the Shays Rebellion – one of reprehension and repression.[7]

The importance of uniting in opposition, of organizing, rather than protesting in isolation, is another aspect of a rural *prise de conscience*. In the case of the Great Rebellion, the tenant farmers vowed "they would stand by each other with Lives and fortunes, would not suffer any particulars of them to compound with their Landlords without the Rest." Unity of opposition also appears as a significant feature of the postwar agrarian movements. The necessity of such a policy was urged on the Massachusetts Regulators in repeated appeals from Daniel Shays, Eli Parsons and other militants. Here it presents itself in the guise of fraternity, and the mutual engagement of all participants is implicit. "We are determined to carry our point. Our cause is yours. Don't give yourself a rest and let us die here, for we are all brethren."[8]

This sort of solidarity was not new; on the contrary, it was a traditional characteristic of peasant uprisings, and in many respects agrarian protest of the postwar years can be compared with earlier movements, both in America and in other countries.[9] Yet the Revolution itself had a significant impact in radicalizing rural discontent at the end of the century. The developing concept of popular sovereignty presupposed responsive government, and if rural agitation was limited in the waning years of the Revolutionary period, it was due to the sensitivity of certain states to the demands and needs of the countryside. Agrarian radicalism in these years may be seen as a test of the Revolution to the extent that it measured the degree and quality of change effected during the period of upheaval. The discrepancy between the political, economic and social expectations, raised by the experience of Independence and constitution-making, and real conditions in the new nation after the war created a situation of growing opposition which developed into rebellion in Massachusetts and Pennsylvania. The Shays Rebellion (1786–1787) and the Whiskey Rebellion (1794) exemplified antagonisms within American society that the Revolution failed to redress and which carried over into the postwar period. Both movements occurred in regions undergoing economic and social transformation. Each resulted from the conjuncture of these changes with the more specific economic questions facing the new state and federal governments – taxation, liquidation of debts, currency regulation and so on – problems inherited from the recent colonial past and aggravated by the process of independence.

The article views agrarian radicalism through the perspective of these two rebellions which were the most highly developed cases of protest in the late Revolutionary period. In its approach it stresses the interests and actions of the participants, rather than studying the subject in a more general historic context. The paper is part of a larger research project in which the author is applying the methods of recent studies on European peasant movements to American agrarian uprisings.[10]

The Shays Rebellion

In the fall and winter of 1786–1787 rebellion swept the Massachusetts countryside. Following a series of county conventions in the summer of 1786, the movement struck out at the judicial system and blocked the inferior and superior courts throughout the western counties for the rest of the year. It was only with the help of a state militia, recruited especially for the purpose of crushing the rebellion, that the uprising was suppressed in the early months of 1787. Its active participants numbered in the thousands; its sympathizers, if we judge from the spring elections of 1787 which overturned the state government, constituted a majority of the voting population.

The movement was given the name of the Shays Rebellion by government supporters who singled out one of its more prominent figures, Daniel Shays, as "generalissimo."[11] The participants referred to themselves as Regulators, a term reminiscent of earlier popular uprisings in America and England and a link with the developing concept of popular sovereignty.[12]

Subsistence farmers formed the bulk of the movement's population.[13] Oath of allegiance lists, the principal source for locating individual par-

90

ticipants in the movement, show an overwhelming proportion of yeomen with respect to gentlemen, although many of the more prominent figures signed "gent." after their names. Among the occupations listed are laborer (which in rural communities of the 1780s meant farm laborer), husbandman, miller, tanner, blacksmith, innkeeper, physician, clergyman, shopkeeper. Military titles (especially lieutenant and captain) appear rather frequently before names, indicating the active association of many Revolutionary war veterans with the movement.

It is difficult to estimate the size of the movement, partly because of the problem of differentiating partisans from sympathetic onlookers. In a letter to Washington, General Henry Knox, who was trying to obtain a federal intervention in the rebellion, judged that at least twenty percent of the inhabitants of the most populous counties were pro-Shaysite.[14] The oath of allegiance lists show well over three thousand signers, and if we add to that those who were indicted for treason and stood trial and those who absconded, the number reaches the proximity of four thousand. What we cannot measure are the silent supporters, although the election returns of 1787 give an indication of their extent.

Partisans of regulation could be found throughout the state, from the coastal counties of Barnstable, Plymouth and Essex, to Berkshire in the west. Yet despite this appearance of geographic heterogeneity, the movement was concentrated in central and western Massachusetts and took its strength from the less "commercial-cosmopolitan" towns of the interior counties, those which, according to Stephen Patterson, constituted a new political force in the Revolutionary seventies.[15] The greatest density of Regulator population was in Hampshire where active participants could be found in all but one town.[16] Many towns here were solidly behind the movement, including Pelham (Shays's town of residence), Whately, Colrain, Amherst, Greenwich, Belchertown, Longmeadow, and South Brimfield, for the most part hill towns above the Connecticut River Valley. In Worcester and Middlesex, too, many of the active towns were a certain distance from the main commercial routes.

In general, then, the movement is constituted from and represents the less developed regions of the agrarian, interior counties, whose interests were identified with the extension of popular democracy in the 1770s and which were to vote Anti-Federalist in the ratification controversy a year after the Shays Rebellion. While not overtly expressing themselves in class-conscious terms, Regulators opposed privilege, minimized deference in their relations with authority, and shared a common set of agrarian values and options which pitted them against the more developed, mercantile centers of the seaboard and the older Connecticut Valley towns.

The grievances of the Shays Rebellion summed up the agrarian discontent of the eighties and reflected to some extent the political demands of the Constitutionalist movement.[17] Repeated appeals for the abolition of the Senate, popular election of magistrates, and more control over civil officers filled the petitions from interior towns and county conventions, echoing the unfulfilled hopes of the seventies. Demands for the amendment of the Constitution, issuing from every part, emphasized a reinforcement of the concept of popular sovereignty, and particularly that aspect concerning public servants' dependency on the popular will. The principle of popular sovereignty was not only upheld in addresses and circular letters but exercised in the practice of county conventions and in the dismissal of representatives who failed to carry out town instructions.[18] Obviously, the question of the delegation of authority was not construed in the same manner by partisans of Regulation and by defenders of order. The latter held that in a republican system authority is resigned to delegates whose decisions are to be obeyed; delegates could be instructed, but not too frequently, "and the instructions should not be binding since most people lived remote from each other and lacked information."[19] The demand to remove the capital from Boston was intended to correct this last point. It was thought that the relocation of the capital somewhere in the interior part of the state would allow not only greater western participation in the legislature, but would also permit the back country to have a larger influence in the affairs of government by their proximity to it.[20]

Among political grievances structural changes were sought at the level of the Senate and the courts. Opposition to the Senate derived in part from a lack of popular control of this body. Senators were elected from a constituency of fifteen or more towns and thus had no immediate local allegiance, nor town instructions. With its high property qualification the Senate was a symbol of aristocracy and, with its veto over the House, the seat of power in the General Court. The structure of government being what it was, people felt "that their votes were not doing them any good."[21]

Partisans of change in the state legal apparatus agreed on their grievances, but differed in their demands. Among the lower tribunals, the Court of Common Pleas was especially unpopular, for it was here that debt suits originated. Moreover, verdicts nearly always were appealed, which meant the accrual of superior court fees with the pursuit of the case. Remedies to the excesses of the judicial system varied from moderate demands for the adjustment of legal fees and reforms within the lower Courts of Probate and General Sessions of Peace (opposition to the

Court of Common Pleas seems to have been unanimous) to the radical solution to abolish the lower courts altogether and the lawyer's profession along with them. Radical criticisms of the court structure were yet another reflection of the desire to extend democracy at the local level and to increase popular autonomy in government, for they would have given the work of the Probate Court and the Registry of Deeds to town clerks and replaced the Court of Common Pleas by committees of arbitration, working with elected rather than appointed justices of the peace.[22]

The economic basis of agrarian discontent is portrayed in a Groton petition to the General Court in the fall of 1786. "The greater part of the common people in this part of the country, although possessed of real Estates, yet have parted with their personal Estates, and are reduced to one & two Cows only, and the income of their hands are insufficient to support their families." Downward mobility is clearly threatening: those with land are losing their personal possessions to meet fiscal and financial obligations, while the landless are often victims of more than seasonal unemployment. The wandering poor, on the increase throughout the state since mid-century, constitute what Douglas Lamar Jones calls "a class of transients" by the 1780s.[23] The situation of Massachusetts subsistence farmers in the eighties can be explained in large part by long range factors. Over the century, demographic increase and growing population density result in a situation of overcrowding in relation to cultivable acreage in certain counties and a corresponding decrease of average landholdings. (Average land per poll in 1786 is one-fifth to one-seventh of that of 1636.)[24] Parcelling of estates and migration, both to rural areas and urban centers, are already practiced before the Revolution in attempts to assure livelihoods, but these measures only partially alleviate the country's growth problems.

While the problem of land was not made explicit in the grievances of the Shaysites, it was an implicit undercurrent of the movement. Petitions encouraging government support for the production of flax, hemp, wheat and the raising of sheep showed a recognition of diminishing crop yields.[25] The dual threat of increasing population and decreasing productive acreage was translated by a desire to find cheaper, better land elsewhere. As long as credit was available, subsistence farmers invested in land, side by side with large speculators (although such small investments did not necessarily guarantee an improvement in the individual's economic or social condition.) Their activities were curtailed by the depression which struck New England in 1783 bringing about a drop in land values and a general price decrease which drove many farmers into

93

debt. According to one witness, the value of land depreciated by more than fifty percent in the following years.[26] Speculators, profiting from the general disarray, bought up promissory notes and debts which they pressed in the lower courts. The peak year for lawsuits in Worcester county was 1784, when some two thousand debt cases were registered, and the following year "94 of 104 of its residents who were sentenced to jail went thither for failing to meet their obligations."[27] Mortgage foreclosures in Berkshire county led to "a continuous elimination of the insecure" in favor of the "more profitable estates" – accentuating the increasing gap between rich and poor, another long range element of change in eighteenth-century America.[28]

The demand for legislation favorable to debtors was a constant theme of rural protest throughout the country in the Confederation years. In Massachusetts discontent was demonstrated in frequent rioting in the western counties from 1781 to 1784. Paper money, as well as an adequate tender law, were the proposed solutions to problems of liquidity and debt, but both propositions met with sharp opposition among merchants and creditors. A motion to issue legal tender was defeated in the spring session of the General Court in 1786. This, along with the vote for increased taxes and supplementary funds to aid the Confederation government, were taken as proof of the state's unresponsiveness to agrarian interests and demands, and prompted the call for county conventions in the summer of 1786.[29] A Hampshire convention of August summed up the multiple grievances stressed throughout the eighties in a program demanding, in priority, reform of the tax structure, the issue of paper money, tender legislation, revision of the Constitution, and, in its insistence upon the unequal burdens born by the people, emphasized the class conflict underlying Confederation society. This theme recurred a short time later in the coastal county of Plymouth, far from the center of agrarian discontent. "The Cry of the People is become great in Consequence of the grievous burthens which they groan under" – and the warning: "the People can not Subsist under it very much Longer but they will rise in open Rebellion against the Law and Government."[30]

The origins of the Shays Rebellion can, in part, be traced back to the agrarian radicalism of the seventies. Massachusetts opposition to British authority in 1774–1775 took a variety of forms which later served as example for agrarian action in the eighties. One ought to exclude from these precedents actions essentially anti-British in nature, such as boycotts of imported goods and anti-loyalist terrorism. There seems to be no equivalent in the Shays Rebellion of the patriots' treatment of tories during the war years. Nor did the Regulators resort to societal violence as a means of achieving unity, as Pennsylvania radicals were later to do. Actions against the judiciary were common, however, both in the seventies and in the eighties. Obstruction of court activities antedates the independence movement, but in the Revolutionary period it was an effective oppositional weapon against authority. Moreover, this type of action was not limited to the courts as institutions; it embraced the magistrature as well.

Another important form of opposition in frequent practice was the recourse to county conventions. Beginning in the summer of 1774, a series of such conventions was held across the state to organize resistance to the Coercive Acts and to dfine the political relationships of the Bay colony with Great Britain. These and later conventions in the seventies served as an important forum for Revolutionary politics. After the adoption of the Constitution of 1780 the legality of future conventions was to be challenged, yet this form of reunion remained important in the interior counties where representation in the General Court was often low. From 1780 to the outbreak of the Shays Rebellion at least a dozen conventions were held in the central and western counties. To a certain extent the western conventions filled a role similar to that of the caucus system in the east, providing a political liaison between the towns and sometimes preparing electoral lists.[31] During the Shays Rebellion such meetings were an instrumental organ in rallying support for Regulation in the early phase of the movement.

It is difficult to determine at what moment the agrarian discontent of the mid-eighties actually developed into a concerted movement of protest. If consultatory action be a criterion of unity, then one may turn to the initiative of the Bristol towns which in July 1786 appealed for a state-wide convention for constitutional amendment when the General Court failed to pass legislation alleviating rural conditions. The unresponsiveness of government to popular grievances was a common chord in initiating the dynamic process of rebellion both in the Shays and the Whiskey movements. Three distinctive phases of action can be discerned in the former: an initial period of seeking redress through petition and assembly, a second stage of recourse to direct action, and a final period of armed conflict. After the Hampshire convention, already mentioned, there seems to have been a hardening of positions within the Regulator movement, with moderates and radicals taking divergent courses of action. The former continued to seek redress through petitions and resolutions; many repudiated the use of force against the judiciary, reaffirmed the legality of county conventions, and urged the interior counties to pack the House and Senate in order to push an active reform program through the General Court. But the convention movement lost its force before the more aggressive course of the militant Regulators who turned to direct action in early September launching a movement which blocked the entire court structure of the western counties for several months. Whether this passage to direct resistance through anti-court action was concerted or spontaneous, its contagious effect across the state demonstrated the degree of popular sympathy behind this move.

The official reaction to court obstruction came rapidly. An emergency session of the General Court was convened in late September and sat throughout part of the period in which the western courts were blocked. The program laid down by this extraordinary session of the legislature and made public in early December in an "Address to the People," contained no structural changes, nor any permanent reforms; neither was it clement in its attitude towards the Regulation. With the suspension of *habeas corpus* arbitrary arrest was henceforth admissible, and the punitive measures of the Riot Act, which applied to groups of three or more, could be enforced an hour after its reading. The issue of warmest debate was an Indemnity Act allowing anyone surrendering up arms and taking an oath of allegiance before January 1, 1787, to go free of prosecution. Those not complying, however, could be tried in any county "where law and Justice may be administered" rather than in their counties of residence.[32] Moreover, the Indemnity Act bore a proviso excluding those who continued to obstruct government in any way after publication of the act (15 November 1786). It is doubtful, therefore, that the men who blocked the Worcester courts a few days later had cognizance of its terms. Warrants for the arrest of many prominent figures in the Regulation, and the use of the Light Horse to round them up showed well enough how the authorities meant to deal with Regulation.

This policy of repression apparently did more to harden attitudes than to quell rebellion, as the following witness affirms: "Sometime in the fall of the Year 1786 I was at Aaron Broads in Holden. Conversation turned upon the Riot act he went & brought it to me & read it he then said now I am determined to fight and Spill my blood and leave my bones at the Court House till the Resurrection."[33]

The Indemnity Act was probably that which best illustrated the fundamental difference in attitude between the forces of authority and those of Regulation (however disparate each may have been within itself). While the supporters of government looked on the movement as a seditious rebellion to overthrow the state, the disaffected areas of the interior counties saw their movement as one of Regulation, giving the sense to this word that the North Carolina insurgents had used in the late sixties. To their way of thinking, their actions were blessed with a sense of public morality. In the absence of good government, they were taking matters in their own hands and trying to halt persecution of debtors until reforms could be enacted through regular legal channels, after the election of a new General Court or after constitutional amendment.

The severity of government reaction to the evolution of events was a decisive factor in shaping the final phase of the Regulation – that of military resistance. By early December the movement had acquired a sort of informal military structure dividing western Massachusetts into seventeen districts, each headed by a prominent member of the Regulation party. This Committee of Seventeen, sometimes called "Shaises Councill", recruited men from the local militia companies in partisan areas.

From the 3rd to the 9th of December between 800 and 1000 Shaysites gathered in Worcester. Their intentions, besides securing the adjournment of court sessions, remain obscure. Rumors were that they intended to march on Boston to release Shattuck and other leaders imprisoned there. Accordingly, the Middlesex regiment was held in readiness to defend Boston against attack, while in the city itself "all things seemed to carry the shew of a garrison."[34] Did the Shaysites hope, as had Prendergast and the New York tenant farmers twenty years earlier, that the city's mechanics and artisans would join cause with them? Although agrarian discontent had reached the eastern county of Barnstable by November,[35] evidence for a rural-urban alliance is lacking. Opposition in Boston hardly seems to have been possible, judging from one man's account: "The powers of government are so united in the metropolis that it is dangerous even to be silent. A man is accused of rebellion if he does not loudly approve every measure as prudent, necessary, wise, and constitutional."[36] Nor did the tone of the city's circular letter to the towns of the interior, condemning resistance and calling for loyalty to the constitution, leave any margin for cooperation. Whatever their aims, the Regulators were held up in Worcester by a blizzard which lasted several days and blocked the roads in every direction.

Within the next two months the Regulation was to be suppressed by a militia, raised mostly in the east, and particularly from Essex County. In the towns of central and western Massachusetts some militia turned out to support government, particularly in the larger centers of the Connecticut River Valley. Many towns, fearing bloodshed and civil war, petitioned the government for a cessation of hostilities and clemency for the offenders. These were the neutral elements whom Bowdoin accused of having contributed to the success of the rebellion by their inactivity.[37] Yet a majority of western towns continued to sympathize with the movement through its last stand against authority, sending men and supplies behind Luke Day, Eli Parsons and Daniel Shays at the battle of Springfield (January 25, 1787) and its follow-up. A contingent of men from Middlesex crossed central Massachusetts to join Shays's troops at Pelham before the retreat and rout at Petersham in the first days of February.[38] Armed resistance continued in Berkshire County through the spring months.

Agrarian resistance in Massachusetts began spontaneously, on all sides, with intent to redress grievances, then to right matters or "regulate," and finally developed into armed rebellion. As a movement the Shays Rebellion was large, heterogeneous and loosely organized, embracing divergent attitudes and encompassing several types of activities and levels of social engagement, from individual protest to crowd action. The latter was the most conspicuous aspect of the movement, drawing the most attention and the sharpest reactions within and beyond Massachusetts. Attitudes within the Regulation ran from the moderate position of conventioners, deploring direct resistance to authority, to the radical stand of certain militants who, perhaps more concerned with resistance than Regulation in the last stages of conflict, called themselves "wood rangers." This term is suggestive of social banditry, which the condition and the comportment of the Berkshire militants resembled during the early months of 1787. Their sporadic border raids from New York and Vermont constituted what Eric Hobsbawm defines as the "rearguard action by backwoods guerillas" in a dying movement.[39]

Conservative supporters of government referred to the Regulators as "banditti" and conceived of the rebellion as a levelling movement seeking to abolish private property, rather than acknowledging the legitimate political and economic grievances of the participants. Yet no evidence has been presented that substantiates these charges or that might indicate designs for some form of reapportionment of property. The grievances of the Regulation were not focused on the equalization or abolition of property rights, but rather on the equalization of social burdens and on the extension of democracy. By robbing the movement of its legitimacy, its opponents could more easily bring their influence to bear in government circles for repression.

Looking backward, one is struck by the clement treatment which the regulators received. By 1788 all were pardoned, including Daniel Shays. Yet the immediate reaction of the Bowdoin government was far from clement. In the spring of 1787, hundreds of people were hunted down and brought in to be indicted for sedition and treason; eighteen were sentenced to death. The final session of the legislature before the spring elections declared Massachusetts in a state of rebellion and passed a Disqualifying Act which disenfranchised all who had participated actively in the movement, as well as anyone giving assistance to it. Regulators were disqualified from holding office, teaching school or keeping taverns for three years, and from jury duty for a year's time. Moreover, many people were not eligible for a pardon under the act, including members of Regulator committees, or those advising them, commissioned officers, conventioners, and several other categories of people. The Disqualifying Act was meant not only to secure the military victory won by General Lincoln's army, but also to assure an electoral victory. Lincoln himself counselled a more moderate policy arguing that many towns would be without government under the terms of the act, – a situation which would give reason to the Regulators' accusation that they had no voice in government.

The defeat of the rebellion and the repressive legislation which followed led many Regulators and sympathizers to flee the state.[40] But in spite of migration and disenfranchisement, sympathy with the Regulator cause brought about a turnover in the House at the spring elections of 1787, replaced several seats in the Senate and put John Hancock back in the office of governor. With a new government, more tolerant to the movement, pardon if not reform was rapidly achieved.

The Whiskey Rebellion

Only four years after the movement for Regulation in Massachusetts, agrarian resistance sprang up beyond the Appalachian mountains in the region of the Allegheny plateau. Here rural discontent centered upon a tax on the distillation of spirits, proposed by Hamilton in his second report on the public credit. The excise tax, as approved by Congress on March 3, 1791, laid a duty of eleven to thirty cents a gallon on all spirits produced "wholly or in part from molasses, sugar or other foreign materials" and nine to twenty-five cents a gallon on alcohol produced from home grown grains.[41] This measure met with widespread opposition from farmers and distillers throughout the country. Even before it became a law, it was condemned by state legislatures in Pennsylvania, Maryland, Virginia and North Carolina. Hostility was particularly vehement in western Pennsylvania where one in every six farmers had a still and whiskey was the most important transportable commodity.[42]

Agrarian opposition led to two federal amendments of the law before culminating in the Whiskey Rebellion of 1794.

The anti-excise movement concerned farmers of five counties in southwestern Pennsylvania (then named Washington, Westmoreland, Allegheny, Fayette and Bedford) and Ohio County, Virginia (now West Virginia). In 1790 the population of the area was about 77,000 out of a state total of 420,000. Immigrants were numerous, especially the Scotch-Irish who seem to have played a dominant role in the uprising. Given their large contribution, it is not surprising to find also that the Presbyterians were the most active supporters of the movement in terms of religious affiliation. The leaders of the rebellion were of various national origins and included a number of important political figures at the state and national level. William Findley, Hugh Brackenridge and Albert Gallatin, among others, were associated with the movement, although they seem to have exercised a moderating influence. Their participation in the meetings of 1794 was aimed at keeping the movement "in bounds."[43] Many of the Mingo Creek Democratic Society seem to have been participants in the Whiskey Rebellion, although the club itself disclaimed direct involvement. Its position may be compared to that of the later Patrons of Husbandry whose members carried on direct political action outside the framework of the society itself. The Whiskey Rebellion, like the Shays Rebellion cut across class lines, but the core of both movements was composed of small farmers whose grievances were expressed by more well-to-do leaders.

Patterns of landownership and labor in the western counties mark the increasing economic and social differentiation in the trans-Appalachian area in the last years of the eighteenth century. J. T. Main has described Bedford County as a region of "considerable land speculation", where (in 1783) over half the land in many townships was held by non-residents and much of the population was propertyless. Farm laborers comprised about one-third of this group. This is in contrast to Washington county, farther west, where Main found "almost no speculative activity," less propertyless men, and where the "wealthiest ten percent of the county's residents (in 1781) owned twenty six percent of the land." In spite of these indications of economic disparity, he concludes that the Pennsylvania frontier was, like that of New England, essentially egalitarian.[44] While not refuting Main's general portrait of subsistence and frontier communities for the early eighties, we would, however, insist more on the social distinctions and changes within this society in the years following the Revolution, when life in the western counties was in the process of development and change.

One indication of increasing social and economic disparity was the problem of land acquisition. Although state laws favored settlement by limiting land sales to four hundred acres per individual and demanding improvements within a short period of time, speculators circumvented the law by purchasing adjacent tracts under assumed names. The planting of fruit trees or construction of a lean-to was sufficient to meet the improvement qualifications.[45] During the Whiskey Rebellion western farmers agitated for federal land offices in the interior which might facilitate credit and supervise the disposal of the public domain against abuses. Their disadvantage before eastern and European capital is seen in the complaint of a western Virginia convention: "A generous land office ought to be opened, in order that citizens in the Western country may have equal privilege of procuring lands with Europeans, and those of our fellow citizens whose situation is not so remote from the seat of government." This same convention passed a resolve to establish a land tax in place of the excise, in hopes that "a direct tax on real property would discourage the men of wealth from engrossing lands profusely, and would afford the industrious men of middle and low class an equal privilege with those of the rich – which ought to be the true object of a republican government." This perception of privilege and class differences is apparent in another resolve calling for equalization of wages in the army.[46]

Although small farmers constituted the majority of the population in the western counties, the existence of indentured servants and slaves was another sign of the inegalitarian nature of society in this region. Slavery lingered in Pennsylvania in spite of legislation for gradual abolition in 1780, and it lasted longer in the western area than elsewhere.[47] Most slaves were domestic, rather than field servants, indentured labor apparently being preferred for farming. Neither slaves nor redemptioners appeared in Massachusetts at the time of the Shays Rebellion, although the tax lists of many of the towns we studied recorded anywhere from one to five "negroes," a few of whom participated in the Regulation. In western Pennsylvania both of these types of labor seem to have been limited to wealthy residents. We do not know what activity, if any, indentured servants may have had in the Whiskey Rebellion, but slaves were sometimes armed to protect their masters' property against the partisans, as was the case with those of General John Neville, federal inspector of revenues for the western counties, whose estate was burned in July 1794.

The heart of resistance to the federal excise was in Washington County, in the southwestern corner of Pennsylvania, the area of greatest population density west of the Appalachians. This region was experiencing rapid transformations. Although essentially a farming economy, industry and commerce were expanding. Two years before the outbreak of the Whiskey Rebellion the town of Washington boasted twenty-three manufacturing trades, Pittsburgh sixteen. Both towns had mechanical societies open to all trades: their principal aims – to ameliorate conditions of work and to encourage the growth of manufactures in the region. In 1791 the Pennsylvania road was opened over the old Forbes trail connecting Philadelphia and Pittsburgh. While travel was very slow (a contemporary traveler estimated the trip accross state at twenty days for conestoga wagons), the overland route was well established by 1794 and a rising local aristocracy was regularly furnished with items of comfortable living.

Small farmers felt out of touch with the economic expansion and the increasing wealth of the western region. They protested that it benefited but a certain class of urban-oriented people, composed of merchants, speculators and professional men, and that prosperity did not filter down to the rural husbandmen. These were, in Jefferson's terms, the "unmonied people;" they lacked ready cash, and like the subsistence farmers of Massachusetts, complained that what currency there was tended to filter into the hands of tradesmen and from tradesmen to the eastern merchants. The excise was to be paid in money, rather than in whiskey – a frequently used medium of exchange in the west. In the 1790s a "hundred-gallon copper still would buy a good farm, two barrels of whiskey a corner lot, a five gallon keg a pound of powder, five barrels for a rifle gun."[48] Moreover, the rate of excise was nearly fifty percent the price of a gallon of ordinary rye whiskey. This tax, then, in its application, tended to strangle the small farmer, forcing him to sell his excess grain at a low price to large distillers who could afford to produce whiskey even at the price of the federal excise.[49]

While the grievances expressed in the Whiskey Rebellion were of an economic nature, the movement itself was an act of political protest against the authority of the new federal government. Extremists apparently toyed with the idea of secession and looked towards their western neighbors beyond the mountains for possible confederates in a new state. The links of western farmers with the interior are demonstrated in frequent demands for free navigation on the Mississippi. They reproached the government for its "mysterious secrecy" on this issue as a "violation of the political rights of the citizens in general, as it declares that the people are unfit to be trusted with important facts."[50] Such criticisms betrayed the sentiment that popular controls on government were slipping and popular sovereignty rapidly becoming a fiction. Indeed, Hamilton, who referred to the people as "a great beast," conceived of the excise tax as a means of reenforcing nationalism and curbing popular democracy by bringing "the power of the federal government to the individual citizens in the states."[51]

The first public meeting of protest in the western counties was held at Redstone Old Fort (now Brownsville) in July 1791. This reunion recognized the right of the government to levy an excise but protested that a tax on whiskey was unconstitutional, since it did not fall equally on all citizens, but rather burdened those of a particular region. A second meeting was held in September at Pittsburgh. Both resulted in petitions for relief and resolutions which were sent to the state and federal legislatures. A Washington County resolution threatened violence and political reprisals if the federal government attempted to apply the law in western Pennsylvania. A state excise law had existed on the books for years, in fact, but had never been exercised beyond the mountains. (Ironically, it had been repealed the very year that the federal law was passed.)

In September of 1791 Robert Johnson, federal collector of revenues for Allegheny and Washington counties, was tarred and feathered as was a deputy marshall shortly thereafter who tried to serve warrants on Johnson's aggressor. Unlike radical opposition in Massachusetts, agrarian protest in Pennsylvania was violent from the outset, and partisans did not hesitate to use threats of violence against their own to force moderate participants into more active roles. Hence, Colonel John Marshall and the lawyer David Bradford who assisted at the Pittsburgh meetings of protest in 1791 and 1792, were to be pushed into leadership in the uprising of 1794 by menaces against their property.[52]

Resistance to the law continued actively throughout 1792 despite congressional reduction of the rate of excise and a presidential proclamation to desist from further obstruction of the act. Although incidents of violence continued against federal collection officers and men registering their stills, many of the larger distillers began to comply with the act. The most unpopular feature of the law still remaining in effect was that offenders had to be tried in a federal court. This meant a three hundred fifty mile journey across the state to Philadelphia at harvest time implying financial loss in crops as well as the costs incurred by the trip and trial. According to some historians "the expenses of such a trial would amount to the selling price of an average western farm."[53]

This clause, amended in June 1794, was the immediate cause for the outbreak of the Whiskey Rebellion, when a federal marshall served summonses on forty offenders whose writs had been issued before the amendment went into effect. Action began in mid-July when the last summons was served in the strongly democratic Mingo Creek settlement of Washington County. General John Neville, wealthiest man in the region and inspector of the excise, accompanied the federal marshall on this mission. Some local people fired shots, causing the two men to flee. The same night some thirty to forty men visited Neville demanding his resignation as inspector, but the General had armed his servants. A short battle ensued in which one of the Mingo Creek men was killed. The following day, a crowd of five hundred local militiamen and others again attempted to force the resignation of Neville. In their efforts, several partisans were wounded, one fatally, and Neville's home and outbuildings were burned.

These incidents, particularly the two shootings, hardened resistance in the western region. Militant opponents of the excise used or threatened violence to draw recalcitrant distillers into opposition ranks. The following excerpt from a letter published in the *Pittsburgh Gazette* is an example of such terrorism: "In taking a survey of the troops under my direction in the late expedition against that insolent exciseman, John Nevill, I find there were a great many delinquents, even among those who carry on distilling. It will, therefore, be observed that I, Tom the Tinker, will not suffer any certain class or set of men to be excluded the service of this my district, when notified to attend on any expedition carried on in order to obstruct the execution of the excise law, and obtain a repeal thereof ... And I do declare on my solemn word, that if such delinquents do not come forth on the next alarm, with equipments ... they will be deemed as enemies ... and shall receive punishment according to the nature of the offense."[54]

Active resistance lasted less than two months before a special commission, appointed by Washington and Governor Mifflin of Pennsylvania, deliberated with the leaders to bring about popular submission. In this short span of time a dual form of protest developed which was not a result of concertation, but seems rather to have sprung from divergent tendencies within the opposition. Militants used direct action, attacking the mails and rallying in mass meetings to determine their potential strength. On August 1st, from four to seven thousand militiamen from the four western counties gathered at Braddock's Field with the rumored intention to burn Pittsburgh. A committee of citizens invited them to the town to eat and drink, and the only arson committed was upon a barn across the river (belonging to Kirkpatrick, commander of the troops who had defended Neville's property).

Another type of action recalls the conventions of the Shays Rebellion. A meeting of delegates from the four western counties of Pennsylvania and from Ohio County, Virginia, was held at Parkinson's Ferry on August 14th to determine a legal course of action. A permanent executive committee of fifteen representatives (three from each county) was elected which became known in the Revolutionary manner as the Committee of Safety. A larger Committee of Sixty was to reconvene in early September after local consultation. The efficacy of moderate resistance was not to be demonstrated, however, for a few days before the meeting at Parkinson's Ferry, Washington issued a proclamation calling for an end to all opposition before September 1st. After meeting with the government commission to discuss submission, the Committee of Safety voted with the larger Committee of Sixty to put the question to the people. Before popular feeling could be adequately tested, however, Washington had issued a second proclamation ordering troops into the field.

In October 1794 an army of 13,000 men, commanded by Governor Henry Lee of Virginia, and accompanied by the President, the Secretary of the Treasury and the Secretary of War, crossed Pennsylvania. At Carlisle, two representatives of the Committee of Safety met the advancing army and tried to dissuade the President from his course of action. They were promised there would be no violence, if there was no resistance. In mid-November two hundred partisans were arrested in the night, and several sent east to Philadelphia for trial. Twenty-two were accused of treason, as compared to several hundred in the Shays Rebellion; four, as compared to eighteen, were sentenced to death. In both movements, all were eventually pardoned, but not before some had served months of prison under the threat of a potential noose.

Conclusion

In the preceding pages we have given a rapid account of agrarian discontent in the post-Revolutionary era through the examples of two popular uprisings. While these movements differed from each other in many particular aspects, a certain number of factors are basic to both. In terms of social composition, economic milieu and regional situation the two movements have much in common. And if the grievances of the Shays Rebellion and the Whiskey Rebellion differ considerably in the forms of expression, similar inequities are the targets of both movements.
The interior counties of Massachusetts, and within these counties the

towns removed from easy commercial access, were those which formed the core of support for the Shays Rebellion. Similarly, it was the back-country of Pennsylvania and Virginia – the counties on the western slopes of the Alleghenies and beyond, which furnished the setting of the Whiskey Rebellion. The population of both movements reflected the composition of society at large to the extent that the bulk of the partici-pants were subsistence farmers, with a diminishing number of artisans, professional men and local political and legal figures involved in each. Veterans of the Revolutionary war and militiamen also were an impor-tant element in these movements. The most active group in the Whiskey Rebellion were the Scotch-Irish. This was not the case in Massachusetts, where the majority of people were of English stock, yet Scotch-Irish participation in the Shays Rebellion was not insignificant. The towns of Pelham and Colrain, both of Scotch-Irish origin, contributed large num-bers of men to the movement, including its leading figure, Daniel Shays.

Opposition in the Shays Rebellion was focused against the state govern-ment, in the Whiskey Rebellion against the federal government. In the earlier movement, the main targets of agrarian discontent were the struc-ture and costs of government and the fiscal policies of the legislature. In the latter, while the immediate issue of conflict was taxation, the prob-lems of equal access to land and markets were strong factors in agrar-ian protest. The limitations on economic and social mobility which were presented in Massachusetts by increasing population density, decreasing crop yields and less available land within many townships, had their parallel in western Pennsylvania, where in spite of richer soils and a flourishing agricultural production, the restrictions on commerce from the closing of the Mississippi and from the imposition of the excise tax menaced the small farmer with ruin. In both regions currency shortages brought severe hardships to many and created a widening gap between the subsistence farmer and the large landowner or the merchant. In Massachusetts paper money and a tender law were among the most fre-quent demands of agrarian radicals. In western Pennsylvania, where whiskey was a commonly accepted medium of exchange, agitation for repeal of the excise tax was the equivalent to these demands.

Both movements had recourse to tactics of protest which had been tried in the Revolution and earlier. Conventions, mass meetings, petitions and resolutions were common to the two, yet in the use of direct action there is a striking difference between the Shays and the Whiskey Rebellion. Although each employed violence, it does not seem to have been with the same intent. In Pennsylvania, violence was discriminate. It was used to halt the enforcement of the excise law, to keep people from complying with the act and to force them to rally to the movement. In Massachusetts, violence was rare and generally defensive. It was used in retaliation, in self-defense and occasionally to secure arms. Although both movements had paramilitary organizations, neither seems to have been ready to engage in offensive warfare. The Regulator movement was markedly opposed to bloodshed, as both its actions in armed conflict and its petitions attest. In spite of the aggressive tone of the Whiskey Rebellion, the partisans gave no opposition to federal troops when they crossed Pennsylvania in the fall of 1794.

Neither movement was without success, although the Whiskey Rebellion seems to have led to more significant changes in local conditions than the Shays Rebellion. Some of the grievances of the Whiskey Rebellion were alleviated within the following decade: navigation on the Mississippi was obtained in the Pinckney Treaty (1795), while the repeal of the Excise Act was one of the first gestures of the Jeffersonian Republicans towards their backcountry constituents. The land problem, however, would remain one of the dominant issues in politics throughout most of the nineteenth century. In Massachusetts, the movement for Regulation brought about a turnover in the state legislature in 1787, but the most important contribution of the new General Court was to pardon the Regulators. The extension of the tender law was a concession to rural grievances, yet imprisonment for debt still existed at the end of the century. While minor reforms were adopted in the legal system, in general the democratic structural changes called for by the Shaysites were ignored. Migration was the prevalent solution to economic hardships. Whether small farmers fared better elsewhere is not always evident. Shays himself died in obscurity in upstate New York some forty years later.

Space does not allow us to discuss the impact of the two movements at the national level, although each had an important influence on national politics. Held up as an example of the tyranny of democracy by conservatives throughout the country, the Shays Rebellion confirmed their suspicions that the nation was on the verge of anarchy. Many felt that the "licentious spirit" of the people needed to be checked by a stronger central government. In this light the Shays Rebellion had a significant bearing on the Constitutional debates of 1787. The Whiskey Rebellion was seen as a threat to the authority of the new federal government by a number of leading Federalists, who thus justified the intervention of the army to suppress the movement. It also served as an excuse for Federalists, including the President himself, to attack the Democratic societies which had placed political adversaries in government in the elections of

1794. These clubs never recovered from the assault and, although they renounced any association with the Whiskey Rebellion, they scarcely outlived the movement.[55]

Rooted in the past in many respects, particularly in their methods of action and their style of address, these two postwar movements were strongly influenced by the Revolutionary doctrines of popular sovereignty and of the equal rights of man. Moreover, in both rebellions a modern note appeared: protest was no longer limited to a specific target or figure but generalized and carried on in the name of a cause. As Eli Parsons put it to the Massachusetts Regulators: "Would to God, I had the tongue of a ready writer, that I might impress on your minds the idea of obligation you, as citizens of a republican government, are under to support those rights and privileges that the God of Nature hath entitled you to. Let me now persuade you, by all the sacred ties of friendship . . . immediately to turn out and assert your rights."[56] For the Regulators and for the opponents of the excise tax, the natural rights of man were no mere rhetoric, but a promise held forth in the American Revolution and still to be achieved.

While we must look to the nineteenth century for examples of clearly class-conscious movements, the process of agrarian politicization is apparent from the early Revolutionary period onward. Signs of it can be seen in both the Shays and the Whiskey Rebellions, in their attacks on privilege, in their awareness of separate agrarian interests, and in the increasing reference to class, rather than to rank or order. Both uprisings symbolize unsettled conflicts at the heart of the Revolution and are movements on the path towards a modern form of protest.

Appendix

A new approach to the analysis of complex structures is now beginning to be used in economics and the social sciences, called Feedback or System Dynamics. Since we believe it could be useful for the understanding of historical events, we have attempted to describe the causal development of agrarian revolts through a very simplified qualitative Causal Diagram.

We consider that the essential causes of both rebellions can be found in the discrepancies developing between the expectations created and enhanced by Independence, and the corresponding unimproved realities. Initially, the discrepancies were voiced through individual complaints (vocal or written). As time passed and complaints did not yield results,

Causal Diagram

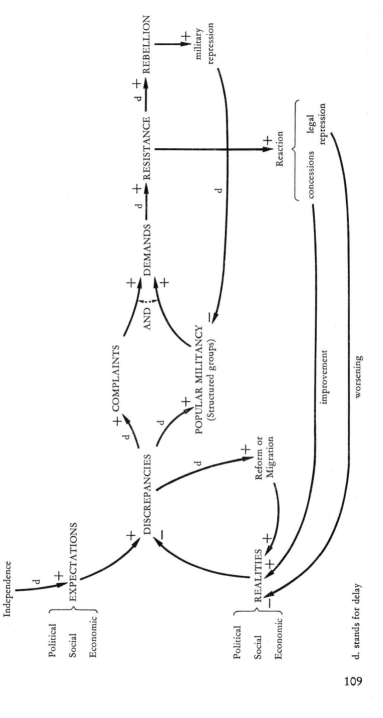

popular militancy developed giving rise to structured protest groups. Through these more or less organized groups complaints were transformed into specific demands. The lack of response from legal and governmental authorities led, after a time *(delay)* to resistance. We then find two reactions from the authorities: on the one hand, concessions which to a certain extent improve realities and should have decreased the discrepancies *(Feedback loop 1);* on the other hand, a legal repression which tends to worsen some of the realities *(Feedback loop 2).* Because of this legal repression, also because of the numerous delays involved in the process, resistance transforms into rebellion, which brings about military repression. The latter is essentially meant, and in the present case succeeds, to destroy what we called popular militancy *(Feedback loop 3).* Although all the discrepancies may and, in fact, do subsist, the disappearance of popular militancy, necessary for transforming complaints into demands, breaks the whole movement. Discrepancies can then be decreased, after a long delay, through reform or migration. Either outlet naturally improves reality, hence decreases discrepancies *(Feedback loop 4).*

Although simple and still only qualitative, this analysis shows four dynamic feedback loops (a loop is dynamic when it brings forth the notion of time, essentially through delays). In further work we intend to develop the study of such loops and, more generally, the use of this approach.

Notes

[1] Cited in Irving Mark, *Agrarian Conflicts in Colonial New York, 1711-1775* (New York, 1940), 136, and in Richard Hofstadter, *The American Political Tradition* (New York, 1948), 6-7.

[2] Carl L. Becker, *The History of Political Parties in the Province of New York, 1760-1776* (Madison, Wis., 1909); Robert E. Brown, *Middle-Class Democracy and the Revolution in Massachusetts 1691-1780* (Ithaca, N. Y., 1955); Louis Hartz, "American Political Thought and the American Revolution," *American Political Science Review,* XLVI (1952), 321–342, and *id., The Liberal Tradition* (New York, 1955).

[3] The expression is that of Berthoff in Rowland Berthoff and John M. Murrin, "Feudalism, Communalism, and the Yeoman Freeholder: The American Revolution Considered as a Social Accident," in Stephen G. Kurtz and James H. Hutson, eds., *Essays on the American Revolution* (Chapel Hill, N. C., 1973), 256–288. Lockridge's changes are in "Social Change and the Meaning of the American Revolution," *JSH,* VI (1972-73), 403-439. On the concentration of wealth see also Robert A. East, *Business and Enterprise in the American Revolutionary Era* (Gloucester, Mass., Reprint 1964). Other references are John M.

Murrin, "Review Essay," *History and Theory*, XI (1972), 226-275, esp. 271; Robert M. Zemsky, *Merchants, Farmers and River Gods* (Boston, 1971); Stephen E. Patterson, *Political Parties in Revolutionary Massachusetts* (Madison, Wis., 1973); Kenneth A. Lockridge, "Land, Population and the Evolution of New England Society 1630-1790," *Past and Present* (Apr. 1968), 62-80, and "Afterthought, 1970," in Stanley N. Katz, ed., *Colonial America: Essays in Politics and Social Development* (Boston, 1971), 483-491.

[4] Especially cogent are Jesse Lemisch, "The American Revolution Seen from the Bottom up," in Barton J. Bernstein, ed., *Towards a New Past* (New York, 1968) 3-45; Staughton Lynd, "Beyond Beard," *ib.*, 46-64, and "Who Should Rule at Home: Dutchess County, New York, in the American Revolution," *WMQ*, 3rd. Ser., XVIII (1961), 330-359; Alfred Young, *The Democratic Republicans of New York* (Chapel Hill, N. C., 1967); Dirk Hoerder, *People and Mobs: Crowd Action in Massachusetts during the American Revolution, 1765-1780* (Berlin, 1971).

[5] See "Violence and the American Revolution," in Kurtz and Hutson, eds., *Essays* (cf. n. 3), 90, 119-120. I use the word "agrarian" synonymously with "rural" as opposed to "urban". After the Revolution agrarian radicalism seems to have been located in regions where village populations varied from 500 to 1500 and where towns were either removed from easy commercial access or were undergoing rapid economic transformation.

[6] The growing number of agricultural laborers and landless poor in the last quarter of the 18th century seems to justify the use of the expression "rural proletariat" although, as I have implied, geographical and social mobility may have been determents to permanence in this group.

[7] Pauline Maier, *From Resistance to Revolution* (New York, 1972), 303-304. A member of the New York Sons of Liberty, John Morin Scott, was a judge at the trial of William Prendergast who received a sentence unusual for the times in its barbarism. That Bostonian Son of Liberty, Sam Adams, felt that it would be a healthy thing to hang a few Shaysites and opposed a general pardon in 1787.

[8] Mark, *Agrarian Conflicts* (cf. n. 1), 136, and Marion Starkey, *A Little Rebellion* (New York, 1955), 101.

[9] I am grateful to Hans-Christoph Schröder for having raised this comparative aspect of agrarian radicalism at the Cologne symposium. His comments and those of many others at the conference have been helpful to me in revising this paper for publication. Several of their criticisms have been incorporated into the article.

[10] Such as those of Boris Porchnev, Eric Hobsbawm, George Rudé, Yves-Marie Bercé and Henry Landsberger.

[11] "Black List", Robert Treat Paine Papers, Massachusetts Historical Society, Boston.

[12] George Rudé, *The Crowd in History, 1730-1848* (New York, 1964), 42, mentions the use of the term "regulator" in England in the 1766 food riots. For usage in the southern states in the 18th century see James Cutler, *Lynch-Law: An Investigation into the History of Lynching in the United States* (New York, 1905), 19-22, 38.

[13] Our preliminary research on the economic status of Regulators within their respective towns shows that Regulator holdings seem to be smaller than those of the average subsistence farm described by Jackson T. Main for the seventies

and eighties, where from 100–200 acres was typical. *(The Social Structure of Revolutionary America* [Princeton, N. J., 1965], 273–274.) Some examples of average Regulator holdings are 90 acres (Pelham); 60 acres (Whately); 62 acres (Amherst); 53 acres (Barre); 69 acres (Shirley), Valuation Lists, 1784. State Library, Boston. However, these figures must still be compared with those of non-Regulator holdings in the same townships.

[14] Robert J. Taylor, *Western Massachusetts in the Revolution* (Providence, R. I., 1954), 147.

[15] The term is that of Van Beck Hall, *Politics Without Parties: Massachusetts, 1780–1791* (Pittsburgh, 1972), ch. 1, who provides a persuasive classification of Massachusetts towns according to a scale establishing their degree of economic and cultural development. Class A towns are the most highly developed, Class C towns the least. The Shays Rebellion derives its force from Class B and C towns. See also Patterson, *Political Parties* (cf. n. 3).

[16] That town was Westhampton. Sources for locating Regulators include the oath of allegiance lists, court records, prison lists, R. T. Paine's "Black List," and other miscellaneous documents, especially legal.

[17] R. J. Taylor, *Western Massachusetts* (cf. n. 14), 148, tends to refute continuity between the two movements on the grounds that most insurgents were debtors, that the leaders of the Constitutionalists opposed the Shays Rebellion (Thomas Allen, Caleb Hyde, Valentine Rathbun, Jonathan Smith), and that, while the grievances may have been similar, the "tone . . . was different . . . The Shaysites were short on political theory and long on military organization." Preliminary research on court records in Worcester County, where debt cases seem to have been the most numerous in the 1780s, has so far not substantiated Taylor's statement (indeed, we found a number of Regulators among the plaintiffs). Nor is it surprising that some of the leaders of the Constitutionalist movement who had welcomed the restoration of civil government in Berkshire by 1780 should repudiate its disruption only a few years later. Finally, the Constitutionalist movement was situated in a period of general search for new government at the height of the independence movement when opposition was more likely to be "long" on theory and military organization not only tolerated but necessary.

[18] Rehoboth, Dec. 25, 1786, for example.

[19] An anonymous Bostonian, cited in Jackson T. Main, *Political Parties before the Constitution* (Chapel Hill, N. C., 1973), 113–114. We have seen the attitude of Jeremy Belknap at the beginning of this article.

[20] In theory the interior towns outnumbered the seaboard towns in the legislature, but in practice they were underrepresented, partly because of the expense of maintaining the delegates in Boston for several weeks. This motive, as well as political reasons, was significant in the demand for the removal of the capital from the coast.

[21] R. J. Taylor, *Western Massachusetts* (cf. n. 14), 143. Samuel Eliot Morison, *Maritime History of Massachusetts, 1783–1860* (Boston, 1941), 36, contends that "maritime Massachusetts controlled the government, by the simple device of apportioning the state senate according to taxable wealth. Every effort of the representatives to relieve the farmers died in the upper house."

[22] See for example the petitions of Dracut (Sept. 29, 1786) and Ware (Jan. 15, 1787), Shays Rebellion Papers, American Antiquarian Society, Worcester; also that of Thomas Grover, cited in George Richards Minot, *The History of the In-*

surrections in Massachusetts in the Year 1786 and the Rebellion Consequent Thereon (Worcester, Mass., 1788), 86.

[23] Douglas L. Jones, "The Strolling Poor: Transiency in Eighteenth-Century Massachusetts," *JSH*, VIII (1974–75), 29.

[24] Lockridge, "Land," (cf. n. 3), 68.

[25] This was especially true of wheat. R. J. Taylor, *Western Massachusetts* (cf. n. 14), 5.

[26] Property estimated at £ 100 in 1783 had declined to £ 40 in three years, "Zenas" (James Sullivan), *Independent Chronicle*, May 11, 1786.

[27] Curtis P. Nettels, *The Emergence of a National Economy, 1775–1815* (New York, 1962), 86–87.

[28] Oscar and Mary Handlin, *Commonwealth: Massachusetts, 1774–1861* (New York, 1947), 61.

[29] The burden of taxation lay most heavily on the agricultural population as most of the state's revenues were collected from direct taxes on polls and estates. In the mid-eighties the poll tax alone constituted nearly 40 percent of state levies. By 1786 this tax was over £ 1 per poll.

[30] Petitions from the town of Plymton, Oct. 2, 1786 and Feb. 12, 1787, Shays Rebellion Papers, American Antiquarian Society (cf. n. 22).

[31] This latter activity, however, was so severely criticized as to be denied by the conventioners themselves on one occasion. J. R. Pole, "Shays's Rebellion: A Political Interpretation," in Jack P. Greene, ed., *The Reinterpretation of the American Revolution, 1763–1789* (New York, 1968), 426–427. By 1788 newspapers were nevertheless publishing electoral lists. J. T. Main, *Political Parties* (cf. n. 19), 119.

[32] This clause recalls the Coercive Acts, but in spite of House pressure for a vote of reconsideration, the act passed *in extenso* supported by a heavy majority of eastern delegates. Well over 80 percent of the coastal and Maine delegates rejected reconsideration, while only 30–40 percent of the western representatives favored it. The last were from the poorest towns. V. B. Hall, *Politics without Parties* (cf. n. 15), 215.

[33] Witness of Robert Furnbush, Trial of Aaron Broad. Shays Rebellion Papers, American Antiquarian Society (cf. n. 22). Broad had opposed the uprising in Holden town meeting, but the Riot Act changed his mind.

[34] Minot, *History of the Insurrections* (cf. n. 22), 88.

[35] *ib.*, 75. Minot notes that "some symptoms of uneasiness began to appear."

[36] Thomas Amory, *Life of James Sullivan* (Boston, 1859), II, 390–391.

[37] Minot, *History of the Insurrections* (cf. n. 22), 45.

[38] Ethel Stanwood Bolton, ed., "Extracts from the Diary of James Parker," *New England Historical and Genealogical Register*, LXIX (1915), 8–17, 117–127, 211–224, 294–308; Seth Chandler, *History of the Town of Shirley* (Shirley, Mass., 1883), 130–131.

[39] Starkey, *Little Rebellion* (cf. n. 8), 173. Eric Hobsbawm, *Social Bandits* (London, 1971), 188.

[40] On March 10, 1787, the General Court resolved to halt migration by a gubernatorial proclamation warning people against buying real estate from Shaysites who had not stood trial. *Acts and Laws of the Commonwealth of Massachusetts* (Boston, 1893), ch. 140, 513.

[41] Pearl E. Wagner, "Economic Conditions in Western Pennsylvania During the Whiskey Rebellion," *Western Pennsylvania Historical Magazine*, X (1927), 193–209, esp. 193.

[42] Robert E. Bright, "The Whiskey Rebellion" (M. A. thesis, Temple University, 1939), 32.

[43] In his *Life of Washington* (Philadelphia, 1804), V, 361, John Marshall noted a deep-seated opposition to government among the Scotch-Irish of western Pennsylvania. "From that section of the state, the Constitution itself had experienced the most decided opposition ... Its measures generally, and the whole system of finance particularly, had been reprobated with peculiar bitterness by many of the most influential men of that district." W. F. Dunaway, *The Scotch-Irish of Colonial Pennsylvania* (Chapel Hill, N. C., 1944), 138, claims that other national groups in western Pennsylvania were as active "in proportion to their numbers." See also Ronald W. Long, "The Presbyterians and the Whiskey Rebellion," *Journal of Presbyterian History*, XLIII (1965), 28–37.

[44] J. T. Main, *Social Structure* (cf. n. 13), 16, 17.

[45] Elizabeth K. Henderson, "The Northwestern Lands of Pennsylvania, 1790–1812," *PMHB*, LX (1936), 131–160.

[46] "Resolves of Ohio County, Virginia," Papers Relating to the Whiskey Rebellion, *Pennsylvania Archives*, 2nd Series, ed. William H. Egle, John B. Linn, and George E. Reed, 19 vols. (Harrisburg, Pa., 1879–1890), IV, 228–229.

[47] "In 1792 there were recorded in Allegheny county 159 slaves; in Washington county, 263; in Westmoreland county, 128." Wagner, "Economic Conditions" (cf. n. 41), 363 and 200.

[48] *ib.,* 202. After repeal of the excise law in 1802 by the Jefferson administration, whiskey continued to be used in lieu of money. See Long, "Presbyterians" (cf. n. 43), 34 n.

[49] According to John Bach McMaster, *A History of the People of the United States from the Revolution to the Civil War* (New York, 1884), II, 189, the rate after amendment in 1792 was 7 cents on a gallon averaging 15.

[50] "Resolves of Ohio County, Virginia," (cf. n. 46), 228.

[51] Solon and Elizabeth Buck, *The Planting of Civilization in Western Pennsylvania*, paperback ed. (Pittsburgh, 1968), 466.

[52] Bradford, reputed to have the finest home in Washington (Pa.), was menaced with arson. Marshall's door was tarred and feathered. Lamar Middleton, *Revolt, U.S.A.* (New York, 1938), 198.

[53] Buck, *Planting of Civilization* (cf. n. 51), 467.

[54] *Pennsylvania Archives* (cf. n. 46), 61–62.

[55] William Miller, "The Democratic Societies and the Whiskey Insurrection," *PMHB*, LXII (1938), 324–349.

[56] Minot, *History of the Insurrections* (cf. n. 22), 147.

The American Revolution and the Modern Concept of "Revolution"

Horst Dippel*

Few words in political rhetoric are more often used whose meaning is less precise, not to say more controversial than that of "revolution". There is not only the clash of different theories of revolution, but a consensus can hardly be reached on the very connotations of the term itself. A greater deal of agreement seems to exist on what the term used to stand for. Derived from the Latin "revolutio", etymologically the word included the idea of revolving on a circular orbit, and ever since Copernicus it has been used as an astronomical term in the natural sciences. During the seventeenth and eighteenth centuries this originally non-historical concept became increasingly applied in the more human, historical field, strictly retaining for the time being its initial meaning. Thus it was associated with a sudden and violent change which had happened at a fixed period in the past resulting from neither a process evolving in time nor from human action, but rather imposed on a people by events over which they had no control.[1]

Although no full agreement on the meaning of "revolution" has been achieved, it is clear that no modern writer considers "revolution" in this context. On the contrary, the prevailing conception is that revolution means conscious, primarily political human action. The term has assumed the grammatical form of a collective singular to denote and to make intelligible a complex set of historical events. It stands for a process of historical change which by its accelerated course is different from evolution and which by its internal dynamics exceeds a conglomeration of reform measures. There is less agreement as to whether we are allowed to speak of "revolution" if there happens only a change in the political structure or whether, of necessity, this change must include a social component in the form of some kind of social emancipation and change in the structure of society.[2] Whatever the details of the change may be, there is a strong feeling that something new is created by it, that the ideas of novelty and innovation are constituents of the revolutionary process. As legitimating factor this assumption divides revolution from justifiable resistance,[3] though there may be some initial convergency of both. Whereas the idea of the former is to begin the world over anew, the application of the right to resist is restricted to the restoration of ancient rights or privileges. This innovatory spirit is expressed in some sort of a revolutionary ideology which is supposed to be a necessary companion of a revolution though there is hardly agreement as to the principles around which this ideology should revolve. Nevertheless, there seems to be no doubt that their implementation is basic to the idea of human progress. Whether, however, revolution necessarily means violence is a question very much debated. There is more agreement on the assumption that the meaning of the term transcends any fixed limits of time and space, with future and global significance.[4]

The connotations of what we may consider the traditional usage of the term "revolution" refer to a retrospective event undertaken to prevent major changes, a Machiavellian *ridurre ai principii*,[5] whereas the modern usage denotes a dynamic process which has perspective on the past and the future. The discrepancy between the traditional and the modern conception of "revolution", and the change from the one to the other resemble the alterations in the usage of numerous other terms which, taken together, form the semantic transformation to the modern world.[6] This period of historical transition is supposed to have been the eighteenth century. Concerning the term "revolution", however, the interpretation generally accepted so far is that the change from the traditional to the modern usage of the term only took place during the French Revolution. Scholars like Eugen Rosenstock, Karl Griewank, Hannah Arendt, and others have assured us that the traditional connotations of "revolution" gave way to a modern usage of the term as a dynamic means of historical change, actively brought about by revolutionaries during the storming of the Bastille on July 14, 1789, when the Duke de La Rochefoucauld-Liancourt corrected the French King with the words: "No, Sire, that is a revolution."[7]

This interpretation of the modern meaning superseding the traditional connotations of "revolution" is in several ways peculiar. First of all, it is in obvious contradiction to the assumption of an evolutionary transition of traditional *topoi* to a modern conception during the eighteenth century without giving specific reasons for this singularity. Secondly, it is an interpretation primarily rooted in the traditions of German or at least continental European historiography and philosophy. Thirdly, this opinion emerged not from an analysis, but generally from a complete disregard of the American Revolution and of the significance it had on the terminological evolution of "revolution". It was this neglect which caused Eugen Rosenstock even to maintain that the American Revolution was renamed "revolution" only after 1789, since according to Rosenstock's view, the American and European contemporaries still possessed the traditional notion of "revolution" until that time.[8]

Rosenstock's opinion, though its internal logic is correct, is historically inaccurate. The term American "Revolution" was used contemporaneously. Accepting this heuristic anticipation we shall have to examine the degree of modernity in the American usage of the term "revolution" during the 1770s and 1780s, and we shall also have to examine the effects of the American Revolution and the American usage of "revolution" on the term in Europe, especially in France and Germany during the years before the French Revolution.

During the colonial time, the American usage generally referred to the Glorious Revolution of 1688–1689 and documented that the Americans thought of themselves as living in a constitutional framework based on revolutionary principles, thus associating the term "revolution" with an altogether positive meaning. Probably the very word was applied to denote internal American events in the conflict with England for the first time in 1775. It was when Richard Henry Lee wrote from Philadelphia on May 21, 1775, to Francis Lightfoot Lee, "There never was a more total revolution at any place than at New York. The Tory's [!] have been obliged to fly, the Province is arming, and the Governor dares not call his prostituted Assembly to receive Ld. Norths [!] foolish plan."[9] In quite similar a vein Samuel Adams asked Benjamin Kent on July 27, 1776, "Was there ever a Revolution brot [!] about, especially so important as this without great internal Tumults & violent Convulsions?"[10]

In very much the same sense the term "revolution" was still later used as "an entire Change of the Governments and Constitutions of thirteen States".[11] This interpretation appears to retain a good deal of the more traditional meaning of "revolution" as *Staatsveränderung, changement d'Etat,* especially when "the Revolution" was fixed to the very moment of the transition from the British colonial administrations to American state governments, as it appeared in a collection "... Containing the Laws now in Force, passed between the 30th Day of September 1775, and the Revolution".[12] Regarding the only beginning dissociation of state and society in a world where government in the Aristotelian tradition was not yet voided of society, statements like these obviously meant more than a mere change of government according to our modern understanding. But a different usage of the term already appeared at this stage. On July 3, 1776, John Adams wrote to his wife Abigail: "When I look back to the Year 1761, and recollect the Argument concerning Writs of Assistance, in the Superior Court, which I have

117

hitherto considered as the Commencement of the Controversy, between Great Britain and America, and run through the whole Period from that Time to this, and recollect the series of political Events, the Chain of Causes and Effects, I am surprised at the Suddenness, as well as the Greatness of this Revolution."[13] Adams's interpretation of the Revolution appears not only to have involved doing away with old governments and instituting new ones, as well as creating new loyalties, it was also a complex set of events, a thoroughly historical process with causes and consequences containing a strong notion of accelerating speed and extraordinary significance. After all, the Revolution was a product of conscious human action, as Edmund Randolph recognized when writing of "those who first kindled the Revolution".[14]

As these ideas indicate the term "revolution" had already assumed several of its modern connotations at an early stage of the American Revolution. Though Adams spoke of the revolution as something which had already happened, the assumption that the revolution was far from being over but still going on, soon gained ground in the years after 1776, thus dissociating the term from the past and integrating it in the present with an open future. It was this new meaning Richard Henry Lee hinted at when he was writing to Thomas Jefferson in May 1779 of "the progress of our glorious revolution".[15] Almost a year later James Madison spoke in quite the same way of "the course of the revolution".[16] The feeling of living right in the center of an ongoing revolution was even more distinct in the mind of Benjamin Rush who late in 1780 clearly spoke of "the present stage of the American Revolution".[17] "Revolution" emerged thus as a category explaining and giving specific importance to a complex set of historical or contemporaneous events in the same manner as this meaning is part of the modern usage of the term.

Rush's wording is important for an additional reason. So far the phrase used was "the revolution", or "the revolution of England", or quite recently "the revolution of America". There is a significant and meaningful change in Rush's and others'[18] speaking of the "American Revolution". This expression, anticipating modern usage, gives evidence of a political event made specific by a precise attribute distinguishing it from similar events in other countries, especially the Glorious Revolution of 1688 to 1689, as well as from different events in one's own country. "Revolution" as collective singular definitely assumed a meaning sharply separating it from past changes, uproars, rebellions and the like.

No doubt, there was a strong initial association of the American Revolution with the right of resistance. Not only was the worsening conflict between the colonies and the mother country from 1763 to the middle of the 1770s marked by the American conception and practice of legitimate resistance, the most famous proclamation of which is the Declaration of Independence with its classic formulation, "That whenever any Form of Government becomes destructive to these ends [i. e. Life, Liberty and the Pursuit of Happiness], it is the Right of the People to alter or to abolish it, and to institute new Government, laying its foundation on such principles and organizing its powers in such form, as to them shall seem most likely to effect their Safety and Happiness." Jefferson had something more in mind than the question posed by the Rhode Island congressional delegates to their governor several years later, "Did America resist the power of Britain to avoid only three pence on a pound of Tea, or was it their Claims, their unlimited claims and the tendency of their Measures, was it not rather Oppression and violence Apprehended and which existed in our well grounded fears and reasonable Jealousy that brought on the present war, than the great weight of Present Injuries?"[19] Jefferson's basic argument in the vindication of the American right of resistance was not that the British government had violated major clauses or the essence of the British constitution, or of the colonial charters, but that it had been destructive to the principles of natural law. The concept of natural law played, however, not only a significant role in modern revolutions,[20] it was also this very idea which enabled the American patriots to associate their Revolution with an even more important aspect, viz. that of novelty and innovation.

How strong this feeling of innovation was is documented by a letter of William Shippen written to his brother Edward on July 27, 1776: "We now have in our Power what never happened to any People before in the World I mean an opportunity of forming a plan of Government upon the most just rational & equal principles; not exposed as others have heretofore been to caprice & accident or the influence of some mad conqueror, or prevailing parties or factions of men but full power to settle our Government from the very foundation *de novo*."[21] Years later David Ramsay, the most important contemporary American historian of the Revolution, concluded that it was Great Britain's inclination "to resist every innovation" which thus "occasioned the revolution", whereas other Americans would have liked to see even stronger innovative principles acting during the Revolution.[22] Quite to the contrary, until this period striving for innovations had been regarded as objectionable and had legitimated the resort to the right of resistance to prevent innovation. Whereas in the traditional meaning innovation may have instigated revolution, this very innovation was now considered a revolutionary goal.

Privately Benjamin Rush had already reasoned on innovation in a letter to John King on April 2, 1783: "We have forgotten in the course of the Revolution *two* things. 1st, That we are a very small society compared with the collected mass of all other societies, and 2dly, That we are a very *modern* society in Pensylvania [!] compared with many others."[23] What Pennsylvania may have been compared with the rest of America, the United States certainly was as compared with Europe.

A whole range of problems derived from the complex term "revolution" are laid bare in these words. There is no doubt that Rush like many other patriots saw in the American Revolution an innovative principle which in his opinion was republicanism. "Our republican forms of government will in time beget republican opinions and manners."[24] The same idea Thomas Jefferson had already voiced several years before, when he spoke of "our political metamorphosis", referring to the people of Virginia having "deposited the monarchical and taken up the republican government".[25]

In their comprehensive understanding of republicanism the American patriots expressed what in a modern sense may justly be called a revolutionary ideology, at the center of which lay the ideas of virtue and of liberty. The change to republican government was taken as a change to more virtue, to more liberty. More virtue meant less corruption, greater security for the first principles of government, and a better human world more appropriate to human nature.[26] Whereas the concept of liberty was not restricted to certain jeopardized constitutional rights or privileges, the patriots soon were convinced to struggle for the general principle of liberty. During the Stamp Act Crisis Richard Henry Lee wrote: "Let us remove from despotism every shew of argument, and let us endeavor to convince the world that we are as firm and unanimous in the cause of liberty, as so noble and exalted a principle demands."[27] The patriots were fully convinced that their conflict with England was of general human importance. They thought of their "defiance to tyranny and its infamous Abettors" as "the cause of Humanity",[28] or, as George Washington put it in plain words: "Our cause is noble, it is the cause of Mankind."[29] But the American Revolution did not only constitute a lesson to the world, there were also concrete consequences, though not of a revolutionary nature, to be expected globally: "Establishing the liberties of America will not only make that people happy, but will have some effect in diminishing the misery of those who in other parts of the world groan under despotism, by rendering it more circumspect, and inducing it to govern with a lighter hand."[30] This conception of the greatness and the significance of their own actions, a consciousness generally associated with a modern understanding of "revolution", induced the patriots to appeal "to a candid world", as Jefferson phrased it in the Declaration of Independence.

The American patriots were not only conscious of the existence of a revolutionary ideology in a modern sense, whose spatial and temporal significance by far exceeded an isolated part of the British Empire at the end of the eighteenth century, giving their country in Rush's opinion the rank of "the only vivid principle of the whole world".[31] There was also a growing awareness of the fact that establishing a *novus ordo saeculorum* in America could not be without social consequences. To be sure, it was the initial intention not to change but to preserve society. But while the Revolution was going on some changes in the social order quite intentionally occurred. Abolishing feudal relicts like primogeniture and entail in Virginia was at least of rhetorical importance. Though there was no native nobility to do away with the patriots could and actually did prohibit all noble titles. What other consequences there were, ever debated in historical literature since Carl L. Becker and J. Franklin Jameson, there was at least an awareness of social consequences in Rush's comment: "The proprietary gentry have retired to their country seats, and honest men have taken the seats they abused so much in the government of our state."[32]

David Ramsay was also fully persuaded that beyond all the drama involved it was this very question of internal social consequences which gave true importance to the American Revolution: "In modern Europe the revolutions of public affairs seldom disturb the humble obscurity of private life, but the American revolution involved the interest of every family, and deeply affected the fortunes and happiness of almost every individual in the United States."[33] Ramsay had no doubts that the consequences of these influences and stimulations originated by the Revolution were to bear their fruits in the future.

It is logical that in view of these expected internal and global consequences of the American Revolution the opinion emerged that this event was not terminated in 1783 or 1787. The ideas of its general human importance and of its internal social consequences, combined in the conception of the Revolution, firmly knit it with the concept of human progress. As early as December 18, 1781, John Adams wrote from Europe to Abigail, "The progress of society will be accelerated by centuries by this revolution."[34] With the same conviction Ramsay closed his interpretation of the American Revolution uttering the wish: "May the Almighty Ruler of the Universe, who has raised you to Independence, and given you a place among the nations of the earth, make the

American Revolution an Era in the history of the world, remarkable for the progressive increase of human happiness!"[35]

The American Revolution had not come to its end in the 1780s but transcended its own limits of time and space, thus making the idea of the future part of its own concept, giving itself an air of permanence. Just as the *Columbian Magazine* of July 1787 referred to the whole course of events since the 1760s as "the present revolution",[36] Benjamin Rush expressed a similar opinion at about the same time with his well known remark: "There is nothing more common than to confound the terms of the American Revolution with those of the late American War. The American War is over: but this is far from being the case with the American Revolution. On the contrary, nothing but the first act of the great drama is closed."[37]

It is not maintained in conclusion of this analysis of the term "revolution" as used in the 1770s and 1780s in America, that the Americans applied the term throughout and exclusively in a thoroughly modern sense. This investigation, however, attempts to show that the American Revolution enlarged the contents of the term "revolution", endowing it with genuinely modern connotations which have hitherto been assumed to be associated with the term only since the days of the French Revolution. Already in America the term was used as a collective singular with a complex as well as an extensive meaning. Certainly, it was comprehended as conscious human action and as a process of historical change with far-reaching, including social, consequences. There was a strong sense of novelty and innovation prevalent and a conglomeration of ideas which may be apprehended as a revolutionary ideology. The implementation of these principles was thought of as being connected with some notion of general human progress which meant that the events transcended the limits of a fixed period and of the own country with future and global significance.

Though the term "revolution" assumed a fuller and more modern meaning in America during the Revolution, not all modern connotations as applied in America were of genuine American origin. In the field of general political and constitutional theory the Americans frequently went back to English thought of the seventeenth and eighteenth centuries, and at least some of the modern connotations of the term "revolution" as used in America had originated in England during and after the Glorious Revolution.

1688–1689 was not the first event to be denoted "revolution" by contemporaries but it then happened for the first time that the term was contemporaneously applied to a revolution in a manner that transcended its traditional meaning.[38] The use of the term as a collective singular may be closely associated with the English interpretation of the Glorious Revolution. When John Evelyn on December 2, 1688, recorded in his diary, "The Popists in offices lay down their Commissions & flie: Universal Consternation amongst them: it lookes like a Revolution",[39] he described part of an event, the whole of which his contemporaries soon came to call "the Revolution".[40] Comprehended in eighteenth-century England as the revolution plain and simple, it retained a good deal of the idea of *Staatsveränderung* in the very way the term was initially used in the American Revolution when the Americans strongly stressed the similarity of both events.[41] But the term did not remain restricted to this meaning.

There was a growing awareness of "revolution" as conscious human action. Bishop Gilbert Burnet, writing about 1705, gives ample proof in his widely read *History of His Own Time* of the change in the notion of "revolution": "The Revolution was brought about, with the universal applause of the whole Nation: Only these last steps began to raise a fermentation."[42] About forty years later, James Ralph wrote in his important *History of England During the Reigns of K. William, Q. Anne, and K. George I* of "Mr. Speke, the principal Transactor in the Revolution", and he quoted the Duke of Buckinghamshire as to the "Part I acted in the Business of the Revolution".[43] More significantly, while analyzing Bishop Burnet's *Enquiry into the Present State of Affairs*[44] and commenting on the actors of 1688–1689, Ralph spoke of "these Revolutioners",[45] using this neologism of 1695 strongly resembling the modern sense of the word "revolutionary". In quite a similar vein Tobias Smollett some years later spoke of Bishop Burnet as "instrumental in effecting the revolution",[46] while David Hume made the revolution fully appear as a political bargain between Whigs and Tories: "The whigs, now the ruling party, having united with the tories, in order to bring about the revolution . . ."[47]

Several other modern notions associated with "revolution" were to turn up in the discussion of 1688 in eighteenth-century England. Though the revolution was founded on the right to resist, it successfully asserted several general principles to secure a more or less liberal political order,[48] and we may regard these "principles of Revolution", as Richard Watson called them, as a first step to what the American patriots developed further as their Revolutionary ideology.

Another aspect David Hume, though still vaguely, associated with "revolution", viz. the idea of innovation, demonstrating that the Glorious Revolution was not restricted to a mere return to England's old liberties but that it created something new. "The revolution forms a new epoch in the constitution; and was probably attended with consequences more advantageous to the people, than barely freeing them from an exceptional administration."[49] Mentioning advantages for the "people" brought about by the revolution involved the idea it had not only causes but also consequences, perhaps even social consequences.

These remarks suggest that during the Glorious Revolution and in the English interpretation of it until the eve of the American Revolution, the term "revolution" had assumed several modern connotations which the Americans were ready to take up during their own Revolution. If the Americans can claim no originality for several connotations as applied during the 1770s and 1780s, their usage, however, accounts for a deeper meaning and expresses a much higher degree of modernity in the term "revolution" than is apparent in the English interpretations of it up to 1776.

Examining the modern notions in the European, i. e. primarily French and German, usage of the term "revolution" during the years of the American Revolution up to 1789, we have to realize that the English interpretation of "revolution" since 1688 had only limited effects. The Glorious Revolution with James II's flight to Louis XIV appeared as a sudden, violent, and essentially anti-monarchical change.[50] The principal modern connotations of "revolution" for decades to come, including the writings of Montesquieu and Rousseau,[51] seem to have been the ideas of conscious human action and of an event with causes and some sort of consequences, which in the second half of the century were vaguely associated with a notion of human progress.[52] But even this limited modern meaning was not generally accepted,[53] being mostly absent in eighteenth-century dictionaries or encyclopedias. In Johann Heinrich Zedler's *Universallexikon* an altogether traditional definition of the term is given: "Revolution is said of a country when the same had suffered a specific change in government."[54] This is nothing like the decisive and conscious political action Zedler linked with the terms rebellion, uprising, revolt, disorder and others.[55] But this same definition was still repeated in Hübner's *Lexikon* during the 1780s.[56] In French dictionaries of the time we also hardly find modern connotations of the term. In the 1772 edition of the *Dictionnaire des mœurs,* there is no article on "revolution",[57] whereas in the 1778 edition of the *Dictionnaire de l'Académie française*, the Copernican and non-historical concepts of "revolution" were advanced including the addition: "It is also figuratively used as change arriving in public affairs."[58]

On the eve of the American Revolution the discussion of the term "revolution" in France and Germany was considerably behind that in England. The reasons for this divergency may not only be seen in the immediate experience of revolution in England and America, making its principles part of the constitutional framework, thus accounting for the positive sense associated with "revolution". The systems of government of both countries were also relatively more open to political participation and individual action than those framed by European absolutism.

With no revolutionary experience of their own before 1789, it was basically through the impact of American events that a discussion of "revolution" arose in France and Germany with the first speculations appearing in 1775 that a revolution in the English North American colonies might take place.[59] But the use of the term was still restricted to the traditional meaning of *Staatsveränderung*. During the following years, three conspicuous ideas became associated in Europe with the American Revolution: the notion of conscious human action; the awareness, at least before 1783, that the events were still unsettled, foreshadowing future consequences; and the idea of liberty as the basic Revolutionary principle. Holbach's assertion that political liberty was often implemented by revolutions[60] now assumed a new meaning while the traditional interpretation of revolution as "the work of nature"[61] soon gave way to a more modern conception.

These modern connotations are the essence of a doctoral dissertation published in 1777 in which for the first time the term appeared in the title of a book on the events in America.[62] Though giving nothing like a precise definition of what he understood by revolution, the author clearly spoke of the American right of revolution and closely linked this revolution with the idea of liberty and with human action.[63]

"Revolution" as conscious human action was also basic to the thinking of Pierre Ulric Du Buisson who after his return from America published his *Abrégé de la révolution de l'Amérique Angloise* in 1778. Du Buisson had not only a strong sense of the actors; he also tried to denote them, calling them "coopérateurs".[64] At the same time he regarded the American events as an historical process evolving in the present with an open future, thus speaking of "la révolution actuelle".[65] It is remarkable to see what happened to these modern connotations in the German translation of the book published a year later. In sharp contradiction to the ideas of its author, the translator rendered the term into the past speaking of a "vorgefallene Staatsveränderung" and changed the cooperators into the depersonalized "cooperating causes".[66] The clash between the traditional and the beginning modern understanding of "revolution" is apparent in this different choice of words.

The Abbé Raynal, who in the early editions of his widely read *Histoire philosophique et politique des établissements & du commerce des Européens dans les deux Indes* had used the term "revolution" in a rather traditional manner,[67] changed his understanding of it in the late 1770s. Just like Du Buisson the "Révolution de l'Amérique" clearly appeared to him not as a singular event at a fixed period in the past but as a contemporary process with an open future. He was conscious of the human action in it, though contrary to Du Buisson he preferred the anonymous French "on" to designate the actors.[68] The genuine contribution of Raynal and his proper theme, however, was the idea of liberty which he firmly knit with the Revolution as its constituent revolutionary principle,[69] a view Raynal set forth more emphatically than any previous European writer had done in this context. It may again be useful to see what happened to this book in its various German translations. While in the Frankfort–Leipzig edition of 1782 the word "révolution" was generally translated as "Revolution" with the noteworthy exception of the title, the translator of a later edition published in 1787 avoided this expression, substituting for it throughout the words "change", "uproar", etc.[70]

"Revolution" as conscious human action was one of the main impressions created by the American Revolution in Europe in this period, with America's adversaries in Germany soon to presume that there was a revolution in the colonies deliberately striven at by rebellious political leaders.[71] August Ludwig Schlözer who expressed an altogether traditional view in his *Vorstellung der Universal-Historie* in the early 1770s, focusing on revolutions of the earth and of mankind passively suffered by man,[72] completely changed his concept of "revolution" during the following years. Publishing a new edition in 1785, he hardly used the term "revolution" any more, now substituting for it the emancipated and consciously acting man, who by his actions brought about change; he confessed that this outlook was alien to him before the American Revolution.[73]

"Revolution" as some form of conscious political action undertaken by men was indeed an interpretation spreading in the late 1770s and 1780s,[74] just as Johann Zinner introduced Samuel Adams as "playing a major part in the present revolution".[75] This "révolution américaine", as the Viennese Count Karl von Zinzendorf wrote in his diary on March 9, 1780,[76] certainly was a contemporary process with a perspective on both the past and the future and no singular *Staatsveränderung* in the traditional sense of the word.

These, however, were not the only modern connotations to emerge in the

European discussion of the American Revolution, which in France as well as in Germany centered on the idea of liberty. The American Revolution assumed significance for Europeans precisely because it was so closely associated with the popular notion of liberty. Because the revolutionary ideology focused on the idea of liberty, a conscious notion of importance, greatness, and novelty was linked with the term "revolution"; its meaning thus exceeded the interpretation of the war years.

These are the main ideas of the anonymous and unpublished "Discours sur la grandeur et importance de la dernière révolution de l'Amérique septentrionale", written in Milan in 1783.[77] The author was well aware of the traditional connotations of the term "revolution" from which he clearly set apart the events in America: "The revolution of North America is of quite a different order."[78] What had happened in America not only had its distinct causes and effects.[79] Basic was his idea of "le caractère de grandeur et de nouveauté" which produced enthusiasts as well as adversaries.[80] With all distinctness the author put his finger on what actually brought forth the controversy, viz. "the new ideas which the revolution that it was, gave birth to on the nature of governments; on the constitution and dependence of colonies; on the narrow limits that separate authority from oppression, resistance from revolt; on the origin, the march, and the means of reunion and consistence of the body politic", which surely would not fail to make their impression in other parts of the world.[81]

At about the same time, a related interpretation of "la Révolution américaine"[82] was given by Matthias Christian Sprengel who first wrote in Germany extensively on the *Revolution von Nordamerika*. It was Raynal who greatly inspired him to tie the American Revolution to the idea of liberty.[83] Though in his opinion the singularity of the events resulted from the sudden establishment of a new extensive republic in a part of the world that had come to the mind of the German public only recently,[84] he clearly apprehended the far-reaching significance of the Revolution. This struggle "for the most sacred rights of humanity, for liberty, and the security of property"[85] was an event whose greatness was matched but by its contribution to the general cause of human progress. Not only the causes set the American Revolution clearly apart from preceding historical events. More important were its consequences which were to be realized in decades still to come[86] and which gave it a definite mark of greatness and the air of permanence. It was this interpretation of the "American Revolution"[87] that met with wide-spread acceptance in the remaining years before the French Revolution, thus contributing to the modern understanding of "revolution" in Europe during this period.[88]

From this analysis we may draw several conclusions. As an event of far-reaching importance the American Revolution had a primary impact on Europe. More than anything else, its most popular catchword "liberty" accounted for the modern connotations of "revolution" in France and Germany in the 1770s and 1780s. Though both countries did not experience a revolution, France and Germany associated a fuller and more modern meaning with the term in the years before 1789 than had been associated with it before 1776. To its new modern connotations belonged the concept of conscious human action in a process of historical change which had a perspective on the past as well as on the future. The term had assumed the form of a collective singular with a complex and extensive meaning. There was no clear-cut idea of the nature of the change brought about or instigated by the Revolution, the reasons for which may be seen in the different reception the American revolutionary ideology had in the different social and political context of European absolutism.[89] There existed, however, the idea of novelty and innovation, expressed in the persuasion that the implementation of these principles had something to do with general human progress and that the significance of the Revolution transcended America and the 1780s.

As we have seen, the modern meaning of "revolution" as understood in Europe had been greatly enhanced by the American Revolution and, although the understanding of the term in Germany was not completely identical with that in France,[90] by 1789 it had come close to the definition which the term had assumed in America during the immediate experience of a revolution. Nevertheless, it must be noted that the specific uses of the term during the American Revolution did not have any noteworthy impact in France or Germany in the 1770s and 1780s. If we disregard Du Buisson, in whose case we may only guess at eventual concrete American influences concerning this point, the modern European usage of the term appears to have been virtually independent of the development the meaning of "revolution" took in America in the same period.

Not all of these modern connotations applied to the term "revolution" in America and Europe during these years originated from the American Revolution. Some of them, on the contrary, dated back as far as 1688, thus documenting an evolution of the term between the Glorious and the American Revolutions. But whereas these modern concepts had an impact on Americans debating their own Revolution, they were less clearly realized on the European continent before 1776. Here, even more than in America itself, it was above all the impact of the American Revolution which accounted for endowing the term "revolution" with a new, i. e. a modern meaning.

Therefore it seems inappropriate to speak of the French Revolution as giving birth to a modern concept of "revolution". Through the experience of their own Revolution in America and via the impact of this event on Europe, the term had already assumed a fuller and more modern content before July 14, 1789, than has thus far been realized. There certainly was a contribution made by the French Revolution; it was, however, not so much to the term "Revolution" itself to which it made some additions, greatly popularizing it among adherents as well as adversaries, but in the field of an elaborated modern theory of "revolution". There was no eighteenth-century predecessor of Barnave,[91] neither in America nor in Europe.

Notes

* For helpful criticism I am indebted to Rainer Tamchina and Rudolf Vierhaus. Special thanks are due to Robert Berdahl who did his very best to transform the manuscript into readable and intelligible English.

[1] Jean Marie Goulemot, "Le Mot *révolution* et la formation du concept de *révolution politique* (fin XVIIe siècle)", *Annales Historiques de la Révolution Française*, XXXIX (1967), 433–434.

[2] Reinhart Koselleck, "Der neuzeitliche Revolutionsbegriff als geschichtliche Kategorie", *Studium generale*, XXII (1969), 831, 833–834.

[3] For a modern strict distinction between both from a juridical point of view, see Karl Friedrich Bertram, *Widerstand und Revolution: Ein Beitrag zur Unterscheidung der Tatbestände und ihrer Rechtsfolgen* (Berlin, 1964), 37–38, and *passim*.

[4] For a general discussion, see Eugen Rosenstock, "Revolution als politischer Begriff in der Neuzeit", in *Festgabe der rechts- und staatswissenschaftlichen Fakultät in Breslau für Paul Heilborn zum 70. Geburtstag, 6. Feb. 1931* (Breslau, 1931), 83–124; Franz Wilhelm Seidler, "Die Geschichte des Wortes Revolution: Ein Beitrag zur Revolutionsforschung" (Ph. D. diss., University of Munich, 1955); Karl Griewank, *Der neuzeitliche Revolutionsbegriff*, 2d ed. (Frankfurt, 1969 [orig. publ. Weimar, 1955]); Hannah Arendt, *On Revolution* (New York, 1963), 1–52; Koselleck, "Der neuzeitliche Revolutionsbegriff" (cf. n. 2), 825–838; Isaac Kramnick, "Reflections on Revolution: Definition and Explanation in Recent Scholarship", *History and Theory*, XI (1972), esp. 26–35.

[5] Cf. J. G. A. Pocock, *The Machiavellian Moment: Florentine Political Thought and the Atlantic Republican Tradition* (Princeton, N. J., 1975), 358–359, and *passim*.

[6] See the introduction by Reinhart Koselleck in Otto Brunner *et al.*, eds., *Geschichtliche Grundbegriffe: Historisches Lexikon zur politisch-sozialen Sprache in Deutschland* (Stuttgart, 1972–), I, esp. xiii-xix. The *Lexikon* is built upon

the assumption that social change from pre-modern to modern history can be understood through the changing meanings of certain key social concepts.

[7] See Rosenstock, "Revolution" (cf. n. 4), 106–107; id., *Die europäischen Revolutionen und der Charakter der Nationen*, 2d ed. (Stuttgart and Cologne, 1951), 325; Griewank, *Revolutionsbegriff* (cf. n. 4), 187, 189, 190–191, 195; Arendt, *On Revolution* (cf. n. 4), 21, 40–41; a more recent example is Kurt Lenk, *Theorien der Revolution* (Munich, 1973), 19–20.

[8] Rosenstock, "Revolution" (cf. n. 4), 113.

[9] For a quite similar remark see also his letter to Gouverneur Morris, May 28, 1775, both in James C. Ballagh, ed., *The Letters of Richard Henry Lee*, 2 vols. (New York, 1911–1914), I, 137, 140.

[10] Harry A. Cushing, ed., *The Writings of Samuel Adams*, 4 vols. (New York, 1904–1908), III, 304.

[11] Elbridge Gerry to James Warren, Nov. 8, 1778, in *LMCC*, III, 483.

[12] So e. g. Elias Boudinot to William Livingston, Aug. 25, 1781, *ib.*, VI, 197–198; [Thomas McKean, ed.,] *The Acts of the General Assembly of the Commonwealth of Pennsylvania ... And an Appendix, Containing the Laws now in Force, passed between the 30th Day of September, 1775, and the Revolution ...* (Philadelphia, 1782); David Ramsay, *The History of South-Carolina, from a British Province to an Independent State*, 2 vols. (Trenton, N. J., 1785), I, v, 128, cf. 79–80, where Ramsay stressed the idea of harmony, unanimity, and regularity in carrying out the Revolution.

[13] For similar remarks in this time, see his letters to Mary Palmer, July 5, 1776, to Abigail Adams, July 10, 1776, and to John Quincy Adams, July 27, 1777, all in L. H. Butterfield, ed., *Adams Family Correspondence*, 4 vols. (Cambridge, Mass., 1963–1973), II, 28, 34, 43, 289. As is well known Adams adhered to this interpretation still in his old age in the 1810s.

[14] To Patrick Henry, Dec. 6, 1786, in William Wirt Henry, *Patrick Henry: Life, Correspondence and Speeches*, 3 vols. (New York, 1891), II, 311. For the idea of conscious human action, see e. g. Thomas Jefferson to George Washington, Apr. 16, 1784, in *LMCC*, VII, 493–494; David Ramsay, *The History of the American Revolution*, 2 vols. (Philadelphia, 1789), II, 313, 316.

[15] May 3, 1779, in Julian P. Boyd *et al.*, eds., *The Papers of Thomas Jefferson* (Princeton, 1950–), II, 262.

[16] To Thomas Jefferson, Mar. 27, 1780, in William T. Hutchinson *et al.*, eds., *The Papers of James Madison* (Chicago, 1962–), II, 6. For "revolution" as historical process, see also Ramsay, *American Revolution* (cf. n. 14), I, 48, II, 124.

[17] To William Shippen, Nov. 18, 1780, in Lyman H. Butterfield, ed., *The Letters of Benjamin Rush*, 2 vols. (Princeton, N. J., 1951), I, 260.

[18] See e. g. the publication of the proceedings of Congress by Gouverneur Morris under the title *Observations on the American Revolution* (Philadelphia, 1779); also William Whipple to Josiah Bartlett, Feb. 28, 1779, in *LMCC*, IV, 83.

[19] Oct. 15, 1782, in *LMCC*, VI, 504; see also the draft by James Duane of ca. Apr. 4, 1781, *ib.*, 45.

[20] See, his numerous historical inaccuracies notwithstanding, Jürgen Habermas, "Naturrecht und Revolution", in his *Theorie und Praxis: Sozialphilosophische Studien*, 4th ed. (Frankfort, 1971), 89–127.

[21] Shippen Papers, XII, 41, Historical Society of Pennsylvania, Philadelphia.

[22] Ramsay, *American Revolution* (cf. n. 14), I, 44, II, 337.

[23] Butterfield, ed., *Rush Letters* (cf. n. 17), I, 298.

[24] To Horatio Gates, Sept. 5, 1781, *ib.*, 265.

[25] To Benjamin Franklin, Aug. 13, 1777, in Boyd *et al.*, eds., *Jefferson Papers* (cf. n. 15), II, 27.

[26] Cf. Gordon S. Wood, *The Creation of the American Republic, 1776–1787* (New York, 1972), 65–70; Pocock, *Machiavellian Moment* (cf. n. 5), 506–552.

[27] To Landon Carter, June 22, 1765, in Ballagh, ed., *Lee Letters* (cf. n. 9), I, 8.

[28] To Gouverneur Morris, May 28, 1775, *ib.*, 140–141.

[29] To James Warren, Mar. 31, 1779, in John C. Fitzpatrick, ed., *The Writings of George Washington*, 39 vols. (Washington, D. C., 1931–1944), XIV, 313.

[30] Benjamin Franklin to François Jean, marquis de Chastellux, Apr. 6, 1782, in John Bigelow, ed., *The Works of Benjamin Franklin*, 12 vols. (New York, 1904), IX, 182–183.

[31] To Thomas Ruston, Oct. 29, 1775, in Butterfield, ed., *Rush Letters* (cf. n. 17), I, 92.

[32] To Charles Lee, July 23, 1776, *ib.*, I, 103.

[33] Ramsay, *American Revolution* (cf. n. 14), II, 293, see also 314–325.

[34] Butterfield, ed., *Adams Family Correspondence* (cf. n. 13), IV, 266.

[35] Ramsay, *American Revolution* (cf. n. 14), II, 356.

[36] *Columbian Magazine* (July 1787), 554.

[37] "On the Defects of the Confederation" (1787), in D. D. Runes, ed., *Selected Writings of Benjamin Rush* (New York, 1947), 26.

[38] For the English usage of the term before 1688, see Vernon F. Snow, "The Concept of Revolution in Seventeenth-Century England", *Historical Journal*, V (1962), 167–174.

[39] E. S. de Beer, ed., *The Diary of John Evelyn*, 6 vols. (Oxford, 1955), IV, 609.

[40] Whereas the term was still used quite traditionally in the plural form in the *Histoire des révolutions d'Angleterre sous le regne de Jacques II. jusqu'au couronnement de Guillaume III.* (Amsterdam, 1689), the events of 1688–1689 were presented as "la Révolution" in [Guillaume de Lamberty,] *Memoires de la dernière révolution d'Angleterre, contenant l'Abdication de Jaques II., l'avenement de S. M. le Roi Guillaume à la Couronne, & plusieurs choses arrivées sous son Régne*, 2 pts. (The Hague, 1702), I, [18], 56, 371, and *passim*.

[41] For a recent example see the new edition of the correspondence between Daniel Dulany and Charles Carroll by Peter S. Onuf, ed., *Maryland and the Empire, 1773: The Antilon – First Citizen Letters* (Baltimore, Md., 1974), 27–28, 66, 88, 103, 130, 187–188, 225–226; also John Adams to his son John Quincy, July 27, 1777, in Butterfield, ed., *Adams Family Correspondence* (cf. n. 13), II, 290.

[42] Gilbert Burnet, *Bishop Burnet's History of His Own Time*, 2 vols. (London, 1724–1734), I, 802, see also 825, II, 2, 13, 14, 23.

[43] [James Ralph,] *The History of England During the Reigns of K. William, Q. Anne, and K. George I*, 2 vols. (London, 1744–1746), I, 1064, II, 8.

[44] Published anonymously: London, 1689.

[45] [Ralph,] *History* (cf. n. 43), II, 23.

[46] Tobias George Smollett, *A Complete History of England*, 3d ed., 7 vols. (London, 1758), VI, 3–4, see also 13.

[47] David Hume, *The History of England*, 3 vols. with the author's last cor-

rections and improvements, repr. of the ed. of 1786 (London and New York,
n. d.), III, 770.

⁴⁸ Richard Watson, *The Principles of Revolution Vindicated. A Sermon
Preached Before the University of Cambridge, May 29, 1776,* in his *Sermons
on Public Occasions and Tracts on Religious Subjects* (Cambridge, 1788),
65–67, see also 71–72.

⁴⁹ Hume, *History of England* (cf. n. 47), III, 773.

⁵⁰ See Goulemot, "Le Mot *révolution*" (cf. n. 1), 430–431, 436. In the age of
absolutism, the anti-monarchical character of the events of 1688–1689 continued to be regarded as apparent, cf. Graf Sigismund von Haslang to Graf
Matthäus von Vieregg, London, Nov. 7, 1788: "Le 4. de ce mois, le Parti des
Whigs, c'est-à-dire, *Anti-Roialistes,* aiant celebré le *Centenaire* de la Revolution
arrivée en l'Année 1688", Kasten schwarz 15 389, Geheimes Staatsarchiv,
München.

⁵¹ For Montesquieu see esp. his *Pensées, Considérations,* and *Esprit des Lois,* in
his *Œuvres complètes,* ed. Roger Caillois, 2 vols. (Paris, 1949–1951), I, 1053,
II, 71, 109–110, 166, 193, 281, 291, 310, 340, 513, 576, 851, 966, 989. For
Rousseau see his *Discours sur les sciences, Discours sur l'inégalité, Fragmens poli-
tiques. Ecrits sur l'abbé de Saint-Pierre,* and his dispatch from Venice, Sept. 2,
1743, all in his *Œuvres complètes,* eds. Bernard Gagnebin and Marcel Raymond, III (Paris, 1964), 6, 170–171, 187, 191, 530, 599, 630, 639, 1068.

⁵² Cf. Griewank, *Revolutionsbegriff* (cf. n. 4), 159–174.

⁵³ See Frederick II's definition of "revolution" as "un événement qui doit faire
changer le système d['une] cour", to Podewils, Aug. 25, 1743, in *Politische
Correspondenz Friedrichs des Grossen,* ed. by the Royal Prussian Academy
of Sciences, 46 vols. (Berlin, 1879–1939), II, 409.

⁵⁴ Johann Heinrich Zedler, *Universal Lexicon,* 64 vols. (Halle and Leipzig,
1733–1750), XXXI (1742), 954.

⁵⁵ See esp. the articles "Aufstand", "Rebellion", and "Revolte", *ib.,* II, 2165,
XXX, 1233–1234, XXXI, 954.

⁵⁶ Johann Hübner, *Reales Staats-, Zeitungs- und Conversations-Lexikon* (ed.
Vienna, 1780), 1077, (ed. Leipzig, 1789), 2065.

⁵⁷ See instead the articles "Changement", "Rebellion", and "Révolte", *Dictionnaire universel, historique et critique des mœurs,* 4 vols. (Paris, 1772), I, 232,
III, 36, 86.

⁵⁸ *Dictionnaire de l'Académie françoise,* new ed., 2 vols. (Nîmes, 1778), II,
460, see also the articles "Rebellion" and "Révolte", *ib.,* 395, 460.

⁵⁹ See e. g. *Wienerisches Diarium,* Apr. 22, 1775; Jakob Mauvillon in Guil-
laume Thomas François Raynal, *Philosophische und politische Geschichte der
Besitzungen und des Handels der Europäer in beiden Indien,* transl. from the
French, 7 vols. (Hanover, 1774–1778), II (1775), 26; Graf Hans Moritz von
Brühl zu Martinskirch to Sacken, Aug. 18, 1775, Locat 2685, conv. XI, fol.
329v, Staatsarchiv, Dresden. For an even earlier but also more vague use of
the word "revolution" with regard to the events in America, see *Teutscher
Merkur* (Mar. 1773), 279.

⁶⁰ [Paul Henri Thiry baron d'Holbach,] *La Politique naturelle: Ou Discours sur les vrais principes du Gouvernement,* 2 pts. (London, 1773), II, 91,
see also I, 79, 113.

⁶¹ See e. g. [Ferdinando Galiani,] *Dialogues sur le commerce des bleds* (London, 1770), 237.

[62] Bengt Lidner, *De iure revolutionis Americanorum* (Ph. D. diss., University of Greifswald, 1777).

[63] *Ib.*, 7, 15.

[64] [Pierre Ulric Du Buisson,] *Abrégé de la révolution de l'Amérique Angloise* (Paris, 1778), 1, see also 430.

[65] *Ib.*, 3.

[66] [Pierre Ulric Du Buisson,] *Historischer Abriß der in Nord-Amerika vorgefallenen Staats-Veränderung,* transl. from the French (Berne, 1779), iii-iv.

[67] See e. g. ed. 7 vols. (The Hague, 1774), III, 1–2, VII, 17.

[68] *Révolution de l'Amérique* (London and The Hague, 1781), 31, 163.

[69] *Ib.*, passim.

[70] See his *Philosophische und politische Geschichte der Besitzungen und Handlung der Europäer in beyden Indien,* 10 vols. (Kempten, 1783—1788), IX (1787), 191, 208, 248, 257–258, 265.

[71] See e. g. [Christoph Heinrich Korn,] *Geschichte der Kriege in und ausser Europa,* 30 pts. (Nuremberg, 1776–1784), III (1777), 39, IX (1777), 70.

[72] 2d ed. (Göttingen, 1775), 219, 221–222, 225, 227, 229, 234, 242–243, 246, 248, 280, 288–289.

[73] New ed. as *Weltgeschichte,* 2 pts. (Göttingen, 1785–1789), I, 42–43, 53, 67, 69, 70, 71.

[74] See e. g. Johannes von Müller, "Beobachtungen über Geschichte, Gesetze und Interessen der Menschen" (1774–1776), in his *Sämmtliche Werke,* ed. Johann Georg Müller, 40 vols. (Stuttgart und Tübingen, 1831–1835), XXXVII, 103, 104; Christoph Meiners, *Grundriß der Geschichte der Menschheit* (Lemgo, 1785), 151.

[75] Johann Zinner, *Merkwürdige Briefe und Schriften der berühmtesten Generäle in Amerika* (Augsburg, 1782), 66.

[76] Diary, XXV, fol. 43, Zinzendorf Papers, Haus-, Hof- und Staatsarchiv, Vienna.

[77] The manuscript is preserved in the Österreichische Nationalbibliothek, Vienna, Cod. 12613.

[78] "Discours", fols. 7v–8, cf. 10–11.

[79] See *ib.*, fols. 6v–7, 43v, 46v.

[80] *Ib.*, fol. 17.

[81] *Ib.*, fol. 65, cf. 69v.

[82] *Ib.*, fol. 29r–v.

[83] Matthias Christian Sprengel, *Allgemeines historisches Taschenbuch ... enthaltend ... die Geschichte der Revolution von Nord-America* (Berlin, 1783), 27–28.

[84] *Ib.*, 27.

[85] *Ib.*, 28.

[86] *Ib.*, 149.

[87] Dietrich Heinrich Stöver, *Historisch-statistische Beyträge zur nähern Kenntniß der Staaten und der neuern Weltbegebenheiten* (Hamburg, 1789), 248–249.

[88] See e. g. Abbé Robin, *Neue Reise durch Nordamerika, in dem Jahr 1781,* transl. from the French (Nuremberg, 1783), [1], 24, 57, 144, 160, 162, 164; Chevalier Deslandes, *Discours sur la révolution dans l'Amérique* (Frankfort and Paris, 1785), 70, 74–75, 83; François Jean, marquis de Chastellux, *Voyage en Amérique,* 191 pages ed. (n. p., 1785), 181–182; *id., Abhandlung über die Vortheile und Nachtheile die für Europa aus der Entdeckung von America*

entstehen, transl. from the French (Halle, 1788), 80–81; Honoré Gabriel Riqueti, comte de Mirabeau, *Sammlung einiger philosophischen und politischen Schriften, die vereinigten Staaten von Nordamerika betreffend,* transl. from the French (Berlin, 1787), 1–2, 153–154, 157; [François Bernard,] *Précis historique de la révolution qui vient de s'opérer en Hollande* (Paris, 1788), 62, 63, 127, 134.

[89] Cf. Otto Vossler, *Die amerikanischen Revolutionsideale in ihrem Verhältnis zu den europäischen, untersucht an Thomas Jefferson.* Beihefte der Historischen Zeitschrift, 17 (Munich, Berlin, 1929), 6–7, 34–37, 66. Cf. R. R. Palmer, "A Neglected Work: Otto Vossler on Jefferson and the Revolutionary Era", *WMQ,* 3rd Ser., XII (1955), 462–471.

[90] For two rather traditional interpretations see Ewald Graf Herzberg, *Abhandlung von den Staats-Revolutionen,* transl. from the French (Schwerin, 1783), 5, 18; Johann Gottfried Herder, *Ideen zur Philosophie der Geschichte der Menschheit,* 4 vols. (Riga and Leipzig, 1784–1791), I, 16–20, 39, 41–42, 169, 246, 309, II, 120, 330.

[91] See Antoine Barnave, *Introduction à la révolution française* (written 1793, first publ. 1843), ed. Fernand Rude (Paris, 1960, repr. 1971).

New Wine in Old Skins? American Definitions of Empire and the Emergence of a New Concept

Norbert Kilian

When the thirteen British colonies in North America issued their Declaration of Independence, they not only rejected George III as their lawful sovereign, but also renounced all further ties with the British Empire.[1] The one seems to be a logical consequence of the other, even by eighteenth-century standards. The term "empire", as Richard Koebner convincingly demonstrated,[2] then retained still much of the Latin *imperium*, implying that somewhere in the body politic there had to be a sovereign, be it king, parliament or both, who was to rule the empire and to whom every part of that empire owed allegiance and submission, the colonies of course not excepted. Considering, however, John Adams' dictum of 1775, that "an Empire is a despotism",[3] it seems odd that Americans after 1776 did not discard the term from their political terminology as unfit and obsolete to describe conditions in the emerging republic in the same way that they dropped monarchy, king, nobility, etc. On the contrary, they began to talk about a rising American empire as soon as independence seemed inevitable. Their empire, however, was not styled after the British Empire, it was rather created in opposition to the political entity they were rejecting – as such, this concept as applied to America became part of the revolutionary ideology. With this they blended the vision of the constant westward move of empires, a movement which was to come to an end in America, where the final and most glorious empire of all would arise.

This paper proposes to study this change in the use of the term "empire" in America more closely. This will be done in four steps: First, the British use of the word will be considered; secondly, the changing American interpretation of the term between 1765 and 1776 will be analyzed, and then I shall attempt to discuss the different uses of the phrase "American empire" before and, in conclusion, after Independence. My findings will be based primarily on American public opinion as expressed in pamphlets and other printed works of the Revolutionary period.

I.

It was not until the end of the French and Indian War that the term "British Empire" was raised "on both sides of the Atlantic, to the level of a concept signifying a political cause, which implied a constitutional system."[4] At the very time, it should be noted, when the first wave of protest and resistance swept through the American colonies in 1765, Englishmen and Americans alike began to discuss the character of their relationship in terms of the "British Empire" meaning thereby the mother country and the colonies taken collectively. Both, however, had a different objective in mind. The *Americans* made use of the term to denote the common interest and strong ties that continued to exist between Great Britain and the colonies in spite of the latters' resistance to British measures after 1763. *English* statesmen and writers, however, used the term to stress the leading role which out of necessity the mother country and Parliament, in particular, had to play to make the various parts of the extensive British Empire act in concert to further the common interest. Accordingly only the center of the Empire was in a position to judge what benefited the whole and what did not. The mother country alone had the perspective and the institutions to act in the interest of her whole Empire, she alone could decide where particular interests had to be encouraged or restricted, depending on whether they worked to the advantage or disadvantage of the whole. This position was shared by the majority of Englishmen up to the beginning of hostilities in America. Thomas Whately stated it very clearly at the beginning of the controversy in 1765: "The British Empire in *Europe* and in *America* is still the same Power: Its subjects in both are still the same people; and all equally participate in the adversity or prosperity of the whole. ... It is an indisputable consequence of their being thus one nation, that they must be governed by the same supreme authority."[5] This quasi-official statement of the British point of view by Grenville's secretary entered the statute book one year later, when, in the Declaratory Act of 1766, it was proclaimed for the first time in British history that the colonies in America were subordinate to "the *Imperial* Crown and *Parliament* of Great Britain".[6] The theory of parliamentary sovereignty was thus given its legal sanction.

Such claims the *colonials* were not ready to accept. They seriously doubted that Parliament had always had the good of the whole Empire in mind when it legislated for the colonies. This suspicion increased considerably when the British government launched its new fiscal policy with the passage of the Revenue Act of 1764. Americans were forced to realize that a good many Englishmen within and without Parliament still favored the old mercantilist doctrine that whatever was good for England was also good for the Empire, or, as some people preferred to put it: What other reasons could there be for founding colonies than to make them subservient to the demands of the mother country?

II.

In 1764 this doctrine which took the subordination of the colonies to the needs of the mother country for granted was no longer acceptable to the colonies as their opposition to the Sugar Act showed. Prompted by a post-war depression they began to demand equality and recognition of their own interests. This they did in the established framework of mercantilism. The colonies were neither ready to develop completely new economic models nor did they confront the mother country with their own brand of mercantilism. Instead they recurred to those recent and more advanced mercantilist doctrines, which viewed different parts of the Empire as economic units with complementary functions. When the colonies sent their raw and staple products to the mother country, they thereby paid for the manufactured goods which they received in return. The northern colonies even went so far as to claim that it did not matter at all from where they procured the money to pay for British manufactures. They therefore demanded unhampered access to foreign markets, particularly the foreign West Indies and southern Europe. In their pamphlets the colonists cited exclusively those passages from mercantilist writers like Josiah Child, Malachy Postlethwayt, Josiah Tucker, William Wood – as well as Cato and Montesquieu where appropriate –, where this "natural relationship"[7] between colonies and mother country was discussed. They neglected, of course, all other aspects of mercantilist thinking in which, by definition, the subordination of the colonies to the mother country was taken for granted.

The colonies wanted recognition of their particular economic needs, and it was this they had in mind whenever they referred to the British Empire.[8] "To represent them as an 'expensive appendage of the British Empire...' is certainly one of the greatest errors;... Every advantage accruing to the colonies by their connection with the mother-country is *amply* – *dearly* – paid for... by the restrictions of their commerce", wrote John Dickinson in 1765.[9] He consequently defined the Navigation Acts as "intended to preserve an intercourse between the mother-country and her colonies, and thus to cultivate a *mutual affection;* to promote the interests of *both* by an exchange of *their* most

137

valuable productions for *her* manufactures, thereby to increase the shipping of both, and thus render them capable of affording aid to each other."[10]

What the colonies claimed was membership in the Empire on an equal footing with the mother country, not a second-class membership. They did not want dramatic changes which would have endangered their remarkable growth. They expected recognition of their growing importance, and the British Empire was the frame of reference in which they voiced their demands. "Let it be demonstrated that the subjects of the British Empire in Europe and America are the same, that the hardships of the latter will ever recoil upon the former. In theory it is supposed that each is equally important to the other, that all partake of the adversity and depression of any. The theory is just and time will certainly establish it . . ."[11] Daniel Dulany, who stated this in 1765, was already advancing to more broadly conceived political demands.

The call for equality in the economic field, which was triggered off by the news of the Sugar Act, was but a foretaste of what the British government would be confronted with when it passed the Stamp Act and the Townshend Acts and thus brought to a test the question of the legal status of the colonies and of parliamentary sovereignty. Both these measures led the colonials to demand political equality within the Empire. In this debate the term "empire" was used as a rhetorical device which was to indicate that in spite of the new political theories proposed by the colonists they still considered themselves as part of the larger community, i. e. the British Empire.[12]

This is not the place to discuss in detail the development of the arguments used by the Americans, beginning with the denial of Parliament's right to lay internal duties to the final point where all legislation without the explicit consent of the colonies was considered illegal. It should be noted, however, that while Americans asserted their rights against parliamentary "encroachments", they were very vague about a positive description of what Parliament did have the right to do. From their point of view this was not even necessary. It was the firm belief of many Americans that they only opposed a novel, unheard-of exercise of power by the British Parliament. When Americans talked about the British Empire, they meant the *status quo* of legal, commercial, and other ties that existed between mother country and colonies. A passage from John Dickinson's *Farmer's Letters* which in 1768–69 motivated opposition as no other publication had done thus far, may illustrate the point: "He, who considers these provinces as states distinct from the *British empire,* has very slender notions of *justice,* or of their *interests.* We are but parts of a *whole;* and therefore there must exist a power somewhere, to pre-side, and preserve the connection in due order. This power is lodged in the Parliament; and we are as much dependent on *Great-Britain,* as a perfectly free people can be on another."[13]

The British Empire among other things still meant protection from out-side interference, loyalty to the king, acceptance of parliamentary legis-lation (with the exception of specific measures which the colonies op-posed), and regulation of trade. Clinging to this concept of the British Empire in the 1760s and early 1770s, they were not just trying to mini-mize the serious difficulties that were to separate them from the mother country only a few years later. They had a far more practical reason for their attitude: As long as they were members of the British Empire they were also entitled to the rights of Englishmen as a birthright inherited from their ancestors. In the beginning of the controversy these rights which could be claimed in a British court were an argument much more convincing to loyal-minded subjects of George III than doctrines of natural law derived from philosophical principles.[14]

The appeal to the rights of Englishmen had helped the colonies to ward off unwanted taxes. They were of little use, however, when Parliament, in reaction to the Tea Party, passed the "Intolerable Acts" and used troops to enforce them. The interference with the internal constitution of Massachusetts the colonies countered by declaring that Parliament had no such power and that they were "entitled to a free and exclusive power of legislation in their several provincial legislatures."[15] The equality they had until then claimed for all the subjects of the Empire was now extended to include the equality of their assemblies with Par-liament. Parliament was no longer to have that "superintending power" it was formerly conceded. This "commonwealth theory of the empire" began to gain ground in the colonies after 1774.[16]

Loyalist writers, wherever they could still publish, launched a vigorous campaign against this new theory and also against the Continental Con-gress for endorsing it. The constitution of the British Empire became a major issue in this campaign. A very characteristic and for our purpose very instructive debate took place in 1774–75 in Massachusetts between Daniel Leonard and John Adams, who in an exchange of letters in the public newspapers justified their respective stands in the controversy as "Massachusettensis" and "Novanglus". Leonard as *Massachusettensis* re-ferred to the British Empire to make sure that his readers never lost sight of the fact that the colonies had always been – and still continued to be – only part of a whole and should not be considered as "distinct a state from Great-Britain as Hanover".[17] Therefore, and this is the essence of the argument which he repeated several times, if "we are a part of the British empire, we must be subject to the supreme power of the state, which is vested in the estates of Parliament, notwithstanding each of the colonies have legislative and executive powers of their own ... which are subordinate to ... the checks, controul and regulation of the supreme authority." He added the sarcastic remark that "this doctrine is not new, but the denial of it is." The doctrine of legislative equality in the assemblies was an absurdity which to Leonard hardly required refutation, for, as he pointed out: "Two supreme or independent authorities cannot exist in the same state. It would be what is called *imperium in imperio,* the height of political absurdity." Statements of this kind were to be repeated over and over again by authors who, in their pamphlets, denied the notion of a federal government.[18]

If it had not been for the "republican party"[19] in the province, everybody in Massachusetts might have admitted the benefits which the colonies had derived from their being part of the Empire, for the "effects of our connection, and subordination... to Britain" Leonard considered obvious: "Our merchants are opulent ... Population is so rapid as to double the number of inhabitants in the short period of twenty-five years: Cities are springing up in the wilderness: Schools, colleges, and even universities are interspersed through the continent ... These are infallible marks not only of opulence but of freedom." To Leonard it was the Empire alone which ensured stability and freedom to the colonies. This the provincial assemblies, were they to act on their own, could not guarantee: "They are but faint sketches of the estates of Parliament," they "have no principle of stability within themselves ... and ... [would] become wholly monarchical or wholly republican, were it not for the checks, controuls, regulations and supports of the supreme authority of the empire."[20]

Never doubting that Britain and her colonies were but parts of a whole, he could meet his republican opponents (e. g. John Adams), who advanced the theory "that government in the dernier resort is in the people", on their own ground: "for admitting" – he writes in his last letter – "that the collective body of the people, that are subject to the British empire, have an inherent right to change their form of government, or race of Kings, it does not follow, that the inhabitants of a single province or of a number of provinces, or any given part under a majority of the whole empire, have such a right. By admitting that the less may rule or sequester themselves from the greater, we unhinge all government."[21]

I have quoted Massachusettensis so extensively to exemplify how effectively the concept of the British Empire could be employed in the political debates and what meaning it had acquired for many people as tension heightened. The patriots were made to look like troublemakers who kept demanding more and more till all lawful government would succumb to anarchy. For selfish reasons they were defying the freest yet strongest government in the world which, in Leonard's words, had "the power to make us subject to the supreme authority of the Empire."[22] Massachusettensis seemed to demand no more than John Dickinson, the "Pennsylvania Farmer," who five years before had contended for the same with the unanimous support of the whole continent. Leonard's proposition – which the Stamp Act Congress of 1765 had already dismissed as impracticable – that the colonies should be represented in Parliament, suggested a willingness to bring about reconciliation and more peaceful times, a quality the demands of the patriots obviously lacked.

In his response *Novanglus* John Adams strove to show that his opponent's interpretation of the British Empire had no foundation in law and that "empire" was, in fact, an inappropriate word to describe the relationship of Britain to her American colonies. Consequently he attempted to avoid the term, although he was not always successful in doing so. In his third letter Novanglus frankly stated that "the terms [!] 'British empire' are not the language of the common law, but the language of newspapers and political pamphlets," and similarly: "This language, 'the imperial crown of Great Britain', is not the style of the common law, but of court sycophants". To him "empire" implied "dominion", something which the colonies never conceded to Parliament. According to Adams it had always been held, "that America is not parcel of the realm, state, kingdom, government, empire or land of England, or Great Britain in any sense which can make it subject universally to the supreme legislature of that island."[23] As Parliament had no right to legislate for the colonies, except where the colonies made a voluntary concession as they had done in the regulation of their trade,[24] the only link that connected the different parts of the Empire was the king. In a very learned though rather dubious legal argument he even stated that the colonies owed their allegiance only to the person of the king and not to the crown, as the latter was held by act of Parliament.[25] He thus created, as Massachusettensis mockingly pointed out, "a King of Massachusetts, King of Rhode Island, King of Connecticut, etc. etc.", who depended on the consent of the respective assemblies. This Adams readily admitted.[26]

It is obvious that Adams tried to get away from the implications which the traditional idea of an empire, centered in Britain, would have on

141

colonial thinking, if allowed to continue unchallenged. Not only did he try to destroy the myth of the British Empire as hitherto maintained, but he even proceeded to give the word a new meaning that would reconcile it with the rising tide of republican thought in the colonies. In so doing, he gave the term such a bend as to make it a ready tool for the rhetoric of the emerging republic.

In his seventh Novanglus letter Adams stated that "we are not a part of the British empire; because the British government is not an empire". According to him only three empires existed at the time in Europe: the German, or Holy Roman, the Russian, and the Ottoman Empire, all of which he considered as despotisms, because it was the will of the prince alone that prevailed. The British government, however, was "a limited monarchy. If Aristotle, Livy and Harrington, knew what a republic was, the British constitution is much more like a republic than an empire. They define a republic to be *a government of laws, and not of men*". As "empire", in another sense of the word, to Adams also meant government,[27] i. e. rule or dominion in general, he could write ten months later in 1776: "... there is no good government but what is republican. That the only valuable part of the British constitution is so; because the very definition of a republic is 'an empire of laws, and not of men'."[28] The term "empire", which only recently had been rejected for its dangerously despotic connotations and for smacking too much of absolute monarchy, was thus reclaimed for the republican ideology. Surprising indeed is the apparent ease as well as the rapidity with which the transition to republican principles was thus accomplished.

There are other examples of this easy transition of ideas and loyalties within the imperial context. Perez Morton of Massachusetts in April 1776 simply declared every part of the Empire outside of America so rotten that the colonies could reap only advantages from a timely separation: "Now is the happy season, to seize again those Rights ... which have been repeatedly and violently attacked by the *King, Lords and Commons of Britain*. Ought we not then to disclaim forever the forfeited Affinity; and by a timely Amputation of the rotten Limb of the Empire, prevent the Mortification of the whole?"[29] His empire would preserve equal rights and leave no room for the mother country and her pretensions. William Smith, the provost of the College of Philadelphia, had similar notions. He saw "one part of a great Empire" opposing the other with a completely different set of values, thus judging actions as virtuous and patriotic, which the other condemned as treasonable – the implication being, of course, that Americans acted the more virtuous parts and thus came to represent the better part of the Empire.[30]

By 1776 two sets of ideas could be associated with the word "empire". On the one hand, there were those of loyalist leanings, who, when talking about the British Empire, had protection, security, lawful government, parliamentary supremacy, and loyalty to the king in mind. On the other hand there were the patriots, who demanded equality of rights, liberty from outside interference, popular sovereignty and, before long, an independent American empire.

The reason why Americans very easily accepted this latter view was not only to be found in the political developments which favored the patriots. It was also due to the fact that it was quite familiar for Americans to talk about an empire in America even before Independence.

III.

When Americans mentioned the Empire before 1776 they sometimes were more specific and meant only that part of the British Empire which lay in North America. In the short time of 150 years this *British* empire in *America* or "empire on this side of the Atlantic"[31] had grown immensely in wealth and population and had expanded over a considerable part of the continent. It had, as one writer said in 1766, acquired "the resources of Empire". Its future development was the object of constant speculation. Extrapolating past developments people calculated that the population in America would double every twenty-five years. On both sides of the Atlantic it seemed an established fact "that this vast Country will, in Time, become the greatest Empire that the world has ever seen."[32] It was openly discussed how many years it would take America's population to exceed that of the mother country and how that would affect mutual relations. Some only saw an increase in trade, others warned the mother country of further taxation measures, because this might disaffect the future larger part of the Empire from the smaller part.[33] As early as 1755, young John Adams talked about the "transfer [of] the great seat of empire into America".[34] Massachusettensis – among others – elaborated on this prospect twenty years later: "After many more centuries", he wrote, when "the colonies may be so far increased as to have the balance of wealth, numbers and powers in their favour, the good of the empire [shall] make it necessary to fix the seat of government here; and some future GEORGE ... may cross the Atlantic, and rule Great Britain by an American parliament". By 1775, however, John Adams had already lost faith in the reigning George and ridiculed the idea as the surest means of driving the colonies into independence.[35]

Although it was occasionally pointed out that a future "American empire" might try to be independent from Great Britain, this idea was dreaded and anticipated with horror.[36] "America ... will become a mighty empire" only "after many revolutions and great distresses," an anonymous writer said in 1768.[37] It seems therefore reasonable to assume that as long as Americans did not discuss independence, which they did not until 1775, the empire in America they were talking about was generally considered to be a part of the more extensive British Empire. Repeatedly the colonials were at pains to point out this fact. Jonathan Mayhew envisioned "a mighty empire" in America, but added in parentheses "I do not mean an independent one". Joseph Reed said in a prize essay written at the College of Philadelphia in 1766 that "the difficulties of an Union for the purposes of empire, are almost insuperable" for the colonies. John Dickinson in his *Essay On The Constitutional Power Of Great Britain over the Colonies in America* still reiterated these thoughts in 1774.[38]

Yet, no one harbored any doubts about "The Rising Glory of America" which was the title of a poem by Philip Freneau and Hugh Henry Brackenridge published in 1772. These verses asked the question "what empires yet must rise" before "Britain's sons shall spread, Dominion to the north and south and west Far from th'Atlantic to the Pacific shores?"[39]

The territorial expansion of the colonies over the whole continent was repeatedly discussed in colonial literature, particularly after the French lost Canada in the French and Indian War.[40] The two young poets were not expounding any strikingly new ideas (that would have been expecting too much from a Princeton commencement exercises address of 1771 anyway). All they were expressing by joining the idea of territorial expansion and empire was that the British Empire in America would eventually extend over the whole continent. Undoubtedly, there was a certain sense of destiny in pronouncements of this kind. "Providence will erect a mighty empire in America" wrote Samuel Adams to Arthur Lee in 1774 with almost religious conviction,[41] explaining that the mother country eventually would depend on America for its existence. Sam Adams's belief may very well have been rooted in the old myth that since antiquity all great empires had been moving from east to west like the sun. Bishop Berkeley had applied this myth to the settlements in America in his poem "On the Prospect of Planting Arts and Learning in America" with its often quoted last stanza:

> Westward the course of empire takes its way;
> The first four Acts already past,

A fifth shall close the Drama with the Day;
Time's noblest offspring is the last.[42]

The point should however be made here that Berkeley was not concerned
with "empire" as a political concept or with territorial expansion. He
was profoundly pessimistic about the future of Britain, where compla-
cency and private interest worked against a badly needed spiritual regeneration. The aim he propounded in the poem was to accomplish this
regeneration in a new society on unspoiled ground.[43]

No prospect could have been more pleasing to the colonial mind; it was
eagerly adopted and propagated. Nathaniel Ames wrote in his almanac
for 1758: "Arts and Sciences will change the Face of Nature in their
Tour from Hence over the Appalachian Mountains to the Western
Ocean." By 1764 empire and progress in the sciences were again combined: "we may anticipate America as the destined seat of science, where
she may found an empire uncontrouled; ... here a new empire arises,
and tho' in its infancy, yet the human mind is in full exertion of all its
faculties, the basis of science large and expanded, and the art of printing
preserving all its investigations." Four years later the concept seemed
firmly established, so that the *American Whig* could address his audience:
"Courage then Americans! Liberty, religion and sciences are on the wing
to these shores. The finger of God points out a mighty empire to your
sons. ..." It should be noted that by then liberty as well as religion had
caught up with the sciences on their journey to the new world, which
Independence did not stop.[44]

IV.

Independence did not basically change the pattern of thought which
had developed around the British Empire in America. It opened, however, new perspectives. Americans were quick to point out, in 1776, that
they were now a new and "Independent empire" which became the new
focus for the already familiar thoughts. "Religion, Learning, and Liberty" continued to flourish there and were the assets of a "new people
rising to empire and renown".[45]

As a result of their being "a distinct empire",[46] a new sense of finality
entered the writings of the former colonists. After commenting on the
"progress of Liberty, of Science and of Empire ... from east to west
since the beginning of time", Timothy Dwight said: "It may as justly be
observed that the glory of empire has been progressive, the last con-
stantly outshining those which were before it". The conclusion to be

drawn from this was "evident": The "Empire of North America will be the last on earth" as well as "the most glorious". Americans were assured that this empire would be the scene of the millenium.[47]

Joel Barlow, the poet, came to a similar conclusion by noting that when the course of empire reaches the "western shore" – meaning the Pacific ocean – "earth-born empires rise and fall no more". To expansionists, echoing earlier statements, these were intriguing thoughts. If the extensive American empire was to be the last and most glorious in the world, it would eventually extend over the whole continent. No one was more explicit than Timothy Dwight, who exclaimed in 1776 in an unparalleled outburst: ". . . the moment our interest demands it, these extensive regions will be our own; . . . the present race of inhabitants [i. e. the Spanish settlers, not the Indians] will either be exterminated, or revive to the native human dignity, by the generous and beneficent influence of just laws, and national freedom". This was in marked contrast to the peaceful empire and the golden age which Freneau envisioned in 1778.[48]

There was yet another line of thought which Americans ardently pursued after Independence. "Exalted to the rank of empire" themselves, they began to reflect on the rise and fall of empires, particularly on what they considered the "downfall of the British empire".[49] This was set in contrast to the rise of the infant American empire. William H. Drayton said in an address to the grand jury of Charlestown, S. C., about the "rise of the American empire": "And thus has suddenly arisen in the world, a new empire, styled the United States of America. An empire that as soon as started into existence, attracts the attention of the rest of the universe, and bids fair by the blessing of God, to be the most glorious of any upon record. – America hails Europe, Asia, and Africa! – She proffers peace and plenty!"

"God Almighty" had already chosen his own people. According to Drayton he "made choice of the present generation to erect the American empire". Loyalists and those who still harbored doubts about the wisdom of declaring Independence were admonished not "to repine that, in our day, America is dissolved from the British state", for this would be impiously ignoring the will of divine providence.

Britain's fate was attributed to more secular causes. Although advancing "that the duration of empire is limited by the Almighty decree", Drayton saw the rise and fall of empires as natural events. Britain "experienced the invariable fate of empire", because she succumbed to riches and luxuries;[50] others attributed her fall from the glory of empire to pride and ambition.[51] Drayton as well as all other Revolutionary writers failed to consider "the invariable fate of empires" with regard to the

American empire. The optimism of the Revolutionary generation apparently ruled out thoughts of this nature – a fact which illustrates more than any other how closely all statements about the rising American empire must be set in the context of Revolutionary rhetoric.

I have already mentioned how John Adams, by reviving Harrington's dictum, made "empire" and "republic" compatible terms. Thereafter the republican character of the American empire was no longer open to discussion. Republicanism, in fact, had become the "link of empire". America was designated the "seat of freedom and the nurse of empire".[52] The Boston Massacre Oration of 1781 celebrated the American republics as the "abodes of empire and liberty". American statesmen were hailed for "the task of forming and defending a free and extensive empire".[53]

Americans were, at the same time, made aware of their unique and incomparable station in the international community as a free people. "To measure the freedom, the Rights and Privileges of the American Empire by those enjoyed by other Nations would be folly."[54] The American empire represented man's advances in "every species of knowledge, natural and moral". Washington struck a similar note in 1783, when he maintained in the *Circular to the States*: "The Foundation of our Empire was not laid in the gloomy age of Ignorance and Superstition, but at an Epocha when the rights of mankind were better understood and more clearly defined, than at any former period."[55]

Washington wrote at a time, when American independence had been secured at Yorktown and the peace treaty of 1783 was ready to be signed. By then, Noah Webster and the Society of the Cincinnati had already become concerned about the "future dignity of the American Empire". Washington himself was widely acclaimed for the "formation and establishment of an empire". The republic, by then risen "into a powerful and polished empire", as one author stated, had begun creating its own heroes – other requisites of empire were to follow in due time.[56]

The quotations presented in this paper seem to suggest that Americans of the Revolutionary period used the term "empire" almost as a household word. This, however, would certainly be a wrong impression. Although there were occasional discussions of the character of the British Empire before 1776,[57] no similar detailed analysis of the nature of the rising American empire was published from 1776 to 1783; references to the term are scattered throughout the bulk of the political writings and public addresses. This apparently haphazard use accounts for the different connotations that have been presented here. Two things stand out: If we take the word of the colonials as our starting point there was no independent American empire before 1775–76. After Independence the term began to appear with a wide range of meanings. These encompassed territorial expansion, republican ideals, the idea of God's chosen people, progress in the arts and sciences, and an equal rank of the United States in the international community of nations. By reducing these rather imprecise ideas to just one aspect, for example to that of territorial expansion, later historians invite the charge of not only reducing a complex set of ideas to a crude belief, but indulge in the questionable practice of transferring backwards concepts which are of much later origin.[58] Modern historians should indeed be cautious about using eighteenth-century quotations when presenting, in their analyses, a more recent concept of "empire".

Notes

[1] When used as a proper name I have capitalized "empire", e. g. as in "British Empire".

[2] Richard Koebner, *Empire* (Cambridge, 1961), 87; in the period under discussion the word was still frequently used in this sense, e. g. [Carter Braxton,] *An Address To The Convention of the Colony* ... (Philadelphia, 1776), 12 (Evans No. 14669), "gaining the empire of the sea."

[3] Charles Francis Adams, ed., *The Works of John Adams* (Boston, 1850–56), IV, 107 (Novanglus Letters).

[4] Koebner, *Empire* (cf. n. 2), 145.

[5] [Thomas Whately,] *The Regulations Lately Made* ... (London, 1765), 39–40.

[6] Koebner, *Empire* (cf. n. 2), 157; italics mine.

[7] [John Dickinson,] *The Late Regulations* ..., in Bernard Bailyn, ed., *Pamphlets of the American Revolution*, I (Cambridge, Mass., 1965), 668–691, is a good illustration of the point. In his footnotes Dickinson quotes extensively from those authors that were usually selected to support the colonists' point of view.

[8] Why the colonies introduced the concept "British Empire" at this point is explained by Koebner, *Empire* (cf. n. 2), 86. There he says that before 1750 its main connotation was "trade, shipping and the navy." Quite early the term "empire" had already been used to describe a "nation extended over vast tracts of land, and number of people," as Koebner, *Empire*, 59, and Gerald Stourzh, *Alexander Hamilton and the Idea of Republican Government* (Stanford, Cal., 1970), 190, both indicate by quoting Sir William Temple. See also James Truslow Adams, "On the Term 'British Empire'," *AHR*, XXVII (1922), 485–489. In the discussion of this paper, Gerald Stourzh also pointed out that in the 18th century an empire was commonly considered a composite entity, where territories with varying degrees of sovereignty and with different jurisdictions coexisted under one head. Such a vast, composite empire was the Holy Roman Empire. Stephen Hopkins, *The Rights of Colonies Examined* (Providence, R. I., 1765), 19–20, in Bailyn, ed., *Pamphlets* (cf. n. 7), I, 519, concluded from the analogy of the British Empire with the Holy Roman Empire that Parliament had no right to tax the colonies: "In an imperial state, which consists of many separate

governments each of which hath peculiar privileges and of which kind it is evident the empire of Great Britain is, no single part, though greater than another part, is by that superiority entitled to make laws for or to tax such lesser part; ... This may be fully verified by the empire of Germany, which consists of many states, some powerful and others weak, yet the powerful never make laws to govern or to tax the little and weak ones, ..." I have not been able to locate additional references to the Holy Roman Empire which bring out this analogy. It would be interesting to know, whether the "Thirteen States in Congress Assembled" still considered themselves a composite empire.

[9] [Dickinson,] *Late Regulations*, 29, in Bailyn, ed., *Pamphlets* (cf. n. 7), I, 686.

[10] *Ib.*, 38 (691); italics Dickinson's.

[11] [Daniel Dulany,] *Considerations on the Propriety of imposing Taxes ...* ([Annapolis,] 1765), 46, in Bailyn, ed., *Pamphlets* (cf. n. 7), I, 649–650.

[12] "British dominions", "British nation" were used in the same sense.

[13] Paul Leicester Ford, ed., *The Writings of John Dickinson*, I (Historical Society of Pennsylvania, *Memoirs*, XIV [Philadelphia, 1895]), 312 (beginning of Letter II).

[14] *JCC*, I, 68. This is the so-called "Declaration of Rights and Grievances" and still makes the point. See also Daniel Shute, *A Sermon Preached Before His Excellency Francis Bernard ...* (Boston, 1748 [i. e. 1768]), 59, "The happiness of THIS PEOPLE in the enjoyment of their natural rights and privileges under providence is provided for by their being a part of the *British* empire, by which they are intitled [*sic*] to the privileges of that happy constitution."

[15] *JCC*, I, 68.

[16] See Randolph G. Adams, *Political Ideas of the American Revolution*, 3d ed. (New York, 1958), 68–85.

[17] [Daniel Leonard,] *Massachusettensis* (Boston, 1775), 6 (Evans No. 14157). See also p. 11: "We had always considered ourselves, as a part of the British empire, and the parliament, as the supreme legislature of the whole." The recent edition of the Massachusettensis-Letters by Bernard Mason, ed., *The American Colonial Crisis* (New York, 1972), which also reprints the bulk of John Adams' Novanglus-Letters, is of little use as it does not reprint both series of letters in full.

[18] [Leonard,] *Massachusettensis* (cf. n. 17), 42, 41.

[19] *Ib.*, 93; see also 23.

[20] *Ib.*, 103; 43–44.

[21] *Ib.*, 114–115.

[22] *Ib.*, 6.

[23] Adams, ed., *Works of John Adams* (cf. n. 3), IV, 37–38, 163.

[24] *Ib.*, 130; see also 158.

[25] *Ib.*, 114; see also 142.

[26] [Leonard,] *Massachusettensis* (cf. n. 17), 43. Adams, ed., *Works of John Adams* (cf. n. 3), IV, 114–115.

[27] *Ib.*, 106–107.

[28] *Ib.*, 194 (*Thoughts on Government*). The quotation is apparently derived from Harrington's *Oceana* as Yehoshua Arieli, *Individualism and Nationalism in American Ideology* (Cambridge, Mass., 1964), 55, points out. References to this statement by Harrington are not uncommon in the colonies, see, for instance, *Four Dissertations, On The Reciprocal Advantages Of A Perpetual Union Between Great-Britain And Her American Colonies* (Philadelphia, 1766),

3 (Dissertation I); [John Dickinson and Arthur Lee,] *The Farmer's and Monitor's Letters* (Williamsburg, Va., 1769), 94 (Evans No. 11239).

[29] Perez Morton, *An Oration; Delivered At the King's Chapel In Boston, April 8, 1776* ... (Boston, 1776), 13 (Evans No. 14892).

[30] William Smith, *An Oration In Memory Of General Montgomery* ... (Philadelphia, 1776), 13 (Evans No. 15084). See also Thomas Paine's statement in William M. Van der Weyde, ed., *The Life and Works of Thomas Paine*, II (New Rochelle, N. Y., 1925), 26 (*A Dialogue Between the Ghost of General Montgomery* ... *and an American Delegate*).

[31] Edmund S. Morgan, ed., *The Stamp Act Crisis: Prologue to Revolution* (Chapel Hill, N. C., 1959), 77 (from the *Providence Gazette*, May 11, 1765); *A Letter To The North American* ... (Barbados, 1766), 11.

[32] [Nicholas Ray,] *The Importance of the Colonies of North America* ... (New York, 1766 [orig. publ. London, 1766]), 5; see also the quotation from Sir William Draper in Richard W. Van Alstyne, *Empire and Independence* (New York, 1965), 42. The first known mention of this rate of increase is found in Benjamin Franklin's *Observations Concerning the Increase of Mankind* as pointed out in J. Potter, "The Growth of Population in America, 1700–1860," in D. V. Glass and D. E. C. Eversley, eds., *Population in History* (London, 1965), 632.

[33] The great future of the colonies is referred to in William Wood, *New England's Prospect* ... (Boston, 1764), iv (Evans No. 9884); Maurice Moore, *The Justice And Policy Of Taxing The American Colonies* (Wilmington, N. C., 1765), 15 (Evans No. 10076); [James Otis,] *A Vindication Of The British Colonies* ... (Boston, 1765), 15 (Evans No. 10117); *Letter To The North-American (cf. n. 31)*, 27; [Stephen Johnson,] *Some Important Observations* ... (Newport, R. I., 1766), 33 (Evans No. 10346), which contains the warning to the mother country.

[34] Adams, ed., *Works of John Adams* (cf. n. 3), I, 23.

[35] [Leonard,] *Massachusettensis* (cf. n. 17), 45; Adams, ed., *Works of John Adams* (cf. n. 3), IV, 121.

[36] The phrase is taken from Malachy Postlethwayt, *The Universal Dictionary of Trade and Commerce*, I (London, 1774), xxiv. Englishmen frequently voiced their fears that America wished "to be an Empire by itself", see the quotations in Van Alstyne, *Empire and Independence* (cf. n. 32), 74, 55.

[37] *The Power And Grandeur Of Great Britain, Founded On The Liberty Of The Colonies* ... (New York, 1768), 22.

[38] Jonathan Mayhew, *Two Discourses Delivered Oct. 25, 1759* ... (Boston, 1759), as quoted in Bailyn, ed., *Pamphlets* (cf. n. 7), 84–85; *Four Dissertations* (cf. n. 28), 101 [J. Reed]; [John Dickinson,] *An Essay On The Constitutional Power of Great Britain* ... (Philadelphia, 1774), 56–62, particularly the extensive footnote.

[39] Fred L. Pattlee, ed., *The Poems of Philip Freneau*, I (New York, 1963), 73.

[40] Franklin's very advanced views on the expansion of the colonies are discussed in Gerald Stourzh, *Benjamin Franklin and American Foreign Policy*, 2d ed. (Chicago, 1969), 54–82.

[41] H. A. Cushing, ed., *The Writings of Samuel Adams*, III (New York, 1907), 102; the letter is dated April 4, 1774.

[42] A. C. Fraser, ed., *The Works of George Berkeley*, IV (Oxford, 1901), 365–66. Werner Goez, *Translatio Imperii. Ein Beitrag zur Geschichte des Ge-*

schichtsdenkens und der politischen Theorien im Mittelalter und in der frühen Neuzeit (Tübingen, 1958), gives an account of the origins of the idea.

[43] Koebner, *Empire* (cf. n. 2), 96; Hans Kohn, *American Nationalism* (New York, 1957), 10–11. The main idea of the poem, as expressed in its title, has very often been disregarded. For a recent example see Loren Baritz, *City on a Hill* (New York, 1964), 94.

[44] Ames is quoted in Jack P. Greene, ed., *Settlements to Society: 1584–1763*, in David Donald, gen. ed., *A Documentary History of American Life*, I (New York, 1966), 380; William Wood, *New-England's Prospect* (cf. n. 33), xvii, the quotation is from the introduction which was written by James Otis, Jr., or Nathaniel Rogers; *American Whig* as quoted in Koebner, *Empire* (cf. n. 2), 172.

[45] The Secret Committee to Silas Deane, October 1, 1776, as quoted in Van Alstyne, *Empire and Independence* (cf. n. 32), 79; Samuel Sherwood, *The Church's Flight Into The Wilderness* ... (New York, 1776), 17 (Evans No. 15082).

[46] Van der Weyde, ed., *Works of Thomas Paine* (cf. n. 30), II, 260.

[47] [Timothy Dwight,] *A Valedictory Address To The Young Gentlemen, Who Commenced Bachelors of Arts, At Yale College, July 25th. 1776* (New Haven, Conn., [1776]), 13, on p. 14 the millennarian aspect is further discussed. For a recent view of millennarian thinking in early Puritan New England see J. F. Maclear, "New-England and the Fifth Monarchy: The Quest for the Millennium in Early American Puritanism," *WMQ*, 3d Ser., XXXII (1975), 223–260.

[48] Joel Barlow, *The Prospect of Peace* ... (New York, 1778), 11 (Evans No. 15729); [Dwight,] *Valedictory Address* (cf. n. 47), 10; Pattlee, ed., *Poems of Philip Freneau* (cf. n. 39), I, 281.

[49] *A Dialogue, Between The Devil and George III* ... (Boston, 1782), 22 (Evans No. 17520).

[50] William H. Drayton, *A Charge, On the Rise of the American Empire* ... (Charleston, S. C., 1776), in Hezekiah Niles, ed., *Principles And Acts Of The Revolution In America*, repr. ed. (New York, 1971 [orig. publ. Baltimore, 1822]), 81–82. It is interesting to note that the American empire apparently did not imply the idea of a strong, centralized government. Judge Drayton is a good example. Although he celebrated the rising American empire in 1776 he opposed the adoption of the Articles of Confederation 16 months later as giving too much power to the central government, *ib.*, 98–114.

[51] See James Murray, *An Impartial History of the War in America* (Boston, 1781 [orig. publ. Newcastle, 1778]), 49 (Evans No. 17241).

[52] Niles, ed., *Principles And Acts* (cf. n. 50), 49; Josiah Meigs, *An Oration Pronounced Before a public Assembly in New Haven* ... (New Haven, Conn., 1782), 4 (Evans No. 17604).

[53] Niles, ed., *Principles And Acts* (cf. n. 50), 52, 26.

[54] Quoted from Willi Paul Adams, *Republikanische Verfassung und bürgerliche Freiheit* (Darmstadt, 1973), 141.

[55] [Dwight,] *Valedictory Address* (cf. n. 47), 12; John C. Fitzpatrick, ed., *The Writings of George Washington*, XXVI (Washington, D. C., 1938), 485; in the Newburgh Address Washington refers also to "our rising Empire", *ib.*, 227.

[56] Noah Webster, *A Grammatical Institute, Of The English Language* ... *Part I* ... (Hartford, Conn., [1783]), 15 (Evans No. 18297); *Observations On A Late Pamphlet, Entituled* [sic], *'Considerations upon the Society or Order of the Cincinnati'*, ... (Philadelphia, 1783), 7 (Evans No. 18073); Meigs, *Oration*

(cf. n. 52), 11; [Charles Henry Wharton,] *A Political Epistle To His Excellency George Washington, Esq.*....(Providence, R. I., 1781), 24; Meigs, *Oration,* 4. Aspects of the empire in America after 1783 are presented in Stourzh, *Hamilton* (cf. n. 8), 189–201, and Julian P. Boyd, "Thomas Jefferson's 'Empire of Liberty'," *Virginia Quarterly Review,* XXIV (1948), 538–554.

[57] A good example is [John Joachim Zubly,] *An Humble Enquiry Into The Nature of the Dependency of the American Colonies* ... ([Charleston, S. C.,] 1769).

[58] Inviting criticism of this kind is, e. g., Walter LaFeber, "Foreign Policies of a New Nation: Franklin, Madison, and the 'Dream of a New Land to Fulfill with People in Self-Control', 1750–1804" in William Appleman Williams, ed., *From Colony to Empire* (New York, 1972), 9–37. Studies about the international aspects of the American Revolution tend to conceive the idea of the American empire too narrowly, see Arthur Burr Darling, *Our Rising Empire, 1763–1803* (New Haven, Conn., 1940). Richard W. Van Alstyne, *The Rising American Empire* (Oxford, 1960), is another example: He concentrates almost exclusively on the territorial aspects of the American empire; his *Empire and Independence* (cf. n. 32), is, however, more broadly conceived.

Reflections on the Army of the American Revolution

Gerhard Kollmann[*]

Among the "ambiguities of the American Revolution" Michael Kammen
– following Gordon S. Wood and Russell F. Weigley respectively –
reckons both an inherent dualism of the concept of equality and a conflict of two military traditions stemming from the War of Independence.[1] These ambiguities are strongly connected with each other. This
is made obvious by the following passage from David Ramsay's *History
of the Revolution of South Carolina.* At the start of the battle at King's
Mountain, one of the American leaders is reported as saying: "When
engaged you are not to wait for the word of command from me. I will
shew you by my example how to fight. I can undertake no more. Every
man must consider himself as an officer, and act from his own judgement."[2] Here we find in essence what may be called a concept of personal responsibility of the individual. Of course even the militia organization did not lack a certain amount of class characteristics.[3] This
observation is valid also for the New England militia organization in
1776.[4] But, nevertheless, the militia came rather close to the concept
of the armed forces as – principally equal – citizens combined for the
defence of their common weal.

Why then was the militia in such ill repute with those responsible for the
shaping of American military politics? As Robert C. Pugh has shown,
bad performance of militia was in no small part due to the inability of
American leaders to work out strategies and tactics adapted to the pecu-
liarities of those troops.[5] But was this inability merely an accident?
Bernard Bailyn, in analyzing the answers of the American Revolution to
the question "whether some Degree of Respect be not always Due from
Inferiors to Superiors", finds "changes in the realm of belief and attitude", a redirection of the flow of authority.[6] This description and its
implications do not fit the regular army. Twenty years ago, Elisha P.
Douglass hinted at what he called "the double paradox" the leaders of
the Revolution found themselves confronted with: "to preserve their
own liberty, the unprivileged masses must be prevented from infringing
on the privileged few; to maintain a government based on consent, a
large proportion of the people must be deprived of the ability to extend
or withhold consent."[7] Although Douglass does not aim at the army,

his description comes very close to what happened there: The bulk of the army's members were divested of their self-determination as citizens. The officers' corps was purged of socially undesirables. At the same time there developed a new group-consciousness among the officers, a consciousness that heightened their self-esteem and tended to establish them as a new quasi-aristocracy – based, as they felt, on due recognition to be paid to their merits. As their military rank, for many of them, meant an elevation they never before could have dreamt of, they often felt insecure about their status, especially so, when their claim to pre-eminence met with the opposition of their compatriots.

At least one of the Revolutionary officers had the misfortune that, his corpse long ago fallen apart, his ghost still must wander about. Unable to find his well-deserved rest, he has to appear ever anew when writers want to show to what a degree equality was practiced in the American army as late as October 11, 1776. For then it happened: a captain of horse "was seen shaving one of his men". Maybe, that poor captain has in the meantime taken his revenge on Joseph Reed, perhaps on some of the later writers too; at any rate, that act of shaving still remains one of the standard examples to describe the relations between officers and men in the early period of the war.[8]

Reed did not need to be so much excited, for things already were in a train that promised better for the future. When Massachusetts organized her army in 1775, she had already departed from the mode of appointing officers that had been established for the militia. On October 26, 1774 the Provincial Congress had ordered preparedness for 25 percent of the colony's militia force. All companies had to choose their subaltern officers, who then had to elect the field grades.[9] After the day of Lexington and Concord, the Revolutionary leaders called for an army of 30,000 men, this time reversing the procedure of appointing officers: the Committee of Safety was to elect the field officers who then appointed their subalterns.[10] Prompted, perhaps, by the necessity of avoiding the appointment of officers of uncertain attachment to the cause of liberty and by the necessity of accelerating the organization of the army, this measure tended to strengthen the position of the higher grades against their subordinates. In May 1775, the Provincial Congress established the pay of privates and non-commissioned officers at twenty shillings hard money or its equivalent, forty shillings in paper. After the adoption of the troops at Cambridge, the Continental Congress followed a rather dubious course. The pay of the privates was left at six and two thirds of a dollar, the New England standard; a distinction on pay was created between privates and non-commissioned officers and between the different ranks of the latter themselves. On these terms Congress tried to recruit companies in Pennsylvania, Maryland, and Virginia.[11] Nevertheless, some months later they tried to get men in New Jersey at five dollars a month.[12] That was the rate common in the middle colonies.[13]

The congressional proposal to New Jersey may be seen as part of the attempts to lessen expenses in general.[14] But this question was even more important. One of its aspects was that the pay for enlisted men – for practical reasons – had to be the same in all the colonies. Equalizing pay meant facilitating recruitment. There seems to have been general agreement on this point, although differences in pay were not abolished till 1776.[15] It also fitted very well in Washington's concept of amalgamating the distinct colonial establishments into what he called "the Troops of the United Colonies."[16] But differences in pay also meant differences in status. So, in fixing the relations between officers' and soldiers' pay, Congress had to determine the principles of military policy. A conference of a congressional committee with high ranking officials from Massachusetts, Rhode Island, and Connecticut together with Washington in October 1775 agreed that pay differences between privates and officers were too low.[17] More interesting than the mere statement of inadequacy were the reasons given for not altering this situation. The conferees concluded "unanimously", "that under the present circumstances the proposition of Lowering the pay of the troops will be attended with dangerous consequences."[18] At the same time a majority of the participants agreed that raising the pay of the officers would be "inconvenient and improper." This reasoning notwithstanding, Congress in November 1775 raised the pay of the subaltern officers by one third.[19] At the bottom of this discussion lay the political question, how great a difference would be compatible with republican principles. The New England politicians favored a relative equality, while the others were inclined towards the establishment of clearer distinctions, thereby to guarantee subordination and discipline.[20]

During winter and spring of 1775–76 the question of pay became entangled with others, as bounties, terms of service, reduction of the number of regiments. The difficulties Washington experienced at Boston, the ill success the American forces had in Canada, and, in the summer of 1776, the disaster at New York, colored the reasoning not only of Washington himself, but also that of Congress. All agreed that there should be a longer term of service and a more severe discipline within the army. The fate of the Canadian expedition confirmed Washington in his earlier observation that his soldiers were unable to perform according to the modes of regular warfare. For this reason they had to be disciplined.

Disciplining them meant bringing "the temper and the genius [of the men] into such subordinate way of thinking as is necessary for a soldier".[21] In a letter to Congress Washington voiced his military-political creed: the troops had to be brought under "proper discipline and Subordination"; "Raw and undisciplined Recruits" had to be transformed into "Veteran soldiers"; to be a disciplined soldier was to be prompted to action not only by natural bravery or hope of reward but – here Washington marked the very point of distinction – by fear of punishment: "A Coward, when taught to believe, that if he breaks his Ranks, and abandons his Colours, will be punished with Death by his own party, will take the chance against the Enemy. ..."[22] Everybody will notice the close proximity of this maxim to the dictum of Frederick the Great: the soldiers "must fear their officers more than any danger."[23] Washington may have been disgusted with what he had found at Cambridge. The failure of the invasion of Canada may be acknowleged as a real motive of Washington's convictions. But, although Montgomery and Schuyler agreed with their commander-in-chief, lack of discipline can be blamed least for that disaster; bad planning and poor finances certainly were of greater weight.[24]

That there was something more fundamental underlying Washington's opinion is shown by the following quotation from the letter cited above: "The Man who thinks little of the one [punishment by his own party], and is fearful of the other [death by the enemy], Acts from present feelings regardless of consequences."[25] These words reveal a concept of human nature based on the belief that the lower strata of society are neither capable of becoming conscious of values nor of acting according to them. From this point of view he could not find anything but an "unaccountable kind of stupidity in the lower class of these people [i. e. the soldiers and some of the officers from New England]."[26] So the army had to be cleared of officers that were no gentlemen and the soldiers had to be made obey orders without thinking of their own. When Roger Sherman denounced long enlistments "as a state of slavery"[27] he recognized exactly what such maxims amounted to. But this sort of opposition was doomed to failure, partly because events in 1776 seemed to show the superiority of the concept of a well-drilled regular army in comparison with citizen-soldiers. Privates were not to "undertake to judge of the motives of a General," as militia general John Cadwallader put it when his troops missed the real sense of his movements. It was doomed to failure also because views such as Washington's reflected the feeling of a wider segment of society.[28]

So it is no wonder that the process of securing property rights and political influence against feared anarchic and licentious behavior of the lower classes[29] was paralleled by the process of securing discipline in the army against what could and would be looked at as anarchic and licentious behavior of the same lower classes. After the war, William Gordon and David Ramsay once more illustrated this view. Gordon quotes an unnamed "gentleman, whose concern in the army gave him the best opportunity of procuring certain information" as saying: "No laws can be too severe for the government of men who live by the sword" and "Absolute tyranny is essential to the government of an army." For this gentleman "every man, from the general officer to the private sentinel, [had to be] content to be a temporary slave."[30] For Gordon and his "gentleman" it was property rights that had to be defended against marauding soldiers. Ramsay too noticed "a rage for plundering" among the "common soldiery", and even among some of the officers. Ramsay echoes Washington, when he bemoans the fact that officers' "commissions were in several instances bestowed on persons who had no pretensions to the rank of gentlemen." He also gave a lucid summary of what can be called the conservative theory of an army: "The unbounded freedom of the savage who roams the woods must be restrained when [man] becomes a citizen of orderly government, and from the necessity of the case must be much more so, when he submits to be a soldier." He also stated very clearly – if from a conservative point of view – the paradox of an army fighting for the realization of liberty, while being held unfree: "The minds of the civil leaders in the councils of America were daily occupied in contemplating the rights of human nature, and investigating arguments on the principles of general liberty to justify their own opposition to Great Britain. Warmed with these ideas they trusted too much to the virtue of their countrymen, and were backward to enforce that subordination and order in their army, which, though it intrenches on civil liberty, produces effects in the military line, unequalled by the effusions of patriotism or the exertion of undisciplined valor."[31]

Judge Advocat William Tudor could feel in perfect harmony with the gentlemen of the army and those civilian ones who followed the line of thinking described by Gordon and Ramsay. To Tudor it was a self-evident truth that "when a man assumes the Soldier he lays aside the citizen, and must be content to submit to the temporary relinquishment of some of his civil Rights."[32] The Blackstonian concept of the soldier amounted to the contrary; according to Blackstone man "puts not off the citizen when he enters the camp."[33] But it has to be admitted that British practice did not follow that enlightened theory.

A valuable ideological asset for the remodelling of the military policy was the traditional concept of the army of republican Rome. Here, so it seemed to eighteenth-century observers, free citizens, for a time, submitted to the most severe discipline in order to serve their *res publica*. Charles Lee who, in 1776, would have liked to live "in the third or fourth century of the Romans", drafted, in 1779, a scheme for a military colony. It is not easy to decide whether Rome, Sparta, or Plato's rigid *politeia* were his models. At any rate, what he produced was no less than an utterly repressive, totalitarian utopia. Neither he nor Alexander McDougall actually would have liked to live there, although McDougall, at the same time, hinted very strongly at Rome as an example for his compatriots. Antiquity, however, might also have provided the American revolutionists with quite a different pattern – a pattern quite in contrast to those noted above, stressing liberty more than discipline, even in the field – that of Athens. Although – or because – this pattern was made use of by those who advocated extension of political rights to the lower classes, those responsible for the army did not like it.[34]

Congress, in October 1776, increased the pay of all officers below the rank of brigadier general, even once more that of the subalterns, without raising that of the privates or the non-commissioned officers.[35] Now, when military policy did not look for the citizen-soldier but for one who was ready to live in a temporary status of slavery, it was but logical to appeal rather to the avidity of the populace than to the patriotic virtues which might have caused the short term enlistments of 1775. Congress tried to do this without paying too much and without lowering the status-relevant pay difference, by offering bounties in cash and promising future rewards in land.[36] But still some politicians felt uneasy in agreeing to what was proposed to them as military necessities. This is illustrated by John Adams. He at the same time advocated long term enlistments as a means to introduce the "most masterly discipline", clung to the ideal of a virtuous citizen army patterned after an idealized perception of republican Rome, and was afraid of the dreadful possibilities of a standing army.[37]

What the recruiting officers now were to look for were people ready to leave their home, family, and connections for a time of at least three years, or for an undeterminable "duration of the war". That such an expectation could not have much of an allurement to reasonably well-to-do people seems obvious. Recruiting wage-earners, day laborers etc. was not without difficulties either, for wages rose steadily, and adventure and financial gain would be achieved more easily aboard the privateers now fitting out to chase the British. To join the rage for prize-money could not be regarded as unpatriotic, for it was the enemy's sea-power that was lessened in this way, and prominent members of the American society, and even of the army, were engaged in this business too, although merely as the owners of these privateers. For those who neither wanted to got to sea nor to serve for a long period of time, the militia offered a possibility to act as a patriot and also to get some bounty money.

Recruiting new soldiers became a hard task.[38] When Washington and Congress, impressed by the "necessity of appointing Gentlemen of Education to military offices as a measure absolutely necessary for saving the Country", undertook a new purge of the officers' corps, they, at the same time, urged compulsory recruiting by drafts.[39] Drafting for military service became rather common in the later seventies, although it practically meant restriction of that service to one year only. Because of the custom of service by substitute, compulsion also was another step in widening the social gap between officers and soldiers.[40] Scarcity of recruits also favored the enlistment of groups ordinarily not included within the circle of desirable soldiers, such as youths, indentured servants, negroes, and deserters from the enemy.[41] Although the policy of both Congress and Washington tended to be against the enlistment of deserters, there was no unanimity on this point within or outside Congress. Actually deserters were enrolled, and as those people seemed to need an especially strong discipline, their enlistment could not fail to influence the behavior of the officers against the other soldiers, too.[42] When the army could be seen as an institution for teaching discipline to "vagrants and disorderly persons", and when the fear of being pressed into service could be greeted as a means for "promoting the spirit of industry in some idle persons" and for "restraining others from disorderly practices", then there could not be much left that might kindle the patriotic feelings of a farmer. So one should not be astonished to find resentment against continental officers. They were said to be "so cruel and severe that the men [would] never be got to serve under 'em."[43] Such recruiting policies were founded on the belief that there existed a certain "class of Men whose tempers, attachments and circumstances disposed them to enter permanently, of for a length of time, into the army."[44] As the war dragged on, this class was located lower and lower on the social scale.

While thus changing the composition of the army, the policies of Congress and of the military leadership were also successful in assimilating the habits of too democratical officers, if ever such had survived the several reorganizations of the army. In 1781, Major General Alexander McDougall could recommend granting empty land in New York to officers of the New England troops on the argument that "the habits of thinking which they have acquired in the army, are more conformable to the genius of our Constitution, than the yeomanry of those States, who will unavoidably come into ours". The levelling spirit of the latter "should be tempered by those of the former".[45]

Washington wanted to keep the soldiers in their place and to emphasize the distinctions of rank. In 1779, the officers of the first New Jersey regiment hinted, among other things, at the poor pay of the common soldiery. They received a strict reprimand from their commander-in-chief. They were told, the opinion that the soldiers' pay was too low was "a doctrine full of dangerous consequences . . . which ought not to be countenanced in any way whatever." The general told his officers how fine their subordinates fared – if compared to the fate of the men in European armies; "any misconception on this point should be rectified." He supposed "every officer incapable of encouraging improper expectations in his men" and hoped "that every exertion [would] be made to suppress them."[46] In 1783, Washington strongly condemned a petition in which soldiers and non-commissioned officers – again from New Jersey – compared the provision Congress had made "for the Gentlemen Officers of the Army" with their own expectations. They called attention to what to them seemed a well known fact: they themselves had been "equal Sufferers with our officers."[47] At the same time, Washington commented favorably on a petition from the Connecticut non-commissioned officers who asked for a distinction between privates and men of their rank in matters of clothing and pay.[48] It seems that the last mentioned petition was the outcome of a certain measure of guiding interference in its preparation by Washington and officers of the Connecticut line.[49]

I certainly do not want to overemphasize the importance of this military policy. In the colonies there never had existed anything like perfect social homogeneity. What had been brought over the Atlantic, and what existed at the time of the Revolution, was a stratified society. But, at least in New England, the ideal of social homogeneity, although not of social and economic equality, had existed. Even if this value was giving way to disintegration, it might still have been used in establishing the new political and social environment. The absence of parts of the community for up to eight years necessarily would have meant an estrangement from what had come to be seen as localisms. The military policy tended to accentuate that estrangement. If there had ever been, at the start of the Revolution, a chance of combining the traditional value of homogeneity with a new – more equalitarian – attitude, this chance remained unused. Even if such a chance did not exist at all, the military policy was bound to accelerate the process of disintegration.[50]

The evolution of distinction of ranks was accepted by the officers. When their status changed, their attitudes and values changed, too. In this development the half pay question was of great importance.[51] The movement for gaining half pay was started in November 1777.[52] Though at first not supported by the commander-in-chief, it gained such momentum that already in December 1777 James Lovell doubted the possibility of introducing what he called "severe Discipline" for the officers without granting half pay and making the officers' commissions vendible.[53] The expectation that these two measures might allow disciplining the officers, too, seems to have been a brainchild of Washington's. As Lovell told his correspondent, Washington was prepared, after having made the commissions desirable, to "cashier without favour or affection till the Army becomes vigorous." Lovell did not place much confidence in Washington's argument, although he despaired of the possibility of putting the army to action without first passing the proposed measures. Actually, he does not seem to have understood what those expectations amounted to, for he combined advocating half pay and salability of the commissions with an idea of his own: the annual election of all officers.[54] So Lovell's letter expresses the ambiguous stand of those more radical politicians, who tried to harmonize their own political convictions with what came to appear to them as military necessities.

Half pay and salability of commissions were more than mere financial stimuli, even though that was the main argument used by Washington.[55] As financial inducement, at least half pay might have been asked for the soldiers, too. But that was an idea that did not occur to the officers, although it was proposed in Congress. Those two measures were symbols of status for men who were shaping their image of themselves after that of the officers of the British army. But there these customs were expressions of the concept of office as an estate, a notion quite contrary to republican principles.[56] Regularity of promotions was another one of those status symbols. Until 1778, as stated by Jedediah Huntington, irregular promotions had been "the Means of loosing many valuable Men who have been superseded for want of attention to this rule."[57] Contrary to Huntington's expectations, promotions remained a constant source of bitterness and a constant cause of resignations.

To the officers, regular promotion also was a point of honor, and honor for them was one of the most important values. It is impossible here to describe the whole range of meaning that could be connected with the term "honor". But some implications of the officers' conception of that term should be noticed. To Montesquieu, it was an aristocratic quality, and as such the principle of monarchies, like that of Great Britain. To

161

the Americans, this notion was not unknown.[58] Although there was no formal aristocracy within the colonies and later states, the term contained an aspect of social pre-eminence, in contrast to lower ranking people. On the other hand, honor also was a principle on which one could defend oneself against infringements committed by government. So it could be used as a foundation of opposition. Thirdly, it meant steadfastness in important decisions which involved someone's whole personality. In this sense the word was used by the signers of the Declaration of Independence, when they pledged their "sacred honour". Among the officers, respect to merit and rank was an aspect no less important than the others. Honor as a principle of defending one's dignity against disregards from below and encroachments from above necessarily had to become not only the means of discrimination against the soldiers, whose honor consisted in obeying orders and staying in the field during battle, but also the basis of defense against actions of superiors. So the appeal to honor meant a guaranty of personal freedom for the officer in deciding his course of action. Aristocratic qualities of the term, and its aptness for preserving a last resort of freedom within the system of subordination on which the army was based, were clearly expressed by Philip Schuyler: "Congress in a variety of instances have forgot that their officers have feelings. I thank God that I am not deprived of mine and that I feel the spirit and resentment of a gentleman at their ill usage, high as some may estimate the dignity of Congress, it is not high enough for a gentleman tamely to suffer unmerited injury, and I will not wear their honors unless with honor to myself."[59]

Honor, to be fully realized, had to be visible to the public. One of the first measures Washington took after his arrival at Cambridge was to make his officers display their respective ranks publicly. Here the connection between honor and discipline becomes very clear.[60] It fitted well into this train of thought that the general officers, in 1780, pointed out to Congress the necessity of their "supporting tables" not too much inferior to those of the officers of the French expeditionary army under Rochambeau.[61] One of the most spectacular consequences of this line of reasoning was the founding of the Order of the Cincinnati after the war's end. The outcry of their countrymen against that society could well have demonstrated to the officers concerned, how far they had estranged themselves from the feelings of their civilian co-revolutionists.[62] Knox is credited with having conceived the first idea of an order like this already in 1776. If so, his reflections could not differ much from those one of the French officers within the American army communicated to Congress, viz. that there was a necessity to make a visible distinction between those who fought for the country and those who either did not touch arms or left their posts.[63] In founding their order, the officers also may have realized that they now belonged to that international brotherhood whose members exchanged courtesies before killing each other. At least from the outside world they were accepted as such. So Washington, in a letter from Poland, was asked to propose some officers of merit, who, together with Washington himself, should be adopted as members of the order "de la Providence divine".[64]

Although the Americans were forbidden to accept that honor, this recognition of their worth must have given them satisfaction. They certainly also could be satisfied, when they compared their status in 1783 to that of 1775, when they were called by that disgraceful name of "rebels", and – when prisoners of war – were denied that discrimination their rank seemed to require.[65] There was no longer any need to show a "ruffled dignity" when asked for the legitimacy of their rank.[66] In 1783, they had got those status symbols as half pay – though finally in the form of "commutation" only – and recognition of their honor as officers, but they also had developed a deep distrust of their fellow citizens. Half pay, in the last instance, had to be made good by those compatriots, too, against whom, when soldiers of the army, they had set up themselves as superior beings, or whom, when politicians of the more radical description, they had to compel by extortion. Their policy of impressing Congress with their merits had been successful, if not by the weight of arguments, at least by the weight of the necessity of holding an army in the field. In sharp contrast to what was declared by William Tudor to be the maxim of army regulations, officers as well as generals had based their argument on their character as "citizens" and so made clear that they did not feel much need to submit to the rules they practiced on their subordinates.[67]

The main topic of the officers' communications to Congress, to their commander-in-chief, to their states, and among themselves, was the financial distress they had to experience in the service. In the course of an enormous depreciation prices climbed rapidly, while Congress only hesitatingly took steps to adapt the pay of their servants to the economic situation. Congress even was unable to pay the army punctually. So, bitter feelings and unrest among officers and soldiers were a constant threat to the successful pursuit of the war. Mutinies and near-mutinies were reported since 1777. Although the hopes cherished by Benedict Arnold, after his treason, and by Sir George Rodney "that upon a certainty of being paid their arrears and a portion of land given after the war, Washington would soon have no army"[68] were disappointed, the possible dangers arising from an unpaid army did not go unnoticed. When, in January 1781, the Pennsylvania troops rose against the conditions of their service, the militia of New Jersey declined to quell the mutiny, because they felt the soldiers had "real grievances which ought to be redressed". The regular troops of that state could not be used against the Pennsylvanians because they seemed to be unreliable, too. A few days after the peaceful settlement of that trouble they also mutinied and had to be brought to order by force; the "ringleaders" were shot. Unrest was noted also among the troops from New York and Connecticut.[69]

The soldiers had no other way of getting rid of the difficulties facing them in the army but mutiny or desertion.[70] The officers could resign, and many of them did just that. When he pressed Congress for granting half pay, Washington stated that between August 1777 and the middle of March 1778 between 200 and 300 officers had quit the army.[71] Later on, this practice lost much of its importance, but it was in use till the end of the war.

When asking for more and better rewards, the officers pointed at the general distress of the army, they reminded Congress of the bitter wants of their families, they hinted at their merits, and compared their situation with that of the civilians; they welcomed steps Congress had taken in favor of other groups and now demanded the same, or even more, for themselves; they found their own dignity at stake and that of the United States in general.[72] There was a marked tendency for singling out their own group against the general situation of the country or the other branches of the civil service. In 1780, according to Washington, the army would already have gone out of existence "had it not been for a spirit of patriotic virtue both in officers and men". When, in 1779, Samuel H. Parsons stated that "as to Virtue and Patriotism, what little ever animated the Country to a noble Resistance ... has become a Stranger to Our Senators and her Vestiges are scarcely found in a Country Village," he hoped, at the same time, that "some small share of her Influence still abides in our Tents."[73] The officers could base their claim to exceptionable merits on their observation, that they not only had shared with their "Fellow Citizens at large every common Misfortune, incident to a State of War," but even had "cheerfully borne the numerous ... Ills, to which the Profession we have adopted is liable", while their civilian compatriots "were solacing themselves at home."[74]

When American patriots lost property by the depreciation of Continental and state money, it seemed to them, as if the patriotism they had proved by investing in American paper, had been made use of as a weapon by those unpatriotic people who either – probably by dark design – had declined investing in those bills and/or now exploited their fellow citizens by high prices of commodities and labor.[75] Some officers also had invested in paper money,[76] and so they shared this grievance with other people. They also had had expenditures in forming their respective units and those expenditures could be viewed as investments, too. But they had to bear even more because they received their pay in that depreciated currency. This aggravation was felt even harder, as they knew that they had "in no shape contributed to the Depreciation of the currency."[77] But that was not all. His exceptionable merits convinced a gentleman of the army that "there [was] Justice due to [him] and every other officer beyond the wages."[78] "Exposed", as the officers felt, "to the rapacity of almost every other class of the community",[79] they had to fight on their own. They even omitted the chance of allying themselves with the civil servants of the states or of Congress, although that group labored under similar circumstances.[80]

The officers felt that after the war they should be received by their fellow citizens "with a full proportion of affection,"[81] but they had reason to believe that such a reception was not too certain. An episode, in 1781, not only evinces the degree of self-esteem of the officers, it also shows that the strategy of combining a number of demands in favor of the officers with some claims in favor of the soldiers was perceived as a mere stratagem by politicians. In a rather strong-worded letter forwarded by Washington to Governor Jonathan Trumbull, Generals Huntington and Parsons marked the measures taken by their state for the relief of officers and soldiers as totally insufficient. "The conduct of government in this and other instances" had convinced them that justice could not be expected, unless their demands were complied with before their services were needed no longer. Once more there appeared the threat of mass resignations.[82] Trumbull did not agree with the officers at all. He could not find their case exceptionable, as "the country, universally" had had "many, very many, embarassments and great difficulties to encounter and struggle through."[83] Parsons now declined any further responsibility "for the fidelity of your troops." As he put it, the troops "considered the neglect and repeated violations of promises made by the State as adding insult to injury."[84] He received a sharp reply in which he was told that "a trifling dispute relative to the detained rations of some of the officers, in which, as such, the soldiery have no interest" was the only matter still unsettled. In a letter to the commander-in-chief Trumbull hinted at the maxim of *"divide et impera"*, and asked, "will we suffer avarice to divide and ruin us and our case?"[85]

To Parsons these letters were the work of his personal enemies among the Connecticut politicians; that there still existed a Connecticut line was due, in his opinion, only to the exertions of himself and the other officers. He also tried to defend his view of the existence of a community of interest between officers and soldiers. But just this defense clearly evinces that there actually was not much ground on which to unite. The statement that the interests of both groups were inseparable is not very convincing. The general's expectation, that the one "class", meaning the soldiers, could not believe that justice should be done to them, when they had to observe injustice done to the other, the officers, only shows that these two groups were viewed as different entities.[86]

Disappointment was to be expected not only from the politicians. Already in 1778 the officers had stated that no trust could be put in the gratitude of the "populace".[87] The sky was dark, indeed, not only for the officers. None of the thirteen states was as happy as Vermont, which was able to waive taxation and instead raise revenue by the sale of confiscated property and empty lands alone.[88] In 1781, Rhode Islanders detected "a Conspiracy ... to prevent the Collection of Taxes and to discourage the recruiting services."[89] If, as Governor William Greene thought, the conspirators had fled to western Massachusetts, they had found a situation even more turbulent. Unrest there had developed into what came near to an open rebellion in 1782, directed primarily against high taxation.[90] Although Gouverneur Morris had expected raising the taxes would drive the poorer classes into the army,[91] he certainly would have found more instances of government difficulties arising from this source. Taxing the people was seen as a panacea to overcome the difficulties of the army by some of its members, too.[92] The realization of half pay or commutation would mean even more taxes. So the officers cannot have been surprised when the final acceptance of commutation by Congress was greeted in New England with what Minot described as a "general outcry".[93] When John Brooks and his fellow representatives of the Massachusetts officers of the Continental Army arrived at Boston, in the summer of 1782, they expected opposition to their claims primarily from "the little people, too many of whom are where they ought not to be."[94] Little people, of course, were not the established politicians of either faction, but the country members of the legislature. One of the members of this delegation even threatened the legislators by hinting at the possibility of a mutiny of the Massachusetts line.[95]

In essence, it was the same sort of argument Parsons had used in 1781. But now it looked even more dangerous, for the officers were reported as being ready to take the lead in such a movement. Actually armed rebellion for enforcing the army's rights had been a topic among the officers at least since May, 1782.[96] And yet, one has to notice that nobody could prove the readiness of the men to wage a new war. Home they might go if not paid their arrears, but there was not much probability of their staying in the field to fight for their officers' half pay.[97] The officers had quelled disturbances among the soldiers, when they had demanded their dues, and even now the officers had to defend themselves against the argument that fulfilling their demands would be a gross injustice to the soldiery.[98] Since 1778, legitimate organization of discontent had been a matter of the officers, undisturbed by soldiers' interference. It was the officers who composed the committees that drafted the lists of grievances, the soldiers were not allowed publicly to reflect on their situation or their status. For "agitators" from the ranks there was no room. Anything like the "Putney Debates" was unthinkable.

That differences existed among the officers as to their relations with their subordinates may be inferred from some land schemes developed within the northern army in the years from 1778 to 1782. Some petitions for Vermont lands contain signatures both of officers and soldiers,[99] while others were signed exclusively by officers.[100] Higher ranking officers tried to emulate the landed aristocracy of New York and of the South. Benedict Arnold aimed at large parts of land, formerly the property of Sir William Johnson.[101] And when Arnold had decided to look for land with the British, Parsons expected the Connecticut officers to "secure the soldiers" who had to settle the lands that might be granted to their superiors by the State of New York.[102] The famous "army petition" for western lands which was submitted to Congress in 1783 was also prepared without participation of the soldiers; the list of signatures lacks any mark of men from the rank and file.[103]

As the size of the expected grant was in relation to the rank of the holder, military differences would have been transformed into social and economic ones. At least at the start of the planning for this petition, the desire of preserving these ranks in a new environment had been voiced even more clearly. An early draft contains the proviso that widows, orphans, and families of disabled associates should receive help by the community, so as to maintain them "in a manner suitable to the heads of them." The children were to be enabled, when grown up, to be on equal footing with those "whose parents at the time of the original formation of the [new] State, were in similar circumstances with those of the former."[104] When General Edward Hand drafted his proposition for a peace establishment of the American army, he expected the garrisons of the western forts to support themselves by the labor of the soldiers and their wives. The soldiers were expected to work the fields "under the direction of their officers", while their wives were "to support themselves by washing ... and mending for the officers and soldiers at rates to be established by the Commanding Officer or a board convened by him for the purpose." In Hand's view, obviously, a thing like the soldiers' right to a decent living for themselves and their families did not exist. He proposed that the soldiers' wives "if they will not work for their maintenance when in health, ... should be considered as nuisances and expeld [from] the Garrison."[105]

The Newburgh addresses, like the settlement plan, were expressions of the officers' fear of the imminent peace.[106] Unable, or unwilling, to step back into their former places, not ready to content themselves with holding positions that could give only local importance and small salaries, some of them were not exactly ambitious "to peddle in trade or starve in public office."[107] Others, with the years of their youth, had lost ability and drive to continue their education.[108] But the officers now had found allies with whose help they could hope to realize their financial expectations. They now belonged to the group of public creditors. As holders of promissory notes they tended to become staunch defenders of government. From their former subordinates they could still claim the deference those had been accustomed to. What a valuable asset their support could be to government may be illustrated by an episode of the Shays Rebellion, as told by Minot: About forty rebels, "with one Luddington their captain, being lodged in house together, were ... surrounded. It was a singular circumstance, that among the government's volunteers, happened to be General Tupper, who had lately commanded a continental regiment, in which Luddington had served as a Corporal. The General, ignorant of the character of his enemy, summoned the party to surrender. How astonished was the Corporal at receiving this summons, in a voice to which he had never dared to refuse obedience! A momentary explanation took place, which but heightened the General's commands. Resistance was no longer made, ... and a surrender was agreed to."[109]

At the end of the war the ambiguities which American military leaders had been confronted with were dissolved. Within the army the officers had established a status in many aspects very similar to that of their European colleagues. In this process they had estranged themselves from the body of their fellow citizens within and outside the army. As to the army as a whole, was it, as Don Higginbotham stated, "in the last analysis ... a republican army"? There is no explicit definition of what the term "republican" is supposed to denote within the context of Higginbotham's description. The verdict seems to be founded on the opinion that the army was "remarkably loyal to the civil authority and the goals of the revolution".[110] But loyalty to civil authority does not necessarily imply republicanism, and if those who shaped the army policy were in accord with the goals of the Revolution, they certainly preferred a rather conservative interpretation of those goals, as far as they were related to the army.[111] There may have been a chance of the army becoming more liberal, perhaps even revolutionary, but such a possibility was being checked consciously and efficiently already since 1775.

Notes

[*] I wish to thank my colleague, Dr. Alfred Kirfel, Rheinbach, who corrected the worst language mistakes in this paper.
[1] Michael Kammen, *People of Paradox: An Inquiry Concerning the Origins of American Civilization,* paperback ed. (New York, 1973 [orig. publ. 1972]), ch. 7, esp. 234–235, 238.
[2] David Ramsay, *The History of the Revolution of South Carolina from a British Province to an Independent State* (Trenton, N. J., 1785), II, 182–183.
[3] Cf. John Shy, "A New Look at Colonial Militia", *WMQ,* 3d Ser., XX (1963), 175–185.
[4] A Militia Man, "Address to the Assembly of Connecticut", Oct. 10, 1776, *AA,* 5, II, 983; cf. John K. Alexander, "The Fort Wilson Incident of 1779: A Case Study of the Revolutionary Crowd", *WMQ,* 3d Ser., XXXI (1974), 589–612, 594.
[5] Robert C. Pugh, "The Revolutionary Militia in the Southern Campaign, 1780–1781", *WMQ,* 3d Ser., XIV (1957), 154–175.
[6] Bernard Bailyn, *The Ideological Origins of the American Revolution* (Cambridge, Mass., 1967), 301–319, quotation 302.
[7] Elisha P. Douglass, *Rebels and Democrats: The Struggle for Equal Political Rights and Majority Rule during the American Revolution* (Chapel Hill, N. C., 1955), 30.
[8] Joseph Reed to Mrs. Reed, Oct. 11, 1776, *AA,* 5, II, 994; Charles K. Bolton, *The Private Soldier under Washington* (New York, 1902), 128; Sidney Kaplan, "Rank and Status among Massachusetts Continental Officers", *AHR,* LVI (1950–51), 319–326, 321; Willard M. Wallace, *Appeal to Arms: A Military History of the American Revolution,* repr. ed. (Chicago, Ill., 1964 [orig. publ. 1951]), 51; Don Higginbotham, *The War of American Independence: Military Attitudes, Policies, and Practice, 1763–1789* (New York, 1971), 101. In autumn 1775, three officers were arrested "for doing something in shoe making and mending," which was done "by the advice and consent of the Commanding officer for the time being and the Colo. of the Regiment." John Brown to Philip Schuyler, Oct. 10, 1775, Papers of Philip Schuyler, 25, New York Public Library, New York.
[9] *The Journals of Each Provincial Congress of Massachusetts in 1774 and 1775 . . .* (Boston, Mass., 1838), 33.

[10] April 14 and 25, 1775, *ib.*, 143, 150; general officers had been appointed by the Provincial Congress Dec. 8, 1774 and Febr. 8, 1775, *ib.*, 35, 89–90.

[11] *Ib.*, 231; resolves of Congress, June 6 and July 7, 1775, *JCC*, II, 89–90, 220–221.

[12] Oct. 7, 1775, *JCC*, III, 285–286.

[13] Richard Smith, Diary, Dec. 12, 1775, *LMCC*, I, 289–290; Louis C. Hatch, *The Administration of the American Revolutionary Army*, repr. ed. (New York, 1970 [orig. publ. 1904]), 75–76.

[14] Smith Diary, Dec. 12, 1775, *LMCC*, I, 289–290; New Jersey delegates to the president of the New Jersey congress, Oct. 7, 1775, *ib.*, I, 223–224; cf. John Adams to J. Warren, Dec. 12, 1775, *ib.*, I, 269.

[15] See Hatch, *Administration* (cf. n. 13), 75–76.

[16] George Washington, "General Orders", July 4, 1775; to the president of the Continental Congress, Aug. 4, 1775; General Orders, Aug. 5, 1775; to David Wooster, Sept. 2, 1775, John C. Fitzpatrick, ed., *The Writings of George Washington from the Original Manuscript Sources, 1745–1799* (Washington, D. C., 1931–1944), III, 309, 391, 402, 465–466.

[17] "Minutes of a Conference …," Oct. 18, 1775, Papers of Samuel Adams, Box 1, New York Public Library, New York; see *AA,* 4, III, 1156.

[18] "Minutes of a Conference," Papers of Samuel Adams. Box 1, (cf. n. 17).

[19] Nov. 4, 1775, *JCC*, III, 322; Hatch, *Administration* (cf. n. 13), 78.

[20] J. Adams to Elbridge Gerry, June 18, 1775, *LMCC*, I, 135–136; Joseph Hawley to S. Adams, Nov. 12, 1775, Papers of Samuel Adams, Box 1 (cf. n. 17); same to J. Adams, Nov. 14, 1775, Charles F. Adams, ed., *The Works of John Adams* (Boston, Mass., 1850–1856), IX, 364; J. Adams to J. Hawley, Nov. 25, 1775, *LMCC*, I, 259–260; cf. Hatch, *Administration* (cf. n. 13), 78.

[21] Washington to J. Reed, Febr. 1, 1776 and Febr. 2, 1776, Fitzpatrick, ed., *Writings of Washington* (cf. n. 16), IV, 299–300, 320–321.

[22] Washington to the president of Congress, Febr. 9, 1776, *ib.*, IV, 315–318, quotation 316.

[23] Quoted by Robert R. Palmer, "Frederick the Great, Guibert, Bülow: From Dynastic to National War", in E. M. Mearle, ed., *Makers of Modern Strategy: Military Thought from Macchiavelli to Hitler* (Princeton, N. J., 1943), 55.

[24] Cf. Higginbotham, *War* (cf. n. 8), 111–112, 115; Jonathan G. Rossie, *The Politics of Command in the American Revolution* (Syracuse, N. Y., 1975), 37–60, esp. 40, 44, 57, 59.

[25] Washington to the president of Congress, Febr. 9, 1776, Fitzpatrick, ed., *Writings of Washington* (cf. n. 16), IV, 316.

[26] Washington to Richard H. Lee, Aug. 29, 1775, *ib.*, IV, 164.

[27] James Duane, "Notes of Debates," Febr. 22, 1776, *LMCC*, I, 360.

[28] Cadwallader's statement in full: "Our Militia is much reduced by Desertion and other Causes – Many persons thought our leaving Princeton was a Retreat – and immediately pushed off to Casulls Ferry and other places, thinking it more safe to retire in small Parties than with the main Body – This Idea has been a great Disadvantage to our Schemes, and ever will, when privates undertake to judge of the motives of a General by his Movements", John Cadwallader to the Council of Pennsylvania, January 10, 1777, Emmet Collection, 8781, New York Public Library, New York. For the second part of the statement made in the text see Richard B. Morris, *The American Revolution Reconsidered,* paperback ed. (New York, 1968 [orig. publ. 1967]), 66–68.

[29] This seems to have been the underlying reason of the strenuous efforts to control the revolutionary mobs; for these efforts cf. Pauline Maier, *From Resistance to Revolution: Colonial Radicals and the Development of American Opposition to Great Britain,* paperback ed. (New York, 1974 [orig. publ. 1972]), *passim; id.,* "Popular Uprisings and Civil Authority in Eighteenth-Century America", *WMQ,* 3d Ser., XXVII (1970), 3–35; *id.,* "The Charleston Mob and the Evolution of Popular Politics in Revolutionary South Carolina, 1765–1784", *Perspectives in American History,* IV (1970), 173–196; Ronald Hoffman, *A Spirit of Dissension: Economics, Politics, and the Revolution in Maryland* (Baltimore, Md., and London, 1973), *passim.*

[30] William Gordon, *The History of the Rise, Progress, and Establishment of the Independence of the United States of America . . .* (London, 1788), II, 332.

[31] David Ramsay, *The History of the American Revolution* (Philadelphia, 1789), I, 331–332; cf. *id., History of the Revolution of South Carolina* (cf. n. 2), II, 143–144; it should be noted that, on the other side of the line, American loyalist officers experienced a very similar sort of contempt because of their being no "gentlemen", see John R. Cuneo, "The Early Days of the Queen's Rangers, August 1776–February 1777", *Military Affairs,* XXII (1958), 65–74, 66–67, 74.

[32] William Tudor, "Remarks on the Rules and Articles for the Government of the Continental Troops", autumn 1775, *PCC,* item 41, II, 1–2.

[33] St. George Tucker, ed., *Blackstone's Commentaries,* repr. ed. (New York, 1969 [orig. publ. 1803]), bk. 1, c. 13, II, 408; William Blackstone's *Commentaries on the Laws of England* were originally published at Oxford, 1765–1769.

[34] Charles Lee to Patrick Henry, July 29, 1776; *id.,* "Sketch of a Plan for the Formation of a Military Colony", 1779, *The [Charles] Lee Papers,* (New York Historical Society, *Collections,* IV–VII [New York, 1872–1875]), II, 177; III, 322–330; for McDougall see Roger J. Champagne, *Alexander McDougall and the American Revolution in New York* (Schenectady, N. Y., 1975), 149–151. For military discipline in Athens and Rome see Johannes Kromayer and Georg Veith, *Heerwesen und Kriegsführung der Griechen und Römer,* in Walter Otto, ed., *Handbuch der Altertumswissenschaft,* 4. Abteilung, 3. Teil, 2. Band (Munich, 1928), 56, 280–282.

[35] Oct. 7, 1776, *JCC,* V, 853; Hatch, *Administration* (cf. n. 13), 79. It should be noted that the evolution of pay differences was paralleled by constant efforts to amend the articles of war, so as to make them more rigid; for this see Maurer Maurer, "Military Justice under General Washington", *Military Affairs,* XXVIII (1964), 8–16, 12–13.

[36] See Hatch, *Administration* (cf. n. 13), 73.

[37] J. Adams to Samuel H. Parsons, Aug. 19, and to Henry Knox, Aug. 25, both 1776, *LMCC,* II, 57, 61.

[38] Samuel Cooper to S. Adams, July 15, 1776, Papers of Samuel Adams, Box 1 (cf. n. 17); S. P. Savage to the same, Aug. 12, 1776, *ib.;* J. Copp to Ph. Schuyler, Sept. 3, 1776, Papers of Philip Schuyler, 30 (cf. n. 8); Esek. Hopkins to committee of Congress, Sept. 10, 30, cf. Nov. 2, 1776, *AA,* 5, II, 282–283, 623; 5, III, 491; William Bradford to the president of Congress Sept. 14, 1776, *AA,* 5, II, 337; Thomas Nelson to John Page, Sept. 18, 1776, Emmet Collection, 1636 (cf. n. 28); Joseph Hawley to Elbridge Gerry, Oct. 13, 1776, Papers of Samuel Adams, Box 1; Benjamin Rush to R. H. Lee, Dec. 21, 1776, Lyman H. Butterfield, ed., *Letters of Benjamin Rush* (Princeton, N. J., 1951), I, 121.

[39] See Elbridge Gerry to Horatio Gates, Sept. 27, 1776, *LMCC*, II, 105–106.

[40] For short information see Higginbotham, *War* (cf. n. 8), 392–393; Bolton, *Private Soldier* (cf. n. 8), 50, 62–63.

[41] See Higginbotham, *War* (cf. n. 8), 391–395.

[42] Cf. report of the Board of War, May 17, 1778, *JCC*, XI, 642–644; resolve concerning foreign officers and soldiers, April 29, 1778, *ib.*, X, 405–409. For estimation and treatment of deserters see Colonel Armand [i. e. Marquis de la Rouerie] to Congress, Dec. 28, 1777, *PCC*, item 164, 366–370; Fitzpatrick, ed., *Writings of Washington* (cf. n. 16), index, s. v. desertion; J. Wood to Thomas Jefferson, Febr. 20, 1781, Julian P. Boyd *et al.*, eds., *The Papers of Thomas Jefferson* (Princeton, N. J., 1950–), IV, 672.

[43] The words are David Ramsay's, see his *History of the Revolution of South Carolina* (cf. n. 2), II, 103. The latter quotation is from David Cobb to Henry Jackson, June 8, 1780, Gaillard Hunt, ed., *Fragments of Revolutionary History: Being Hitherto Unpublished Writings of the Men of the American Revolution* (Brooklyn, N. Y., 1892), 149; cf. William Shephard to John Hancock, June 20, 1781, Massachusetts Archives, CCIII, 336, Massachusetts State Archives, Boston.

[44] So Washington in 1778, quoted by Higginbotham, *War* (cf. n. 8), 392; cf. Robert Morris and Richard Peters to Washington, Aug. 13, 1781, *LMCC*, VI, 178.

[45] Alexander McDougall to George Clinton, March 12, 1781, *LMCC*, VI, 26.

[46] Memorial of the officers of the 1st New Jersey Regiment, April 17, 1779, *PCC*, item 152, VII, 325–327; Washington to William Maxwell, May 10, 1779, Fitzpatrick, ed., *Writings of Washington* (cf. n. 16), XV, 32–33.

[47] Petition of non-commissioned officers and privates of the New Jersey line, April 9, 1783, *PCC*, item 152, XI, 227; Washington to the president of Congress, April 18, 1783, Fitzpatrick, ed., *Writings of Washington* (cf. n. 16), XXVI, 330–334.

[48] Petition of the Sergeants of the Connecticut line, May 1, 1783, *PCC*, item 152, XI, 291–294; Washington to the president of Congress, May 21, 1783, Fitzpatrick, ed., *Writings of Washington* (cf. n. 16), XXVI, 448–449.

[49] See Washington to the president of Congress, April 18, 1783, *ib.*, XXVI, 332; Jedediah Huntington to Washington, April 25, 1783, *PCC*, item 149, III, 337–338.

[50] Cf. David Syrett, "Town Meeting Politics in Massachusetts, 1776–1786", *WMQ*, 3d Ser., XXI (1964), 352–366; Kenneth Lockridge, "Land, Population, and the Evolution of New England Society, 1630–1790", *Past and Present*, XXXIX (Apr. 1968), 523–544; Michael Zuckerman, "The Social Context of Democracy in Massachusetts", *WMQ*, 3d Ser., XXV (1968), 523–544; Edward M. Cook, "Social Behavior and Changing Values in Dedham, Massachusetts, 1700–1775", *WMQ*, 3d Ser., XXVII (1970), 546–580.

[51] Half pay was the officers' pension as introduced by the British in the 17th century; for a short outline see William H. Glasson, *Federal Military Pensions in the United States* (New York, 1918), 24–43; Hatch, *Administration* (cf. n. 13), 79–85.

[52] See Fitzpatrick, ed., *Writings of Washington* (cf. n. 16), X, 125n.

[53] James Lovell to S. Adams, Dec. 20, 1777, Papers of S. Adams, Box 2 (cf. n. 17).

[54] *Ib.*

[55] See Washington to the president of Congress, Dec. 23, to E. Gerry, Dec. 25, both 1777; to the Committee with the Army, January 29, to the president of Congress, April 10, to John Banister, April 21, to A. McDougall, April 22, to Gouverneur Morris, April 25, to Henry Laurens, April 30, all 1778, Fitzpatrick, ed., *Writings of Washington* (cf. n. 16), X, 196–197, 201, 363–365; XI, 139, 158, 239–240, 285, 298, 307, 327–328.

[56] For the proposal made in Congress see John Fell, Diary, Aug. 12, 1778, *LMCC*, IV, 363. John Brooke suggested the ideological foundation of half pay and the vendibility of commissions with the British.

[57] Jedediah Huntington to Jabez Huntington, January 16, 1778, Albert C. Bates, ed., *Correspondence of the Brothers Joshua and Jedediah Huntington during the Period of the American Revolution* (Connecticut Historical Society, *Collections*, XX [Hartford, Conn., 1923]), 395.

[58] Paul M. Spurlin, *Montesquieu in America, 1760–1801* (Baton Rouge, La., 1940), 146.

[59] Schuyler to Duane, Aug. 15, 1777, Bancroft Collection, Schuyler Transcripts, 415–416, New York Public Library, New York. Cf. McDougall to Schuyler, March 14, 1776, Papers of Ph. Schuyler, 28 (cf. n. 8); Nathanael Greene to Washington, April 24 and 26, 1778, Jared Sparks, ed., *Correspondence of the American Revolution* ... (Boston, Mass., 1853), II, 272–274, 279; Benedict Arnold to same, May 5, 1779, and Knox to same, March 27, 1781, *ib.*, II, 291, III 276; Parsons to Lovell, May 22, 1779, Charles S. Hall, *Life and Letters of Samuel Holden Parsons*, repr. ed. (New York, 1968 [orig. publ. 1905]), 241; general officers to Congress, July 11, 1780, *PCC*, item 43, 259; same to same, *ib.*, item 41, VII, 259–266.

[60] Hatch, *Administration* (cf. n. 13), 14.

[61] See general officers to Congress, July 11, 1780, *PCC*, item 43, 259; cf. Ebenezer Huntington to Andrew Huntington, Aug. 2, 1781, "Letters of Ebenezer Huntington, 1774–1781", *AHR*, V (1899–1900), 702–729, 728; Champagne, *Alexander McDougall* (cf. n. 34), 162.

[62] See Wallace E. Davies, "The Society of the Cincinnati in New England, 1783–1800", *WMQ*, 3d Ser., V (1948), 3–25; Sidney Kaplan, "Veteran Officers and Politics in Massachusetts, 1783–1787", *WMQ*, 3d Ser., IX (1952), 29–57.

[63] Colonel Armand [i. e. Marquis de la Rouerie] to Congress, Dec. 28, 1777, *PCC*, item 164, 366–367.

[64] Jean de Heintz to Washington, May 13, 1783, *ib.*, item 152, XI, 443–446.

[65] See Douglas S. Freeman, *George Washington: A Biography* (New York, 1948–1957), III, 526–527.

[66] See "Journal of Lieutenant John Charles Philip von Krafft, 1776–1784" (New York Historical Society, *Collections*, XV [New York, 1883]), 135, May 11, 1781.

[67] See Nathaniel Greene, "To the officers of the Pennsylvania line", March 29, 1782, Bancroft Collection, Greene Letterbooks, II, 165–167, New York Public Library, New York (Greene here denies his officers the right to argue on that principle); general officers to Congress, July 11, 1780, *PCC*, item 43, 259.

[68] Sir George Rodney to Lord George Germain, Dec. 22, 1780, *Report on the Manuscripts of Mrs. Stopford Sackville of Drayton House, Northamptonshire*, Historical Manuscripts Commission, *Ninth Report*, part III, 2d ed. rev. (Hereford, 1904–1910), II, 193.

[69] Parsons to J. Wadsworth, January 14, to Washington, January 12, to Mrs. Parsons, January 31, to Governor Trumbull, Febr. 5, all 1781, Hall, *Parsons* (cf. n. 59), 321, 323, 335–336, 324–326. The story is told by Carl Van Doren, *Mutiny in January: The Story of a Crisis in the Continental Army* (New York, 1943).

[70] For desertion see Arthur J. Alexander, "Desertion and Its Punishment in Revolutionary Virginia", *WMQ*, 3d Ser., III (1946), 383–397.

[71] Washington to the president of Congress, March 24, 1778, Fitzpatrick, ed., *Writings of Washington* (cf. n. 16), XI, 139.

[72] See petition of the officers of the northern army, Sept. 13, 1778, *PCC*, item 41, VII, 195–204; petition of officers of the Connecticut line to their state, Oct. 3, 1778, *ib.*, item 66, I, 443–446; memorial of the general officers (read in Congress Sept. 18, 1779), *ib.*, item 41, VII, 259; resignation of New York officers, Febr. 5, 1780, Hugh Hastings, ed., *Public Papers of George Clinton, First Governor of New York, 1777–1804* (Albany, N. Y., 1899–1914), V, 478–480; memorial of general officers to Congress, July 11, 1780, *PCC*, item 43, 259–263.

[73] Washington to the president of Congress, April 3, 1780, Fitzpatrick, ed., *Writings of Washington* (cf. n. 16), XVIII, 208–209; Parsons to Gates, Dec. 8, 1779, Papers of Horatio Gates, microfilm, arranged by dates, New York Historical Society, New York.

[74] Memorial of the general officers (read in Congress Sept. 18, 1779), *PCC*, item 41, VII, 259. Note the fact that the officers talk of their service as a "profession".

[75] Cf. Ramsay, *History of the Revolution of South Carolina* (cf. n. 2), II, 83–84, 93, 96–97.

[76] Actual investments do not seem to have been either common or very heavy. Parsons, in 1779, owned cash and certificates of about $ 20,000, see Hall, *Parsons* (cf. n. 59), 291. The matter seems to need more attention.

[77] Memorial of the general officers (read in Congress Sept. 18, 1779), *PCC*, item 41, VII, 259.

[78] Parsons to –, January 26, 1782, Dearborn Collection, bMS Am 1649.6 (153), Harvard University Library, Cambridge, Mass.

[79] Memorial of the general officers, July 11, 1780, *PCC*, item 43, 262.

[80] Cf. Elizabeth Cometti, "The Civil Servants of the Revolutionary Period", *PMHB*, LXXV (1951), 159–169.

[81] Knox, draft of a congratulatory address of the Massachusetts line to Governor John Hancock, 1780, Papers of Henry Knox, V, 97, Massachusetts Historical Society, Boston, Mass.

[82] Parsons to Washington, June 26, 1781, Hall, *Parsons* (cf. n. 59), 370–371.

[83] Governor Trumbull to Washington, July 9, 1781, *ib.*, 373.

[84] Parsons to Governor Trumbull, July 10 and 12, *ib.*, 375–376.

[85] Trumbull to Parsons, July 16, 1781, to Washington, July 17, 1781, *ib.*, 377–379.

[86] Parsons to Trumbull, July 26, 1781, *ib.*, 380–381.

[87] Petition of officers of the northern army, Sept. 13, 1778, *PCC*, item 41, VII, 195–204.

[88] Ira Allen, "History of Vermont", in *Records of the Governor and Council of the State of Vermont* (Montpellier, Vt., 1873–1880), II, 61–62.

[89] William Greene to John Hancock, May 3, 1781, Massachusetts Archives, CCIII, 283 (cf. n. 43).

[90] For general accounts of western Massachusetts during the Revolution see Lee N. Newcomer, *The Embattled Farmers: A Massachusetts Countryside in the American Revolution* (New York, 1953), and Robert J. Taylor, *Western Massachusetts in the Revolution* (Providence, R. I., 1954). My sketch is based on the following sources: memorial of the towns of Worcester County, April 4, 1781; committee of both houses, "address to the inhabitants of the Commonwealth", n. d., Massachusetts Archives, CXLII, 335, 285 (cf. n. 43); William Gordon to Edward Pope, June 7, 1782, Elisha Porter to Governor Hancock, June 18, 1782 (two letters), E. Pope to Governor Hancock, July 4, 1782, *ib.*, CCIV, 171, 160, 160½, 169; David Sewall to S. Adams, Oct. 10, 1783, Papers of Samuel Adams, Box 6 (cf. n. 17); Joseph Hawley to E. Wright, April 16, 178[2], Bancroft Collection, Papers of Joseph Hawley, New York Historical Society, New York, folder for the year 1787 [!]; same to Caleb Strong, June 7 and 24, 1782, *ib.*, Box 1.

[91] Gouverneur Morris, "To the inhabitants of America: Plan for Finances of the Country", draft, n. d., Papers of Gouverneur Morris, 819, fol. 6 r, Columbia University Library, New York.

[92] Timothy Pickering to Richard Peters, January 4, 1781, Papers of Timothy Pickering, V, 203, Massachusetts Historical Society, Boston, Mass.

[93] George R. Minot, *The History of the Insurrections in Massachusetts ...* (Worcester, Mass., 1788), 17. Minot, of course, is referring to Massachusetts.

[94] John Brooks to Knox, Sept. 8, 1782, Papers of Henry Knox, X, 13 (cf. n. 81). For the mission and its results see memorial of the officers of the Massachusetts line, July 1782, *ib.*, IX, 67; Brooks to Knox, Oct. 17, 1782, Samuel Osgood to Knox, Dec. 4, 1782, *ib.*, IX, 67, and X, 130–131; cf. the literature cited in n. 106.

[95] Rufus Putnam to the speakers of both houses Oct. 18, 1782, Papers of Samuel Adams, Box 6 (cf. n. 17).

[96] See Louise B. Dunbar, *A Study of 'Monarchical' Tendencies in the United States from 1776 to 1801*, repr. ed. (New York, 1971 [orig. publ. 1922]), 42.

[97] Alexander Hamilton, in March 1783 [!], was sure that the "soldiery would abandon their officers", Hamilton to Washington, March 25, 1783, as quoted by Richard H. Kohn, "The Inside History of the Newburgh Conspiracy: America and the Coup d'Etat", *WMQ*, 3d Ser., XXVII (1970), 187–220, 198.

[98] No author, no title, n. d., "Those who say that the Soldier does not receive an Equal reward ...", Papers of Samuel Adams, Box 6 (cf. n. 17).

[99] Mary G. Nye, ed., *Petitions for Grants of Lands, 1778–1811, State Papers of Vermont*, V (Brattleboro, Vt., 1939), 152–153, 153–154, 289–290.

[100] *Ib.*, 155, 244.

[101] Arnold to Schuyler, Nov. 30, 1778, and Febr. 8, 1779, Bancroft Collection, Schuyler Transcripts, 603, 709 (cf. n. 59); John Jay *et al.* to Governor Clinton, Febr. 3, 1779, Hall, *Parsons* (cf. n. 59), 283.

[102] Parsons to Clinton, Febr. 21, 1780, Hall, *Parsons* (cf. n. 59), 282.

[103] Petition of officers in the army for lands, June 16, 1783; *PCC*, item 42, VI, 65–71.

[104] Octavius Pickering, *Life of Timothy Pickering* (Boston, Mass., 1867–1873), I, 458–459.

[105] Edward Hand, Proposition for a Peace Establishment, two drafts, n. d.,

Papers of Edward Hand, II, 54 and 55, Pennsylvania Historical Society, Philadelphia; the quotations are from the second draft.

[106] For the Newburgh affair see Hatch, *Administration* (cf. n. 13), ch. 8; Merrill Jensen, *The New Nation: A History of the United States during the Confederation* (New York, 1950), 157–164; Forrest McDonald, *E Pluribus Unum: The Formation of the American Republic, 1776–1790* (Boston, 1965), 23–30; Kohn, "Inside History of the Newburgh Conspiracy" (cf. n. 97); Paul D. Nelson, "Horatio Gates at Newburgh 1783: A Misunderstood Role", *WMQ*, 3d Ser., XXIX (1972), 143–151, with a rebuttal by Richard H. Kohn, *ib.*, 151–158.

[107] The words are Pickering's: Pickering to Hogdon, April 6, 1783, Pickering, *Pickering* (cf. n. 104), I, 456.

[108] N. Fitch to G. Clinton, April 14, 1784, Hastings, ed., *Public Papers of George Clinton* (cf. n. 72), VIII, 137–138.

[109] Minot, *History* (cf. n. 93), 117–118.

[110] Higginbotham, *War* (cf. n. 8), 412–413.

[111] The relation of the army to the structure of late 18th-century American society was the most important topic of the discussion of this paper. I agree with Richard Buel, Jr. and Duncan J. MacLeod that both structures were related to each other. I just intend to show that the army as an extension of society (Buel) had to show the marks of just this society being, as it was, on the verge of moving from a post-feudal to a pre-"capitalist" stage of historical development. Nevertheless, I disagree with Erich Angermann's remark that the concept of the citizen in uniform came up with the French Revolution. The citizen army was a topic quite common in American propaganda; as to reality, the concept, still, is far from being secured in practice. That is just the reason why it is necessary to look back at the critical moments of the development of western culture in order to ask whether the right choices were taken at those times. As to Richard Buel's remark that, on lower levels, the actual everyday life of officers and men might have differed greatly from the picture given above, personal contact certainly also was of influence in shaping the officers' attitude and behavior. But this behavior would have had to acknowledge the bounds set by the framework as it is described in the text.

The American Revolution: The Triumph of a Delusion?

James H. Hutson

This paper will take as its point of departure that tour de force of recent American scholarship, Professor Bernard Bailyn's series of books on the ideological origins of the American Revolution.[1] Professor Bailyn's conclusions, that a heretofore undetected set of convictions – which he ascribes to the influence of British "opposition ideology" – triggered the American Revolution, I find convincing. What I wish to do is to examine those convictions from a perspective which he did not employ, that of psychology and social psychology, and to demonstrate that they are susceptible to an interpretation different from his own – an interpretation which may deepen our understanding of the American Revolution.

Professor Bailyn believes in taking men at their word, in assuming that they believe what they say, even if what they say appears to be bizarre or fantastic. Bailyn represents Americans as saying that the cause of the Revolution was the policy of the British ministers of state, who conducted "a constant, unremitted, uniform" conspiracy,[2] nurtured in corruption, to deprive them of their liberties, to enslave them, no less.[3] Historians have known for decades – as opponents of the Revolution declared at the time – that this notion was absurd.[4] The British ministries of the Revolutionary Era were shifting coalitions whose principal discernible goal was the preservation of power. How could reasonable people believe them capable of fiendish malevolence, cunningly concerted and sustained, year in, year out?

Reasonable people! No one has ever denied or questioned that Revolutionary Americans were reasonable people. To even suggest the contrary has been unthinkable. Thus, when American historians in the 1930s and 40s appraised the complaints of Revolutionary leaders that they were victims of a conspiracy to enslave them, they assumed that the leaders, being reasonable people, did not believe what they were saying and were spreading chimeras to inflame their less sophisticated countrymen and to enlist them in the controversy with Great Britain: cries of conspiracy were, in other words, dismissed as propaganda.

Professor Bailyn will have none of this. The fears which Revolutionary leaders professed were authentic, he asserts – "real fears, real anxieties." No less forcefully does he insist that Revolutionary leaders were "profoundly reasonable people."[5] The result is a paradox: the American Revolution was caused by profoundly irrational beliefs working on and through profoundly rational people. Bailyn resolves this problem by arguing that the conspiratorial conviction which caused the Revolution, when examined in the context of its own time and when considered as the product of an historical process, makes sense and is only apparently irrational.

Bailyn's thesis is familiar: a group of British Whig "opposition" writers and publicists in the age of Walpole, drawing for inspiration on the heroes of Commonwealth England, developed a theory of politics, which, though scorned in their own land, was immensely attractive to eighteenth-century Americans; "opposition" writers stressed the vulnerability of liberty to the aggressions of the holders of political power, operating through conspiracy and corruption; their apprehensions about conspiracies to subvert liberty were not, Bailyn claims, "neurotic fantasies but . . . realistic responses to the recent history and existing condition of public life in England";[6] these apprehensions infected Americans because the endemic political conflicts in the colonies between the executive and the legislative branches made them seem plausible; therefore, when the British began to administer the colonies with unaccustomed vigor at the end of the Seven Years' War, their actions were refracted through the prism of "opposition" ideology, which depicted them as lurid steps in a conspiracy to enslave the colonies; such an intolerable "design" was resisted in arms.

The most telling recent critiques of Bailyn's thesis have come from Professors Jack Greene and Richard Bushman. Both accept Bailyn's contention that in the years after 1763 Americans interpreted British actions in a conspiratorial framework. But neither find much evidence that "opposition" ideology produced this interpretation or that it was "determinative of the policital understanding" of Americans in the mid-eighteenth century.[7] Bushman, examining the literature of political conflict in Massachusetts between 1692 and 1741, finds that, although the "opposition" writers were known in the Bay Colony, their principal theme, the corruption of the legislature by the executive, was conspicuous by its virtual absence from the political dialogue. He concludes that in Massachusetts political problems were defined by parochial concerns rather than by "opposition" ideology.[8] Greene challenges Bailyn's account of the cirumstances which allegedly enabled the "opposition" ideology to take such a tenacious grip on the American mind: the pervasive political conflict in the colonies. According to Greene, in only three or four colonies was the political conflict intense enough to sear the "opposition" ideology into American consciousness. Elsewhere, he argues, "opposition" ideology, before 1763, can at best be considered supplemental to "the older tradition of the seventeenth-century opposition to the Stuarts."[9]

It is by no means certain, then, that "opposition" ideology caused the belief in the British conspiracy which burgeoned in America. The belief in a ministerial conspiracy to enslave was patently false – a delusion. Not just any delusion but a persecutory delusion, the prime symptom of the paranoid condition.[10] If the conspiratorial conviction is considered, not as a theme in intellectual history (as Professor Bailyn views it) but as a product of psychological processes, a different explanation of its causes – and, derivatively, of the causes of the American Revolution – may be obtained.

Bailyn himself entertained the possibility, if only fleetingly, that the flourishing of "opposition" ideology was a manifestation of a large scale paranoid disorder. Viewing the ideology from the perspective of one whom it buffeted and destroyed – Thomas Hutchinson – Bailyn pronounced it "morbid, pathological, paranoiac."[11] Other intellectual historians have had similar impressions: to Gordon Wood "opposition" ideology displayed a "paranoiac" mistrust of power; to Winthrop Jordan it appeared, in New England, at least, as "radical paranoia."[12] But these writers have not pursued these perceptions. The reasons for their reluctance are, I believe, both professional and patriotic.

First, the professional reasons. Intellectual historians are constrained from admitting that ideas under their examination are pathological, for once they concede this, they risk losing control of their subject matter to the psychologist; secondly, efforts to apply psychology to history in American scholarship have thus far been so unfortunate – the Freud-Bullitt biography of Woodrow Wilson is perhaps the most familiar fiasco – as to frighten off "reputable" scholars. Now, the patriotic reasons. Since the American nation is the product of the American Revolution, theories which discredit the Revolution seem to impugn the American experience. Was the Revolution caused by a pandemic of persecutory delusions? Then, the United States was conceived, not in liberty, as Lincoln would have it, but in madness, an idea which strikes most American historians as being more or less blasphemous. But there are even greater difficulties to ascribing the Revolution to a paranoid delusion. The most familiar theory of the etiology of paranoia is Freud's, formulated in 1911, that the disorder is a defense against homosexuality. To claim, therefore, that paranoia is the ideational engine driving the Revolution is to attribute it to a massive homosexual panic, a notion which appears to sink beneath blasphemy to obscenity.

179

Even though applying psychology to the American Revolution might yield results which appear tasteless to some and even though the participants in this symposium were extremely pessimistic about the power of psychology – or of any other discipline, for that matter – to explain episodes of collective emotion, I shall attempt a psychological interpretation of the coming of the Revolution. The first step is to examine the conviction that American Revolutionary leaders were "profoundly reasonable." In the scope of a short paper it is, of course, impossible to consider the leaders of all the colonies. A look at Massachusetts and a glance at Virginia must suffice. The leaders of Massachusetts were anything but reasonable men. James Otis, considered mad by some as early as 1760,[13] tottered on the edge of insanity throughout the decade. In 1771, a Massachusetts court declared him a "Lunatick" and sent him into confinement "bound hand and foot." A year earlier, drunk and distracted, he had bawled out to his former adversary, Thomas Hutchinson, that he was "cruelly persecuted."[14] The whig leader of Western Massachusetts, Joseph Hawley, was a victim of an hereditary mental disorder – apparently a manic-depressive psychosis with persecutory delusions – which "killed" his grandmother and caused his father to cut his throat with a razor in 1735. The malady overtook Hawley in 1760 – his biographer describes him as succumbing to a fit of "mild insanity" – recurred throughout the decade, and totally and permanently incapacitated him in 1776.[15] The one biographer who has undertaken a psychological study of Samuel Adams has found him "non-rational," "not entirely normal," "probably ... a neurotic; in any case nervously unstable." Adams is represented as being afflicted with a massive "inferiority complex". During the conflict with Great Britain he is said to have created "an imaginary world," which he constructed "through the principle of projection," the defense mechanism operative in paranoia.[16] The "inequalities" of John Adams' temper were conspicuous to his contemporaries. Benjamin Franklin, for example, believed that on occasion Adams was "absolutely out of his senses," while Jonathan Dayton claimed that he suffered from a "derangement of intellect" serious enough to disqualify him from public service.[17] Recent historians have pronounced Adams a "neurotic personality," have found him burdened with a "handful of vigorous complexes, from hypochondria to mild paranoia."[18] His latest biographer has revealed that he suffered three nervous "breakdowns" between 1771 and 1783.[19] Professor Bailyn himself, in 1962, described how Adams "became paranoiac" in the "intense heat of domestic politics."[20]

The Lees of Virginia, to whose political alliance with the Adamses some historians only half facetiously attribute the Revolution, were hardly models of rationality. Arthur Lee, in fact, presents a textbook case of paranoid symptomatology. His suspicions were pathological: "He has confidence in no body. He believes all Men selfish – And, no Man honest or sincere."[21] "His jealous disposition," wrote a contemporary, "led him to apprehend designs injurious to him in every one he dealt with."[22] He had "a Sick Mind," wrote another contemporary, "which is forever tormenting itself, with its Jealousies, Suspicions, and Fancies."[23] A letter Lee wrote to Samuel Adams of June 10, 1771, Professor Bailyn pronounced "perhaps the most paranoid ... in the entire literature of the American Revolution."[24] Like Joseph Hawley, Lee seems to have been plagued by problems which ran in his family. His sister, Alice Lee Shippen, her "imagination disorder'd," was forced into confinement in the Pennsylvania countryside during the Revolutionary period.[25] A favorite nephew, Francis Lightfoot Lee, went mad in the prime of life.[26] And his brothers, Richard Henry Lee included, do not appear to have entirely escaped the family affliction.

A brief look at the whig leadership in the most important hotbeds of anti-British sentiment reveals it to have been prone to emotional instability, predisposed to psychological problems, vulnerable to them under the goad of an appropriate precipitant. In his famous analysis of the Schreber case in 1911, Freud declared that the "strikingly prominent features in the causation of paranoia ... are social humiliations and slights."[27] Psychologists of all schools have endorsed this observation, so that today there is a consensus that the precipitant of the paranoid condition is any event which damages an individual's self-esteem.[28] The Stamp Act damaged America's self-esteem on a massive scale, by putting Americans on notice that they were not what they thought they deserved to be: full-fledged Englishmen. Professor Jack Greene has recently called attention to the powerful mimetic impulse which developed in colonial America during the eighteenth century, the passion of the colonists for imitating the culture and manners of England. Painfully aware of their own cultural inferiority vis-à-vis England, the colonial elite attempted to transcend it by identifying itself with the metropolis.[29] The part played by the Seven Years' War in this process has not, I believe, been fully recognized. Americans appeared to have considered that their contributions to the war effort – which they consistently depicted in heroic terms of spilling rivers of blood and exhausting their treasures[30] – entitled them to acknowledgment by the British of the equal status to which they aspired. But far from legitimating their aspirations, the experience of the Seven Year's War deflated them. The influx of British army officers and officials into the colonies to prosecute the war resulted, as Robert Weir has recently observed,[31] in the first large-scale commingling of the British and colonial elites. The superciliousness of the British toward the colonials, their refusal to treat them as anything like equals deeply wounded American self-esteem. Then came the Stamp Act, which by depriving the colonists of the fundamental rights of Englishmen to taxation by their representatives and trial by their peers, brutally announced that Americans were not authentic Englishmen. The act, therefore, was more than a public law. It was also an assault on the identities which the American elite had assumed, a rejection of them personally, and a relegation of them to a status of inferiority. As a blow to America's self-esteem, the Stamp Act served the psychological role of a precipitant and in its wake the paranoid delusions that Britain was conspiring to enslave Americans began to flourish.

John Adams illustrates the manner in which the Stamp Act precipitated delusions in an American leader who was predisposed to experience them. The paranoid condition seems always to have lain just below the surface of Adams' personality. In April 1759, for example, he confided to his diary that he "used to dread J[ames] O[tis] and B[enjamin] K[ent] because I suspected they laughed at me."[32] And in April 1764 he wrote his fiancée, Abigail Smith, of "some who would heartily rejoice to hear that both of Us [JA and his brother] were dead of Small Pox provided no others would be raised up in our stead to be a Terror to evil Doers."[33] In 1765 the Stamp Act is passed. Adams interprets it as aggression against him personally. "I have had Poverty to struggle with," he complained on December 18, 1765, "Envy and Jealousy and Malice of Enemies to encounter – no Friends, or but few to assist me, so that I have ... just become known ... when this execrable Project was set on foot for my Ruin as well as that of America in General."[34] And up wells the conviction of a malign conspiracy against the colonies. "There seems to be a direct and formal design on foot to enslave all America," Adams writes in his *Dissertation on the Canon and Feudal Law* (1765).[35]

The experience of Adams appears to have been repeated throughout the colonies in 1765. But going beyond a description of the interaction of precipitant and predisposition to establish the true "cause" of the paranoid disorder, in Adams and his contemporaries, is difficult for the historian, because there is no agreement among psychologists about the etiology of paranoia. Disciples of Freud still insist on the rectitude of the master's theory, that paranoia is a defense against homosexuality, but an impressive body of literature has grown up challenging it.[36] Other theories about the causes of paranoia range from deficiencies in role playing skills[37] to cognitive impairments[38] to contentions that paranoid symptomatology reflects "real" persecution inflicted on the victim during his nonage.[39] Advocates of these competing theories claim that verification can be obtained in the laboratory or in the psychiatric interview, but since neither facility is accessible to the historian, he must fall back to a position on which there is a consensus among psychologists (trusting that, unlike pre-Copernican cosmologists, the consensus to which he is assenting is correct).

The position on which there is virtual unanimity among psychologists is that the mechanism of symptom formation in paranoia is projection. "The role of projection in paranoid or paranoidally tinged disorders," writes the Freudian analyst Niederland, "is recognized virtually everywhere in our science today, in analytic as well as nonanalytic quarters."[40] From a different perspective Dr. David Shapiro writes that projection "is so central to our understanding of paranoid pathology and symptoms that it has almost come to define what is called 'paranoid' in psychiatry."[41] What is projection? It is the process by which internal feelings, impulses, or ideas, which are unacceptable to or repudiated by the ego, are attributed to external persons or objects; the attributes thus ascribed to external figures become, in turn, the substance of the attributor's delusions. Projection is called the "mirror-defense,"[42] because the external figure faithfully reflects the intolerable feelings of the attributor; "the patients' own inclinations," writes Dr. Lawrence Kolb, "are mirrored in the particular motives and intentions attributed to others."[43] In the case of the American Revolutionary leaders, the entity on which they projected their unacceptable feelings was the British ministry. By examining the delusions entertained about the ministry, we can open a window into the minds of the American leaders and obtain that "interior view" which Professor Bailyn sought by mastering the pamphlet literature of the Revolution.[44]

Considered as a product of projection, the delusion that the British ministry was trying to enslave America indicates that Americans were troubled by their own impulses to enslave or subjugate (in the broadest sense by their aggressive instincts). The problem of race, "white over black" as Winthrop Jordan calls it, is never far below the surface of any issue in American history. The Revolutionary period was no exception. "During the closing years of the colonial period," writes Benjamin Quarles, "abolitionist sentiment increasingly found its basis in the philosophical doctrines of the eighteenth-century Enlightenment."[45] Freedom and liberty tripped from every white man's tongue, trailed from every white man's pen. Yet before every white man's face were black slaves. The contrast between profession and practice was sharpened by the Stamp

Act, which, in denying Americans the identity they sought as Englishmen, demeaned them and seemed to suggest that they shared an inferiority with other groups on the North American continent – blacks, especially.[46] The merest suggestion that white Americans might, in some way, be associated with their black slaves seems to have increased for them the repugnance of slavery, which was, besides, a constant reproach to their professed ideals. The opposition to slavery accordingly intensified, finding its most eloquent voice in the religious leaders of the northern and middle colonies, but spreading as is well known, throughout the South. Slavery, declared Patrick Henry, was "repugnant to humanity ... inconsistent with the Bible, and destructive to liberty",[47] and statements no less emphatic can be quoted from Washington, Jefferson, Laurens, and other southern leaders.[48] Yet as unpalatable as slavery was to the Revolutionary leaders, they dared not disturb it, for as a South Carolinian wrote in 1774, its abolition would "complete the ruin of many American provinces."[49] The "solution" Americans found to the problem in the wake of the Stamp Act was to attribute slavery to the British ministry; a vivid example of the technique was Jefferson's celebrated philippic, deleted from the Declaration of Independence, which blamed the existence of American slavery on George III.

Treating the fears Americans entertained of the British ministry as products of projection may provide a solution to what J. H. Plumb has recently called "one of the greatest conundrums of American history," the fact that the men who rebelled from Britain in the name of freedom did not abolish slavery in their midst.[50] Psychologically, the American Revolutionary leaders abolished slavery twice; first, by expelling it from their psyches and attributing it to the British; next, by defeating it, now that it was identified as a British war aim, in battle. The struggle with Britain was so long, bloody, and exhausting that John Adams believed that a man could only engage in one revolution in a lifetime. Put in the terms in which Americans defined their Revolution, he was saying that a generation has energy enough for only one crusade against slavery. For slavery to be abolished in fact, a new generation of Americans, which had not spent its energies opposing it (no matter that it was a fight against a proxy) must mature and come forward, as it did in the nineteenth century.

The designs projectively imputed to the British ministry are susceptible to another interpretation, too. By the end of the Seven Years' War the American colonists, conscious of the exuberant growth of their population and economy, had become, as the tory George Rome put it, "intoxicated with their own importance."[51] It now appeared to Americans that they were the primary contributors to the strength of the British Empire, that, as the circumspect Dickinson wrote in 1765, "the foundations of the power and glory of Great Britain are laid in America."[52] It followed that if America separated from Britain, the latter could hardly survive. She "could not exist" without America, Richard Henry Lee declared in 1774; she would suffer "national Ruin," a "national Bankruptcy and a Revolution in favour of Arbitrary Power." If Britain lost America, it might be enslaved by being delivered up "weak & defenceless to its natural enemies," ending up, perhaps, as a "province of France."[53] Benjamin Franklin expressed the colonists' thinking on the matter when he wrote in 1767 that America "must become a great country, populous and mighty; and will, in less time than is generally conceived, be able to shake off any shackles that may be imposed on her, and perhaps place them on the imposer."[54] As if reading the Americans' minds, the French merchant, Joseph Mandrillon, stated the proposition best: "The New World, once our slave, but in large part peopled by our emigrants, will come in its turn to put us into chains. Its industry, strength and power will grow as ours diminish; the Old World will be subjugated by the New. . . ."[55]

The idea of America wresting independence from Britain — not to mention causing her enslavement — was totally unacceptable to the colonists, bound as they were to Britain by the symbolic leading strings of a child-mother relationship. In such a psychological context independence was equated with a betrayal of parents, with "PARRICIDE," as an indignant Briton reminded the colonists.[56] Independence, therefore, was "unthinkable," something which an early New York governor was "unwilling to name."[57] No accusation was more likely to inflame Americans than the charge that they were hankering after independence: "Nothing can be more wicked or a greater slander on the Whigs," wrote John Adams as Novanglus in 1775, "because there is not a man in the province, among the Whigs, nor ever was, who harbors a wish of that sort."[58] And yet it is obvious to the historian that the colonists were, in fact, aspiring toward independence. Occasionally, someone would let the cat out of the bag, as Samuel Adams did in 1769, when a tavern keeper reported him exhorting his companions to: "take up arms immediately and be free . . . the times were never better in Rome than when they had no king and were a free state."[59] But, as J. M. Bumsted has recently observed, the evidence is more frequently found in the passion and the persistence with which the independence-wish was denied, a conspicuous case of people protesting too much.[60] The Stamp Act, in signaling a British rejection of the identity to which Americans aspired, seems to have provoked the Americans to counter by rejecting Britain; that is, it quickened the impulse toward independence, the consequence of which Americans believed would be the enslavement, or something very much like it, of Britain. The feelings being unacceptable to Americans, they attributed them to the British, whom they represented as plotting to enslave them.

One other insight into the minds of American leaders can be obtained by looking into the mirror which the British ministry held up for their projections. David Shapiro attributes fears of being enslaved – he calls them "the threat of aggressive destruction or subjugation of will" – to the "unstable autonomy" of those who conceive them, by which he means individuals who are in constant fear of being overpowered by their own instincts, which fear they project outward.[61] What Gordon Wood calls the "obsession" of American leaders with "luxury, vice, and corruption,"[62] their exaggerated fear of succumbing to these ogres, suggests personalities with "unstable autonomy," a condition to which the inability of American leaders to obtain acknowledgment of their status as Englishmen must have contributed. Problems of personal autonomy – can we say, with Erik Erikson, identity? – seem also to be indicated by the projective content of American delusions.

Recently, the American psychiatrist, Morton Schatzman, a disciple of R. D. Laing, has proposed a theory of the causation of paranoia which does not presuppose the operation of projection. On the basis of a fresh interpretation of the Schreber case, Schatzman concludes that delusions are not fanciful creations of a defense mechanism but are authentic descriptions of traumatic conditions to which their victims were subjected during their upbringing. If a person claims that so-and-so is trying to enslave him, Schatzman believes he is recollecting early experiences in which he suffered "real" oppression. His theory affords the possibility of understanding the delusions of American leaders in terms of their childhoods.[63]

The study of childrearing in colonial America has only recently begun to engage the attention of scholars; therefore, little reliable information about the topic exists. The most popular current thesis seems to be that of Philip Greven, who, in a study of Andover, Massachusetts, argued that the first generation of settlers, by withholding land and other means of independent subsistence from their offsprings until a late age, forced them to be psychologically dependent (although it has never been clear to me why the parental manipulation Greven describes did not produce rebelliousness, instead). Greven conjectured that with the exhaustion of land the third generation parents could no longer impose deferential behavior on their children and that these, the American Revolutionary generation, became perforce independently disposed.[64] Greven's thesis has been corroborated, to some extent, by a recent article which claims that the theoretical foundations for parental autocracy were destroyed by the publication of Locke's *Thoughts Concerning Education* (1693); by the middle of the eighteenth century, it is argued, the "liberal" practices prescribed in Locke's volume produced a free spirited generation which could not brook subservience to Great Britain.[65]

There is more than a little evidence to suggest, however, that habits of patriarchalism were extremely pertinaceous in colonial America. In seeking the cause of the Revolution, Gordon Wood has pointed to a "social crisis within the ruling group";[66] although Wood does not specifically examine how childrearing might have contributed to this crisis, there is considerable evidence of familial conflict besetting the Revolutionary generation. Frequent complaints by parents of the rebelliousness and insubordination of their children[67] suggest that attempts to impose rigid patriarchal discipline were being made, but were being regarded as tyrannical. Moreover, many of the practices recommended by Locke – the daily plunging of small children into ice water, for example[68] – have the look of a form of torture no less traumatic than the devices which Schreber *père*, in the name of good posture, inflicted on his son. It appears, then, that Americans of the Revolutionary generation may have felt oppressed by their upbringing and could have reexperienced the oppression as slavery imposed by the British ministry.

Interpreting the delusions of American leaders by psychological methods gives us this reading of their "interior" condition: they were tormented by their enslavement of blacks and by their aspirations toward independence, and its ramifications; their personal autonomy may have been unstable; and they may have been deeply scarred by unpalatable childrearing techniques. These conditions prevailed in all the colonies and occurred in individuals singly or in combination; when a powerful precipitant like the Stamp Act, which devastated the colonists' quest for British identity, interacted with them, delusions of persecution, of enslavement, were created by the process of projection. The language in which the delusions were articulated was the "opposition" ideology, which was one of the several intellectual systems familiar to Americans and which, because of its emphasis on conspiracy, was peculiarly compatible with the substance of their concerns. The "opposition" ideology, in other words, served to rationalize these concerns.

After the Stamp Act, the delusions of American leaders spread through the mass of American society so quickly as to appear to be generated spontaneously. The spread of delusions of persecution through groups of people has long been familiar to psychologists; "paranoid reactions", write Slater and Roth, "show a particular tendency to spread by psychological contagion."[69] The phenomenon of diffusion of delusions is called, in the psychological literature, "*folie à deux*"; the spread of delusions on a massive scale, recent writers suggest, should be called "*folie collective.*"[70] *Folie à deux* means "communicated insanity" or "socially shared psychopathology," but such definitions are misleading to the extent that they suggest that all who harbor contagious delusions are deranged. L. S. Penrose corrects such a misapprehension by pointing out that "an erroneous or irrational idea ... may be held by all or a great majority of the members of a group without making them individually of disordered mind." It is a "curious paradox," adds Penrose, that the "capacity to share the delusions of the crowd is a sign of individual health"; the mentally ill, he reminds us, are always "out of touch" with the community at large.[71] Thus, the fact that large numbers of Revolutionary Americans shared a delusion about the British ministry does not compel us to assume that we are dealing with a population of lunatics.

Folie à deux comes into being through "the process of suggestion."[72] "Suggestion," according to an authority, "is a process of communication resulting in the acceptance with conviction of the communicated proposition in the absence of logically adequate grounds for its acceptance."[73] The literature on suggestion states that its successful operation depends on at least three conditions: lack of knowledge about, as well as of standards by which to judge, the propositions in regard to which suggestion is made; "the impressive character of the source from which the suggested proposition is communicated"; and "a strong disposition in the subject to fit observations into a pre-existing mental context."[74]

Each of these conditions obtained in the American colonies in the 1760s and 1770s. It is easy to overestimate the colonists' knowledge of British politics. Information from Britain reaching the seaport towns was, at best, five or six weeks late. The great majority of Americans – up to 90 percent – did not, however, live in seaports but in the isolation of farms and small villages. For them, accurate information about what was happening in British political circles was virtually nonexistent. There was need, a minister in Danbury, Conn., wrote, "to enlighten the people of a country town not under the best advantages for information from newspapers and other pieces wrote upon the controversy."[75] The great bulk of Americans shared the difficulties of this minister and his parishioners. Successive British ministries did not help matters, for they made no attempt to inform the American public about the motives, often reasonable enough, for their actions. The conception of government's role in eighteenth-century Britain simply did not include explaining programs to the public – least of all to a colonial public[76] – and, therefore, there was deep ignorance in America about British intentions. There was, in other words, no authoritative explanation of British politics to compete with the delusive, distorted version being offered by whig leaders in America. Because of the esteem in which the majority of Americans held these leaders, it was their version which was accepted; put another way, the principle of "prestige suggestion" came into operation, by which the prestige of the suggestor obtained credence for his suggestion.

Ordinary Americans were also receptive to the view of the British as conspirators, because this view satisfied their psychological needs. In studying the function of opinions, scholars have found that in certain circumstances they serve the end of "externalization." Externalization is the process by which an idea is espoused because it solves, or at least alleviates, an "unresolved inner problem."[77] It appears that many Americans espoused the notion that Britain was trying to enslave them because they were just as troubled as their leaders by their inner feelings about slavery, about independence and its ramifications, and about their uncertain autonomy and perceived in the ideas about slavery projectively propagated by their leaders solutions to their own problems.

Another reason why Americans may have been receptive to paranoid delusions derives from discoveries of psychologists about the relationship of paranoia and movement. Several writers have found that the uprooted – immigrants, refugees, displaced persons, people who move from community to community – are particularly susceptible to paranoid delusions.[78] Summarizing the literature on the subject, the Norwegian psychiatrist Retterstöl states that "change of environment appears to constitute one of the more important insecurity-provoking factors with regard to the outbreak and development of the paranoid psychosis."[79] Since Revolutionary America consisted of a nation of movers – both immigrants from abroad and internal migrants – it may have been peculiarly susceptible, on that account, to a mass delusion.[80]

Finally, Revolutionary Americans may have been susceptible to delusions of persecution because of the acute economic distress which afflicted their society. In 1763 and again in 1772 the American colonies suffered economic "depressions," caused by international credit crises.[81] Mass economic dislocation has frequently produced mass persecutory delusions and it seems more than coincidental that the two phenomena occurred simultaneously in America in the 1760s and 1770s.

If the conviction that the British ministry was conspiring to enslave America is considered as a delusion explicable by the principles of psychology rather than a theme in intellectual history, does the American Revolution, which Professor Bailyn attributed to the force of that conviction, become a bizarre, singular episode in American history? Or in world history? By no means. At few periods during modern history has Europe been entirely free of mass persecutory delusions: the witch craze of the sixteenth and seventeenth centuries;[82] the recurrent fears of Catholic plots in seventeenth- and eighteenth-century England, one of which exploded into the Gordon Riots of 1780;[83] the Great Fear of 1789 in France, whose resemblance to the fear preceding the American Revolution is, in many ways, so remarkable;[84] the mass fears in both France and Germany during the Revolutions of 1848;[85] and the tragic delusions in Germany in the 1930s.

Mass delusions of persecution have not been strangers to the United States either, however. They have, in fact, been so common in American history that Richard Hofstadter could write a celebrated book on *The Paranoid Style in American Politics*.[86] In the 1790s many Americans felt they were the objects of a malign conspiracy managed by the so-called Bavarian Illuminati and hardly a decade afterward passed without the flourishing of widespread fears that evil conspirators were undermining the fabric of American life: Masons, Catholics, Wall Street Bankers, Jews, Communists, etc. The British ministry was a charter member in this company. Mass delusions predated the Revolution, however. "One confessing witch, for example, reported that a gathering of 'about six score' witches in Salem village had decided to 'pull down the Kingdom of Christ and set up the Devil's Kingdom.'"[87] Substitute British ministry for six score witches and this statement from 1692 would be interchangeable with many of those in the 1760s and 1770s. Whatever else Salem witchcraft was, it was a mass persecutory delusion.[88] The Great Awakening was many things, too, but with its hysterical emphasis on the aggressive inroads of Satan on Christian America it also partook of a mass delusion.

Delusions, to appropriate a famous statement of the 1960s, are as American as cherry pie. It should not be surprising (or scandalous), then, if the event which founded the American nation was the product of a delusion.

Notes

[1] Bernard Bailyn, ed., *Pamphlets of the American Revolution 1750–1776*, (Cambridge, Mass., 1965); *id.*, *The Ideological Origins of the American Revolution* (Cambridge, Mass., 1967); *id.*, *The Origins of American Politics* (Cambridge, Mass., 1968); *id.*, *The Ordeal of Thomas Hutchinson* (Cambridge, Mass., 1974).

[2] *Id.*, *Thomas Hutchinson* (cf. n. 1), 206.

[3] *Id.*, *Ideological Origins* (cf. n. 1), ix; *Id.*, *Origins of American Politics* (cf. n. 1), 11, 95.

[4] Ian Christie, for example, pronounces it "a chimera". Bailyn, *Ideological Origins* (cf. n. 1), 149.

[5] *Ib.*, ix, 18.

[6] *Id.*, *Origins of American Politics* (cf. n. 1), 53.

[7] *Ib.*, 56. Gerald Stourzh, *Alexander Hamilton and the Idea of Republican Government* (Stanford, Cal, 1970), 36, 133 ff., also disputes Bailyn's broad claims on behalf of "opposition" ideology; he calls attention rather to the influence of "an empirical science of international politics that flourished in the epoch between Machiavelli and the French Revolution," an important practitioner of which was Montesquieu.

[8] Richard Bushman, "Corruption and Power in Provincial America", in *The Development of a Revolutionary Mentality*, Library of Congress Symposia on the American Revolution [1] (Washington, D. C., 1972), 63–91.

[9] Jack P. Greene, "Political Mimesis: A Consideration of the Historical and Cultural Roots of Legislative Behavior in the British Colonies in the Eighteenth Century", *AHR*, LXXV (1969–1970), 337–60, here 359.

[10] In this paper the terms "paranoid condition", "paranoid disorder", and "paranoia" are used interchangeably, as a literary device to avoid repetition. I am fully aware that paranoia is not properly a generic term, but a specific clinical entity. American Psychiatric Association, *Diagnostic and Statistical Manual of Mental Disorders*, 2nd ed. (Washington, D. C., 1968), 37–38.

[11] Bailyn, *Thomas Hutchinson* (cf. n. 1), 2.

[12] Gordon S. Wood, *The Creation of the American Republic, 1776–1787* (Chapel Hill, N. C., 1969), 17; Winthrop D. Jordan, *White over Black: American Attitudes toward the Negro, 1550–1812* (Chapel Hill, N. C., 1968), 292.

[13] John C. Miller, *Sam Adams: Pioneer in Propaganda* (Stanford, Cal., 1960), 96.

[14] Clifford K. Shipton, *Biographical Sketches of Those Who Attended Harvard College in the Classes 1741–1745, with Biographical and Other Notes*, Sibley's Harvard Graduates, XI (Boston, 1960), 281–283.

[15] E. Francis Brown, *Joseph Hawley: Colonial Radical* (New York, 1931), 94–95, 171.

[16] Ralph V. Harlow, *Samuel Adams: Promoter of the American Revolution*, 2nd ed. (New York, 1975), 38–39, 64–65, 118, 170–171.

[17] Benjamin Franklin to Robert Livingston, July 22, 1783, Albert H. Smyth, ed., *The Writings of Benjamin Franklin*, 10 vols. (New York, 1907), IX, 62; the Dayton quotation is from Alexander de Conde, *The Quasi-War* (New York, 1966), 291.

191

[18] Richard B. Morris, *The Peacemakers* (New York, 1965), 192; Page Smith, *John Adams* (Garden City, N. Y., 1962), I, 71.

[19] Peter Shaw, *The Character of John Adams* (Chapel Hill, N. C., 1976), 64–66, 150–152, 189–191.

[20] Bernard Bailyn, "Butterfield's Adams: Notes for a Sketch", *WMQ*, 3rd Ser., XIX (1962), 252.

[21] L. H. Butterfield, ed., *Diary and Autobiography of John Adams*, 4 vols. (Cambridge, Mass., 1961), II, 347.

[22] "Silas Deane's Narrative Read before Congress, [Dec. 1778]," The Deane Papers, 5 vols. (New York Historical Society, *Collections*, XIX–XXIII, for the years 1886–1890 [New York, 1887–1891]), IV, 175.

[23] Quoted in H. James Henderson, "Congressional Factionalism", *WMQ*, 3rd Ser., XXVII (1970), 249.

[24] Bailyn, *Thomas Hutchinson* (cf. n. 1), 193 n.

[25] Ethel Armes, ed., *Nancy Shippen: Her Journal Book ...* (Philadelphia, 1935), 179–180, 195, 208, 215, 218, *passim.*

[26] Robert S. Gamble, *Sully: The Biography of a House* (Chantilly, Va., 1973), 61–72.

[27] James Strachey, ed., *The Standard Edition of the Complete Psychological Works of Sigmund Freud*, XII (London, 1953), 60.

[28] As Slater and Roth put it: "psychogenic precipitants are also important, and these are most often of the type that provide an assault on the patient's self esteem." Eliot Slater and Martin Roth, *Clinical Psychiatry*, 3rd ed. (London, 1969), 148–149.

[29] Jack P. Greene, "Search for Identity: An Interpretation of the Meaning of Selected Patterns of Social Responses in Eighteenth-Century America", *JSH*, III (1969–1970), 190–220.

[30] See Edwin G. Burrows and Michael Wallace, "The American Revolution: The Ideology and Psychology of National Liberation", *Perspectives in American History*, VI (1972), 192, 202.

[31] Robert M. Weir, "Who Shall Rule at Home: The American Revolution as a Crisis of Legitimacy for the Colonial Elite", *Journal of Interdisciplinary History* (forthcoming).

[32] Butterfield, ed., *Diary of John Adams* (cf. n. 21), I, 83.

[33] L. H. Butterfield, ed., *Adams Family Correspondence* (4 vols., Cambridge, Mass., 1963–1973), I, 23.

[34] Butterfield, ed., *Diary of John Adams* (cf. n. 21), I, 264–265.

[35] Charles Francis Adams, ed., *The Works of John Adams,* reprint ed. (New York, 1969), III, 464.

[36] For a defense of the Freudian theory, see Anthony C. Carr, "Observations on Paranoia and Their Relationship to the Schreber Case", in William G. Niederland, ed., *The Schreber Case* (New York, 1974), 159–162; for a summary of the literature challenging Freud's interpretation, see David D. Swanson *et al., The Paranoid* (Boston, 1970), 261–265.

[37] Norman Cameron and Ann Magaret, *Behavior Pathology* (Boston, 1951), 406–407.

[38] For this and other theories about the causation of paranoia, see Swanson *et al., The Paranoid* (cf. n. 36), 268 ff.

[39] Morton Schatzman, *Soul Murder* (New York, 1974).

[40] William G. Niederland, "Paranoia: Theory and Practice", *Psychiatry and Social Science Review* (Dec. 8, 1970), 4.

[41] David Shapiro, *Neurotic Styles* (New York, 1965), 68.

[42] Henry P. Laughlin, *The Ego and Its Defenses* (New York, 1970), 221, 226–227.

[43] Lawrence C. Kolb, *Noyes' Modern Clinical Psychiatry*, 7th ed. (Philadelphia, 1968), 404.

[44] Bailyn, *Ideological Origins* (cf. n. 1), vi.

[45] Benjamin Quarles, *The Negro in the American Revolution* (Chapel Hill, N. C., 1961), 33.

[46] Greene, "Search for Identity" (cf. n. 29), 191n; Burrows and Wallace, "The American Revolution" (cf. n. 30), 280.

[47] Quoted in Quarles, *The Negro in the American Revolution* (cf. n. 45), 35.

[48] Wrote George Washington to Robert Morris, Apr. 12, 1786: "There is not a man living who wishes more sincerely than I do, to see a plan adopted for a gradual abolition of it", *ib.*, 187. "I have long deplored the wretched State of these men", John Laurens declared to his father, Feb. 2, 1778, "the bloody wars excited in Africa to furnish America with Slaves. The Groans of despairing Multitudes toiling for the Luxuries of Merciless Tyrants". Replied Henry Laurens on Feb. 6, 1778: "this by no means intimates that I am an Advocate for Slavery – you know I am not". Laurens Papers, University of South Carolina, Columbia, S. C.

[49] Bailyn, *Ideological Origins* (cf. n. 1), 236.

[50] J. H. Plumb, review of Edmund S. Morgan's *American Slavery, American Freedom*, in *New York Review of Books* (Nov. 27, 1975).

[51] Burrows and Wallace, "American Revolution" (cf. n. 30), 221.

[52] Bailyn, ed., *Pamphlets* (cf. n. 1), 687.

[53] *LMCC*, I, 3; John Adams to Edmund Jenings, July 18, 1780, Adams Papers microfilm, Reel 352. All references to the Adams Papers are to the microfilm edition published by the Massachusetts Historical Society, Boston, which owns the originals. John Adams to Henry Laurens, Dec. 8, 1778, *ib.*, Reel 93; the Continental Congress to the Inhabitants of Great Britain, July 8, 1775, in James H. Hutson, ed., *A Decent Respect to the Opinions of Mankind* (Washington, D. C., 1976), 108; John Wendell to Benjamin Franklin, Oct. 30, 1777, Franklin Papers, American Philosophical Society, Philadelphia.

[54] To Lord Kames, Apr. 11, 1767, Smyth, ed., *Writings of Franklin* (cf. n. 17), V, 21.

[55] Quoted in R. R. Palmer, "The Impact of the American Revolution Abroad", in *The Impact of the American Revolution Abroad*, Library of Congress Symposia on the American Revolution [4] (Washington, D. C., 1976), 8.

[56] Burrows and Wallace, "American Revolution" (cf. n. 30), 190.

[57] Bailyn, *Ideological Origins* (cf. n. 1), 118n.

[58] Quoted in Merrill Jensen, *The Founding of a Nation: A History of the American Revolution, 1763–1776* (New York, 1968), 514.

[59] Bailyn, *Thomas Hutchinson* (cf. n. 1), 127.

[60] J. M. Bumsted, "'Things in the Womb of Time': Ideas of American Independence, 1633 to 1763", *WMQ*, 3rd. Ser., XXXI (1974), 533–564.

[61] Shapiro, *Neurotic Styles* (cf. n. 41), 80–84.

[62] Wood, *Creation of the American Republic* (cf. n. 12), 113.

[63] Schatzman, *Soul Murder* (cf. n. 39).

[64] Philip J. Greven, Jr., *Four Generations: Population, Land, and Family in Colonial Andover, Massachusetts* (Ithaca, N. Y., 1970), 280–282.

[65] Burrows and Wallace, "American Revolution" (cf. n. 30), 255–267.

[66] Gordon S. Wood, "Rhetoric and Reality in the American Revolution", *WMQ*, 3rd Ser., XXIII (1966), 27.

[67] Burrows and Wallace, "American Revolution" (cf. n. 30), 266.

[68] Mary Cable, *The Little Darlings* (New York, 1975), 53.

[69] Slater and Roth, *Clinical Psychiatry* (cf. n. 28), 149.

[70] Two recent articles on *folie à deux* are: Kenneth Dewhurst and John Todd, "The Psychosis of Association – Folie À Deux", *The Journal of Nervous and Mental Disease*, CXXIV (Nov. 1956), 451–459, and Ernest M. Gruenberg, "Socially Shared Psychopathology", in Alexander H. Leighton *et al.*, eds., *Explorations in Social Psychiatry* (New York, 1957), 201–229. The term *"folie collective"* is Dewhurst and Todd's.

[71] L. S. Penrose, *On the Objective Study of Crowd Behavior* (London, 1952), 59.

[72] Dewhurst and Todd, "The Psychosis of Association" (cf. n. 70), 456.

[73] William McDougall, *An Introduction to Social Psychology*, 29th ed. (London, 1940), 83.

[74] *Ib.*; Kurt and Gladys Lang, *Collective Dynamics* (New York, 1961), 222.

[75] Bailyn, *Ideological Origins* (cf. n. 1), 129.

[76] *Id., Origins of American Politics* (cf. n. 1), 101–102.

[77] M. Brewster Smith, *et al.*, *Opinion and Personality* (New York, 1956), 43.

[78] Libuse Tyhurst, "Displacement and Migration", *American Journal of Psychiatry*, CVII (1951), 561–568; Neil A. Dayton, *New Facts on Mental Disorders: Study of 89,190 Cases* (Springfield, Ill., 1940), chapter 9; F. F. Kino, "Aliens' Paranoid Reactions", cited in Dewhurst and Todd, "The Psychosis of Association" (cf. n. 70), 453.

[79] Nils Retterstöl, *Paranoid and Paranoiac Psychoses* (Oslo, 1966), 127.

[80] In this context, Greven's description of the impact of the Great Awakening on the residents of Andover, Mass., is most provocative: Andover was immune to the Awakening, but those Andover citizens who moved to other towns were caught up in it and became New Lights. If a religious revival is considered as a mass delusion, Greven's evidence supports the psychologists who see a connection between mobility and susceptibility to delusion, Greven, *Colonial Andover* (cf. n. 64), 279.

[81] Marc Egnal and Joseph A. Ernst, "An Economic Interpretation of the American Revolution", *WMQ*, 3rd Ser., XXIX (1972), 17, 28.

[82] See H. R. Trevor-Roper, *The Crisis of the Seventeenth Century* (New York, 1968), 90–192.

[83] *Ib.*, 165.

[84] Georges Lefèbvre, *The Great Fear of 1789* (New York, 1973).

[85] *Ib.*, 54–55; the fear in Germany in 1848 was mentioned by Erich Angermann.

[86] Richard Hofstadter, *The Paranoid Style in American Politics, and Other Essays* (New York, 1965).

[87] Quoted from Paul Boyer and Stephen Nissenbaum, *Salem Possessed: The Social Origins of Witchcraft* (Cambridge, Mass., 1974), 188.

[88] Write Slater and Roth, *Clinical Psychiatry* (cf. n. 28), 149: "the spread by contagion of delusional ideas may, however, take place on a much larger scale. In primitive communities whole villages have come to be dominated by, for example, a belief that they were subject to machinations of witches".

Notes on Participants

Erich Angermann, Professor of Anglo-American History at the University of Cologne (1963), was born in 1927 in Chemnitz, Saxony; Dr. phil. (1952) and Habilitation (1961) at the University of Munich, visiting professor at St. Antony's College, Oxford (1970–71). Author of *Robert von Mohl (1799–1875): Leben und Werk eines altliberalen Staatsgelehrten*, Politica, VIII (Neuwied, 1962); "Ständische Rechtstraditionen in der amerikanischen Unabhängigkeitserklärung," *Historische Zeitschrift*, CC (1965); *Die Vereinigten Staaten von Amerika*, dtv-Weltgeschichte des 20. Jahrhunderts, VII (Munich, 4th ed. 1975 [1st ed. 1966]); "Early German Constitutionalism and the American Model," XIVth International Congress of Historical Sciences (San Francisco, Cal., 1975), and other publications; co-editor of (with Günter Kahle) *Handbuch der Amerikanischen Geschichte*, 2 vols. (forthcoming).

John Brooke, editor of *The Yale Edition of Horace Walpole's Memoirs* (1975), was born in 1920; he has served as senior editor of the Royal Commission on Historical Manuscripts, London (1964), and is member of the advisory committees of *The Yale Edition of Horace Walpole's Correspondence*, *The Writings and Speeches of Edmund Burke*, and *The Yale Edition of the Private Papers of James Boswell*. Author of *The Chatham Administration, 1766–1768* (London, 1956); *King George III* (London, 1972); co-author of (with Sir Lewis Namier) *The History of Parliament: The House of Commons*, 3 vols. (London, 1964); *Charles Townshend* (London, 1964).

Richard Buel, Jr., Professor of History at Wesleyan University, Middletown, Conn. (1962), was born in 1933 in Morristown, N. J., received his Ph. D. from Harvard University (1962), and is associate editor of *History and Theory* (1970); he held ACLS (1966–7, 1974–5), Charles Warren (1966–7) and National Endowment of the Humanities Fellowships (1971–2). Author of "Democracy and the American Revolution: A Frame of Reference," *WMQ*, 3d Ser., XXI (1964); *Securing the Revolution: Ideology in American Politics, 1789–1815* (Ithaca, N. Y., 1972), and other publications.

Edward Countryman, Lecturer in History at the University of Warwick, Coventry, England, received his Ph. D. from Cornell University, Ithaca, N. Y. (1971), and was formerly lecturer at the University of Canterbury, New Zealand. Author of "The Problem of the Early American Crowd," *Journal of American Studies*, VII (1973); "'Out of the Bounds of the Law': Northern Land Rioters in the 18th Century," in Alfred Young, ed., *The American Revolution* (DeKalb, Ill., 1976); "Consolidating Power in Revolutionary America: The Case of New York, 1775–1783," *Journal of Interdisciplinary History*, VI (1976).

Horst Dippel, born in 1942 in Düren, Rhineland, holds a fellowship of the Deutsche Forschungsgemeinschaft (1976); he received his Dr. phil. from the University of Cologne (1970) and was subsequently associated with the Institut für Europäische Geschichte Mainz (1970), the Max Planck-Institut für Geschichte at Göttingen (1972), the Historische Seminar der Universität Hamburg (1973), and the Deutsche Historische Institut Paris (1975). Author of *Deutschland und die amerikanische Revolution: Sozialgeschichtliche Untersuchung zum politischen Bewußtsein im ausgehenden 18. Jahrhundert* ([Ph. D. diss.] Cologne, 1972, English translation forthcoming); "Die Theorie der bürgerlichen Gesellschaft bei Benjamin Franklin," *Historische Zeitschrift,* CCXX (1975); "Benjamin Franklin" and "Thomas Paine", in Kurt Fassmann, ed., *Die Großen der Weltgeschichte,* VI (Zurich, 1975); *Americana Germanica, 1700–1800: Bibliographie deutscher Amerikaliteratur,* Amerikastudien/American Studies. Eine Schriftenreihe, XLIV (Stuttgart, 1976), part of the dissertation.

Joseph A. Ernst, Professor of History at York University, Toronto (1968), was born in 1931 in Brooklyn, N. Y., and received his Ph. D. from the University of Wisconsin (1962) as a student of Merrill Jensen's. He is the author of such recent publications as *Money and Politics in America, 1755–1775: A Study in the Currency Act of 1764 and the Political Economy of Revolution* (Chapel Hill, N. C., 1973); and co-author of (with Marc Egnal) "An Economic Interpretation of the American Revolution," *WMQ,* 3d Ser., XXIX (1972); and (with H. Roy Merrens) "'Camden's turrets pierce the skies!': The Urban Process in the Southern Colonies during the Eighteenth Century," *ib.,* XXX (1973).

Claude B. Fohlen, Professor of North American History at the Sorbonne, Paris (1967), was born in 1922 in Mulhouse, France, and received his Docteur ès Lettres in 1954; he was formerly at the University of Besançon (1955) and visiting professor at Yale, Harvard, and Stanford Universities and the University of California at Berkeley. He is author of *L' Amérique Anglo-Saxonne de 1815 à nos jours,* Nouvelle Clio, XLIII (Paris, 1965, 2nd ed. 1969); *La société américaine 1865–1970,* Sociétés Contemporaines, IV (Paris, 1973); *Les Noirs aux Etats-Unis,* Que sais-je?, 1191 (Paris, 5th ed. 1975); "The Impact of the American Revolution on France," in *The Impact of the American Revolution Abroad,* Library of Congress Symposia on the American Revolution [4] (Washington, D. C., 1976); and other publications.

Marie-Luise Frings, assistant at the Anglo-Amerikanische Abteilung in Cologne, is a native of Aix-la-Chapelle; she has just received her Dr. phil. from the University of Cologne (1976) with an as yet unpublished thesis on Henry Clay's "American System" and the sectional controversy, 1815–1829.

Hans Rudolf Guggisberg, Professor of History at the University of Basel, Switzerland (1969), was born in 1930 in Berlin, received his Dr. phil. at Basel (1956), and taught at various universities (Vanderbilt and Columbia, 1961–2, 1966; Cologne, 1966–7; Free University of Berlin, 1967–9); he held fellowships at Yale (1960–61) and the Institute for Advanced Study at Princeton (1974 to 1975). Among other publications in both European and American intellectual and religious history, he is author of *Sebastian Castellio im Urteil seiner Nachwelt vom Späthumanismus bis zur Aufklärung*, Basler Beiträge zur Geschichtswissenschaft, LVII (Basel and Stuttgart, 1956); *Das europäische Mittelalter im amerikanischen Geschichtsdenken des 19. und des frühen 20. Jahrhunderts, ib.*, XCII (1964); *Alte und Neue Welt in historischer Perspektive: Sieben Studien zum amerikanischen Geschichts- und Selbstverständnis* (Bern and Frankfurt, 1973); and *Geschichte der USA*, 2 vols., Urban-Taschenbücher, CCIX–CCX (Stuttgart, 1975).

Dirk Hoerder, associated with the John F. Kennedy-Institut at the Free University of Berlin, was born in 1943 in Eutin, received his Dr. phil. from the Free University of Berlin (1971), and held Kennedy Memorial and Charles Warren Fellowships at Harvard University (1973–75). He is author of *People and Mobs: Crowd Action in Massachusetts during the American Revolution, 1763–1780* ([Ph. D. diss.] Berlin, 1971); *Society and Government, 1760–1780: The Power Structure in Massachusetts Townships* (Berlin, 1972); and "Boston Leaders and Boston Crowds, 1765–1776," in Alfred F. Young, ed., *The American Revolution* (DeKalb, Ill., 1976); "Crowd Action in Revolutionary Massachusetts, 1765–1780," in Charles Tilly and Edward Shorter, eds., *Studies in Social Discontinuity* (forthcoming autumn 1976).

James H. Hutson, Coordinator, American Revolution Bicentennial Program, Library of Congress, Washington, D. C. (1972), was born in 1937 in Bridgeport, W. Va., and received his Ph. D. from Yale University (1964); formerly he served as assistant editor of the *Papers of Benjamin Franklin* (1963) and editor of publications at the Institute of Early American History and Culture (1969). He is author of *Pennsylvania Politics, 1746–1770* (Princeton, N. J., 1972), "Benjamin Franklin and the Parliamentary Grant for 1758," *WMQ*, 3d Ser., X (1966), and other publications, as well as co-editor of (with Stephen G. Kurtz) *Essays on the American Revolution* (Chapel Hill, N. C., 1973).

Barbara Karsky, a native of Baltimore, Md., is teaching American History and civilization as Maître Assistant at the University of Paris VII; she received a Doctorat du 3e cycle from the Sorbonne and is now working on a thesis for a Doctorat d'Etat on "Protest and Rebellion: Agrarian Radicalism in the Early National Period". She published "L'Abolition de l'Esclavage aux Etats-Unis et l'Opinion Française," *Revue d'Histoire Moderne* (Dec., 1974).

Norbert Kilian, teacher of history and English, was born in 1942 in Königsberg; he was an assistant at the Anglo-Amerikanische Abteilung in Cologne until 1975 and is working on a thesis on the significance of the British Empire in American radical thought, 1763–1776.

Gerhard Kollmann, teacher of history and German near Cologne, was born in 1943; he received his Dr. phil. from the University of Cologne with an as yet unpublished thesis "Revolution und Kontinuität: Eine Untersuchung der Pläne und Ansätze zur Organisation der Gebiete zwischen Appalachen und Mississippi, 1774–1784" (1974).

Zofia Libiszowska, Professor of Modern History at the University of Lodz, received her doctor's degree from the University of Lodz in 1950; she is author of *Opinia poleska wobec Rewolucij Amerykánskiej w XVIII vieku* (Lodz-Wroclaw, 1962); *Misja polska w Londynie, 1769–1795* (Lodz-Wroclaw, 1967); and *Francja Encyklopedýstów* (Warsaw, 1973).

Duncan J. MacLeod, Fellow of St. Catherine's College, Oxford, and University Lecturer in American History (1972), received his Ph. D. from the University of Cambridge and was formerly Lecturer in American History at University College, London (1968). He is author of *Slavery, Race and the American Revolution* (Cambridge, 1974).

Jackson Turner Main, Professor of History at the State University of New York at Stony Brook, N. Y. (1966), was born in 1917 in Chicago; he received his Ph. D. from the University of Wisconsin (1949) and taught, among other institutions, at Stanford University and the University of Maryland. He is author of *The Antifederalists: Critics of the Constitution, 1781–1788* (Chapel Hill, N. C., 1961); *The Social Structure of Revolutionary America* (Princeton, N. J., 1965); *The Upper House in Revolutionary America, 1763–1788* (Madison, Wis., 1967); *Political Parties before the Constitution* (Chapel Hill, N. C., 1973); *The Sovereign States, 1775–1783* (New York, 1973), and other publications.

Günter Moltmann, Professor of History at the University of Hamburg (1967), was born in 1926 in Hamburg, received his Dr. phil. from the University of Hamburg (1956), and was formerly both a Professor of History and Political Education at the Teachers' Academy at Bielefeld and a Lecturer in American History at the University of Hamburg (1961); he was an ACLS Fellow at the University of Chicago (1965–6), guest professor at Indiana University, Bloomington (1970–71), and a Charles Warren Fellow at Harvard University (1973). He is, among other publications, author of *Amerikas Deutschlandpolitik im zweiten Weltkrieg: Kriegs- und Friedensziele 1941–1945,* Beihefte zum Jahrbuch für Amerikastudien, III (Heidelberg, 1958); "Die weltpolitische Lage 1936 bis 1939: Die USA," in Oswald Hauser, ed., *Weltpolitik 1933–1939* (Göttingen, 1973); *Atlantische Blockpolitik im 19. Jahrhundert: Die Vereinigten Staaten und der deutsche Liberalismus während der Revolution von 1848/49* (Düsseldorf, 1973); also editor and co-author of *Deutsche Amerikaauswanderung im 19. Jahrhundert: Sozialgeschichtliche Beiträge,* Amerikastudien/American Studies. Eine Schriftenreihe, XLIV (Stuttgart, 1976).

J. R. Pole, Reader in American History and Government at Cambridge University (1963) and Vice-Master of Churchill College, was born in 1922 in London, received his Ph. D. from Princeton University, and is a Fellow of the Royal Historical Society; he has taught at University College, London (1953 to 1963), Princeton, Berkeley, in Chicago, and in Ghana. He is author of *Political Representation in England and the Origins of the American Republic* (Berkeley, Cal., 1966); *Foundations of American Independence, 1763–1815* (Indianapolis and New York, 1972); *The Decision for American Independence* (Philadelphia, 1975), and other publications, as well as editor of *The Advance of Democracy* (New York, 1967); and *The Revolution in America, 1754–1788: Documents and Commentaries* (London, 1970).

Hans-Christoph Schröder, Professor of History at the Technische Hochschule Darmstadt (1974), was born in 1933 in Rathenow, received his Dr. phil. from the University of Cologne (1966), and was on the staff of the Max Planck-Institut für Geschichte at Göttingen (1966–74). He is author of *Sozialismus und Imperialismus: Die Auseinandersetzung der deutschen Sozialdemokratie mit dem Imperialismusproblem und der ,Weltpolitik' vor 1914* (Hannover 1968, 2d ed. forthcoming); "Das Eigentumsproblem in den Auseinandersetzungen um die Verfassung von Massachusetts, 1775–1787," in Rudolf Vierhaus, ed., *Eigentum und Verfassung: Zur Eigentumsdiskussion im ausgehenden 18. Jahrhundert,* Veröffentlichungen des Max-Planck-Instituts für Geschichte, XXXVII (Göttingen, 1972); *Sozialistische Imperialismusdeutung: Studien zu ihrer Geschichte,* Kleine Vandenhoeck-Reihe, 375S (Göttingen, 1973), and other publications.

Jan Willem Schulte Nordholt, Professor of American History at the University of Leiden (1966), was born in 1920 at Zwolle (Netherlands). He is author of *The People That Walk in Darkness* (London, 1960, Dutch ed. 1956); and *Abraham Lincoln* (Arnhem, 1959). He is now working on a book on *The Impact of the American Revolution on the Dutch Republic.*

Gerald Stourzh, Professor of Modern History at the University of Vienna (1969), was born in Vienna in 1929 and formerly Professor of American History at the Free University of Berlin (1965). Among his publications are *Benjamin Franklin and American Foreign Policy* (Chicago, 1954, 2d ed. 1969); *Alexander Hamilton and the Idea of Republican Government* (Stanford, Cal., 1970); "William Blackstone: Teacher of Revolution," *Jahrbuch für Amerikastudien,* XV (1970); and *Vom Widerstandsrecht zur Verfassungsgerichtsbarkeit: Zum Problem der Verfassungswidrigkeit im 18. Jahrhundert* (Graz, 1974); he is co-editor of (with Ralph Lerner and H. C. Harlan) *Readings in American Democracy* (New York, 1959, 2d ed. 1966).

Aladár Urbán, Professor of History at the University of Budapest, was born in 1929 and received his Ph. D. from the Hungarian Academy of Sciences (1965). He is author of *Európa a forradalom forgószelében, 1848–49* (Budapest, 1970); and *A nemzetőrség és honvédség szervezése 1848 nyarán* (Budapest, 1973), summary in German: "Die Organisierung des Heeres der ungarischen Revolution vom Jahre 1848," *Annales Universitatis Scientiarum Budapestinensis,* Sectio Historica, IX (1967) and XIII (1972); he is now working on a book, in Hungarian, on military problems of the American Revolution.

Hermann Wellenreuther, assistant at the Anglo-Amerikanische Abteilung in Cologne (1970), was born in 1941 in Freiburg (Breisgau), received his Dr. phil.

from the University of Cologne (1968), was a Harkness Fellow (1968–70), and held a fellowship of the Deutsche Forschungsgemeinschaft for his current studies of the political structure of England in the mid-18th century. He is author of "The Political Dilemma of the Quakers in Pennsylvania, 1681–1748," *PMHB*, XCIV (1970); *Glaube und Politik in Pennsylvania 1681–1776: Die Wandlungen der Obrigkeitsdoktrin und des* Peace Testimony *der Quäker*, Kölner Historische Abhandlungen, XX (Cologne and Vienna, 1972); "Urbanization in the Colonial South: A Critique," *WMQ*, 3d Ser., XXXI (1974); "Land, Gesellschaft und Wirtschaft in England während des Siebenjährigen Krieges," *Historische Zeitschrift*, CCXVIII (1974); "'The Wisdom to Secure the Entire Absolute and Immediate Dependency of the Colonies': Überlegungen zum Verhältnis zwischen der Krone und den englischen Kolonien in Nordamerika, 1689 bis 1776," in Hans-Ulrich Wehler, ed., *Zweihundert Jahre Amerikanische Revolution und moderne Revolutionsforschung*, Geschichte und Gesellschaft, special issue 2 (Göttingen 1976).

Index of Names

Jürgen Gebhardt

Die Krise des Amerikanismus

Revolutionäre Ordnung und gesellschaftliches Selbstverständnis in der amerikanischen Republik

ca. 400 Seiten. Brosch. ISBN 3-12-910360-0

Das 200jährige Ordnungsexperiment „Amerika" ist der Gegenstand dieser sozialwissenschaftlich und historisch grundlegenden Analyse. „Amerikanismus", der Begriff eines ursprünglich revolutionären Selbstverständnisses der USA, wird vorgeführt im Drama seines Wandels von der „Wahrheit" der Revolution zum Mythos in der Krise.

Ernst Klett Verlag, Stuttgart

Industrielle Welt, Band 14

Peter Marschalck

Deutsche Überseewanderung im 19. Jahrhundert

Ein Beitrag zur soziologischen Theorie der Bevölkerung
128 Seiten. Kartoniert. ISBN 3-12-905480-4
In der deutschen Geschichte des 19. Jahrhunderts spielte – neben den politischen, sozialen, wirtschaftlichen und technischen Umwälzungen – die natürliche und vor allem die räumliche Bevölkerungsbewegung eine besondere Rolle.
Die Problematik der Wanderungen wird von Peter Marschalck einer theoretischen Analyse unterzogen. Seine Forschungsergebnisse unterscheiden sich von den bisher vorliegenden durch eine integrale Betrachtung der Gründe, Strukturen und Folgen der Wanderungen.

Ernst Klett Verlag, Stuttgart

Stuttgarter Beiträge zur Geschichte und Politik, Band 8

Detlef Junker

Der unteilbare Weltmarkt

Das ökonomische Interesse in der Außenpolitik der USA 1933–1941

307 Seiten. Linson. ISBN 3-12-904700-X

Der Autor analysiert die außenpolitische Reaktion der Weltmacht USA auf die beiden großen Herausforderungen ihres politisch-ökonomischen Systems in den dreißiger Jahren: die Weltwirtschaftskrise und den Versuch Deutschlands, Japans und Italiens, mit dem globalen Status quo zugleich den offenen, ungeteilten Weltmarkt zu zerstören.

Er schildert auf breiter Quellengrundlage den Kampf zwischen Internationalisten und Isolationisten um *Inhalt* und *Reichweite* der amerikanischen Außenpolitik, rückt das ökonomische Moment undogmatisch in den Mittelpunkt und sieht die entscheidende Ursache für den Kriegseintritt der USA in den Zweiten Weltkrieg in der *globalen Definition des nationalen Interesses der USA* durch die Internationalisten um Präsident Franklin D. Roosevelt.

Die ständige Auseinandersetzung mit bisherigen Deutungsversuchen wie z. B. mit Vertretern der Isolationismus-These und der „new left interpretation" ist ein integraler Bestandteil der Arbeit. Diese Diskussion wird von Junker mit empirischen und geschichtstheoretischen Argumenten geführt.

Ernst Klett Verlag, Stuttgart